"Remember that success requires half luck and half brains."

"I heard this from my good friend Abe Plough and it has since become one of my favorite sayings."

Kemmons Wilson

HALF LUCK

AND

HALF BRAINS

The Kemmons Wilson, Holiday Inn Story

Kemmons Wilson
With
Robert Kerr

PUBLISHED IN NASHVILLE, TENNESSEE,
BY HAMBLETON-HILL PUBLISHING, INC.

Royalties from the sales of this book will go directly to the Wilson Foundation, a grant-making foundation offering selective financial assistance to worthy community-based programs in the areas of youth, education, religion and community development.

Library of Congress Cataloging-in-Publication Data

Wilson, Kemmons.
Half Luck and Half Brains: The Kemmons Wilson, Holiday Inn Story / Kemmons Wilson with Robert Kerr. — 1st ed. in the U.S.A.

ISBN 1-57102-506-5

Publisher: Van E. Hill
Managing Editor: Robbin Brent
Book Layout and Design: R Brent and Company

Dedication

I dedicate this book
in loving memory
of my mother
Ruby Lloyd Wilson

To my wife Dorothy

My five great children and their spouses
who are like my own:
Spence and Becky Wilson
Bob and Susan Wilson
Kem and Norma Wilson
Betty and Jack Moore
Carole and Bill West

And to my 14 grandchildren

KEMMONS WILSON'S TWENTY TIPS FOR SUCCESS

1. Work only a half a day; it makes no difference which half–it can be either the first 12 hours or the last 12 hours.
2. Work is the master key that opens the door to all opportunities.
3. Mental attitude plays a far more important role in a person's success or failure than mental capacity.
4. Remember that we all climb the ladder of success one step at a time.
5. There are two ways to get to the top of an oak tree. One way is to sit on an acorn and wait; the other way is to climb it.
6. Do not be afraid of taking a chance. Remember that a broken watch is exactly right at least twice every 24 hours.
7. The secret of happiness is not in doing what one likes, but in liking what one does.
8. Eliminate from your vocabulary the words, "I don't think I can' and substitute, "I know I can."
9. In evaluating a career, put opportunity ahead of security.
10. Remember that success requires half luck and half brains.
11. A person has to take risks to achieve.
12. People who take pains never to do more than they get paid for, never get paid for anything more than they do.
13. No job is too hard as long as you are smart enough to find someone else to do it for you.
14. Opportunity comes often. It knocks as often as you have an ear trained to hear it, an eye trained to see it, a hand trained to grasp it, and a head trained to use it.
15. You cannot procrastinate–in two days, tomorrow will be yesterday.
16. Sell your wristwatch and buy an alarm clock.
17. A successful person realizes his personal responsibility for self-motivation. He starts himself because he possesses the key to his own ignition switch.
18. Do not worry. You can't change the past, but you sure can ruin the present by worrying over the future. Remember that half the things we worry about never happen, and the other half are going to happen anyway. So, why worry?
19. It is not how much you have but how much you enjoy that makes happiness.
20. Believe in God and obey the Ten Commandments.

ACKNOWLEDGEMENTS

$\mathcal{O}$ver the years I have been approached many times by writers and would-be writers who tried to convince me to write my life story. My answer was always the same — I'm too busy living my life to take time to write about it. I want to thank my three sons, Spence, Bob and Kem Jr., for convincing me to write this book. It was a lot more fun than I anticipated.

Some men are blessed with good looks, charm, great athletic abilities or born into wealth. I, on the other hand, have been blessed with wonderful women in my life, even though I lack all the attributes beforementioned. My mother, without a doubt, influenced my life more than any other person and deserves all the credit for any measure of success that I have attained. My wife, Dorothy, deserves a special place in heaven for putting up with me and all of my shenanigans for more than fifty years. My daughters, Betty and Carole, have always made me feel like the world's number one Dad and their support has been unwavering. It is hard to believe that throughout my long business career I have had only three secretaries. Fairie Morris, Sue Todd and Dottie Bonds have contributed more than long hours and endless typing to my career. They each possessed the ability to juggle ten projects at once, made sure I was where I was supposed to be, and could handle any situation that arose. In short, they made the "Boss" look good.

This book could not have been conceived without the help of many, many friends, partners, business associates and family members. These individuals shared memories, read drafts and offered insights, supplied photos and provided their talents and assistance in research. I appreciate everyone's faith and encouragement in this project and thank them all.

I want to thank Robbin Brent of RBRENT & Company for her assistance and expertise in editing.

I am grateful to Bill Holcombe and his great staff at Wilson Graphics for all their help and patience in putting this book together. I'm sure Bill's ulcer had absolutely nothing to do with the many changes I made in the production of this book. A special thank you to Rusty Vance and his staff at Vance Commercial Color Lab for the excellent job in creating all the photo pages.

As I enter my eighty-third year here on this earth, I feel I must give thanks every day for the many blessings I have received throughout my life. I thank God, our creator and maker of the universe, for without Him, nothing is possible.

TABLE OF CONTENTS

MAJOR AWARDS OF KEMMONS WILSON

Hall of Fame - 1961 - *American Motel Magazine*

Hall of Fame - 1961 - *Hospitality Magazine*

Golden Plate Award - 1965 - American Academy of Achievement

National Image Award - 1966 - Real Estate Board of Memphis

Master of Free Enterprise Achievement Award
- 1968 - Jr. Achievement

One of 1000 Makers of Twentieth Century
- 1969 - *London Sunday Times*

Horatio Alger Award - 1970 - Horatio Alger Association

Businessman of the Year - 1970 - Religious Heritage of America

National Human Relations Award
- 1972 - National Conference of Christians and Jews

Hall of Fame - 1975 - American Society of Travel Agents

National Business Hall of Fame
- 1982 - *Fortune Magazine* - Jr. Achievement

Entrepreneur Award - 1982 International Franchise Association

Memphis Business Hall of Fame
- 1984 - Memphis Area Chamber of Commerce

International Achievement Award
- 1984 - World Trade Club/San Francisco

International Executive of the Year
- 1985 - Sales and Marketing Executive International

Outstanding Business Leader Award
- 1985 - Northwood Institute

Hall of Fame - 1989 - International Franchise Association

Outstanding Citizen Award - 1992 - Civitan International

Hall of Leaders - 1991 - Travel Industry Association

Cook Halle Award - 1992 - Carnival Memphis

Entrepreneurial Hall of Honor - 1992 - Pink Palace Museum

HONORARY DEGREES OF KEMMONS WILSON

University of Alabama - Doctorate of Laws - 1968

Rhodes College - Doctorate of Business Administration - 1972

Northwood Institute - Doctorate of Laws - 1973

William Woods College - Doctorate of Humanities - 1978

Christian Brothers University - Doctorate of Humanities - 1979

Spence, Bob, Kem, Betty and Carole Wilson
Ribbon-cutting ceremony of the first Holiday Inn—1952

PROLOGUE

$\mathscr{A}$ugust, 1952. It is a hot Saturday afternoon out on Highway 70, the main route into Memphis from the east.

The five blue-eyed children of Kemmons and Dorothy Wilson are all dressed up in their Sunday best. The boys sport crew-cuts, bow-ties and jackets; the girls wear babydoll dresses, perms and freshly polished white shoes.

In stairstep order, ages 9 to 3, Spence, Bob, Kem, Betty and Carole line up to cut the ribbon on their Daddy's latest business venture. The grand opening of his new motel has attracted so many onlookers, police have closed the busy highway to traffic.

The Wilson children's father is a perpetually busy man, a stout man with pumpkin-colored hair and steel-blue eyes, who is always launching something new around Memphis. But none of the children can know how dramatically this particular afternoon will change not only the course of their lives, but the very landscape of modern America.

The heat of the Memphis summer keeps them fidgeting in their dress clothes. Mayor Frank Tobey of Memphis is scheduled to do the ribbon-cutting. But when he fails to show on time, Dorothy says, "Kemmons, let the children do it." Kemmons agrees.

As the photographer's finger touches the shutter button, Carole looks behind her. Spence teeters on the edge of his shoes. Bob looks down. Only Betty looks at the camera. Kem snips his scissors a count before the others.

The flash goes off. And by dramatic happenstance, a quintessential moment in 20th-century popular culture is captured forever.

To one side of where the children stand on the sidewalk, but slightly out of the picture, stretches a long parking lot. It is lined with big Chevrolets and Fords, their flowing fins and massive chromework emblematic of the golden age of Detroit's automakers.

To the other side of the children gleams a 120-room motel billed as the largest and finest in the South. The five ranch-style wings of the red-brick, green-roofed structure sprawl over seven acres on Highway 70. The motel has been built in front of Kemmons' lumberyard, which supplies his homebuilding operations.

Towering behind and 55 feet above the five small Wilson children is a bright, green-and-yellow, porcelain-enamel sign. It is framed on one side and across the top with a stream of flashing lights that forms a giant arrow directing the eye toward the motel. A marquee announces single rooms for $4, doubles for $6. Perched on a pedestal at the very top of the sign, a pulsating star establishes a beacon for travelers.

The tall sign is a crucial element in Kemmons' vision for the motel. His earlier years of operating movie theaters taught him the value of having a marquee out front to draw in the crowds.

And there it is, in flowing white script against a green background on the huge motel sign: the name of this brand-new creation that Kemmons wants the world to see.

Holiday Inn

On that very spot, the state of Tennessee would one day erect a historical marker. The Smithsonian Institution would acquire a Holiday Inn sign for its permanent collection of Americana. The Sunday Times of London would select Kemmons as one of the people it considered "The 1000 Makers of the 20th century."

All that and much more came later. But even at that moment in 1952, looking at Kemmons and Dorothy's children and the parking lot full of automobiles and the Holiday Inn sign looming overhead, you could see the future.

Like instant icons, those images represented the major trends just beginning to pulse through postwar America. The economy had retooled from its wartime effort into a consumer market that would change the country and the world. Faster than ever before, American families were growing larger, more mobile and more affluent.

Enter Kemmons Wilson, a man with a plan to tap into it all. Kemmons Wilson, Memphis builder and developer, supersalesman and general wheeler-dealer. The only son of a mother left widowed and penniless when her baby was nine months old. A man who had been forced to quit high school to eke out a living for himself and his mother in the heart of the Depression.

Like so many other American men of his generation, Kemmons had returned from World War II to raise a family and make his fortune. In the 1950s, the Baby Boom was rewriting the nation's demographic charts at a record rate of more than 4 million births a year. America was entering the age of Davy Crockett caps and Hula-Hoops, of a marketplace dominated by the needs and desires of young, active families.

Kemmons knew that American families would be taking to the road, looking for fun and comfort at an affordable price. Construction would soon be under way on a $76-billion, federal interstate-highway system, which would make travel easier and even more popular coast-to-coast.

After all, it had been a cross-country vacation trip with his children the year before that had inspired Kemmons to build his Holiday Inn in the first place. Pulitzer-prize-winning author David Halberstam, in his bestseller *The Fifties*, would call it "the vacation that changed the face of the American road."

Kemmons discovered that most motels were second-rate — "wayside cabins" they were often called. Even worse, from Kemmons' point of view, they charged an extra $2 apiece for every child: "It made my Scottish blood boil."

Kemmons told Dorothy he was going to build 400 motels across the country to give families a brand name they could trust anywhere they traveled. Motels that would never charge extra for children. She laughed, which only made him more determined.

By the time he got back home, Kemmons had put the tape measure he always carried to enough motel rooms to know exactly how he wanted to lay out his own motel in Memphis. He sketched it out, then asked Eddie Bluestein, a draftsman friend, to draw up the plans.

One evening, about the time Bluestein was completing the plans, he happened to see on television a showing of "Holiday Inn," the old Bing Crosby/Fred Astaire movie in which Crosby introduced the song "White Christmas." On a whim, the draftsman scrawled the words "Holiday Inn" across his drawing.

"That's a great name," Kemmons said when he saw it. "We'll use it."

Kemmons fully expected his first motel to be a success from the start. He had learned that not a single new hotel room had been built in Memphis since 1929, even though the city's population had doubled. He knew how to build the kind of motel he wanted, having completed the first Holiday Inn $45,000 under budget.

He knew he could offer his rooms for 15-20 percent less than the established hotels and still make a profit, because he could build a motel room for half what they could. Kemmons also knew families increasingly preferred stopping at a motel in the outlying areas of cities, rather than fighting the traffic into congested downtown areas where most older hotels were located.

Kemmons knew what he and his wife wanted in a motel room, and he knew the things his children wanted. So his Holiday Inns would have swimming pools. In every room there would be televisions and air conditioning — both still luxuries in 1952. There would be plenty of parking right next to the rooms, clean restaurants, free ice, baby-sitters, drugstores, service stations, doctors and dentists on call.

"Kemmons saw that if children are happy, the parents are happy," Dorothy would later recall.

And Kemmons knew something the rest of the world would soon discover: The sleepy, mom-and-pop motel industry was about to become big, big business. He was convinced the motel business was "the greatest untouched industry in America."

Bottom line, Kemmons Wilson knew he had his ducks in a row on this venture. He might appear to some as a headstrong risk-taker. But as he liked to say, "I don't do a whole lot of wishful thinking. I'm a dreamer, but I'm a practical dreamer."

He never doubted he could pay back the ever-larger loans he would take out for his Holiday Inns and other projects. "I borrowed certainly a billion dollars in my life, and paid it all back with interest. Nobody ever lost a nickel loaning me money," Kemmons says today.

The late John Martin, Kemmons' first attorney, liked to joke that "Kemmons Wilson is the biggest borrower in history. Only the United States government was bigger than Kemmons when it came to borrowing."

But Kemmons had no fear of debt because he woke up every morning charged with boundless confidence. The late Wallace Johnson, the Memphis homebuilder who became Kemmons' first partner in taking Holiday Inn national, remembered that from the very start, "There was enthusiasm in Kemmons' voice."

Out of that enthusiasm, Holiday Inn grew into one of the largest corporations in the world, in fact the largest business of its kind in history. By the 1970s, a new Holiday Inn was being built somewhere every two and a half days, and a new room every 20 minutes. By offering franchise ownerships on the grandest scale imagined at that point, Kemmons figures, "Holiday Inn made more millionaires than about any company that has ever been around."

The worldwide, multibillion-dollar corporation created jobs for thousands upon thousands of people. Time magazine once put Kemmons on its cover and called him "The Man with 300,000 Beds."

Yet, it all began for Kemmons Wilson in a town so small it's one of the few places he never opened a Holiday Inn. Within a year after he was born in 1913 in Osceola, Arkansas, his father died of what was probably Lou Gehrig's Disease.

This boy who was victim of such unfortunate circumstances couldn't have inspired many to expect big things from him. But even though Kemmons may have started life with the odds stacked against him, he had the good fortune to be the only son of Ruby Lloyd Wilson.

Better known to everyone as "Doll," because she stood just 4-foot-11, she was the source of her son's confidence, his work ethic, and his enthusiasm. Even when she and Kemmons were so poor they had to live on a few pounds of dried butter beans for a week at a time, she promised him he was destined for achievement.

"When I was just a kid, she told me, 'Kemmons, some day you will be an important man. There's nobody who can do anything that you can't do better,' " he recalls.

"There is no doubt my mother was the major influence in my life. She told me every day I could do anything I wanted to if I just worked hard enough. And she drove that in my head so hard, she finally convinced me I *could* do anything."

Though Doll Wilson died in 1968, she lived long enough to see the things she told her son come true. Doll not only witnessed Holiday Inn's rise to worldwide success, she established its trademark decorating theme, dominated by greens and yellows, her favorite colors.

It has been said that what John D. Rockefeller did for gasoline and Henry Ford did for automobiles, Kemmons did for lodging: standardizing a product and making it available to the masses at a reasonable price anywhere they went. "You can cater to the rich people, and I'll take the rest," Kemmons once told a high-end competitor. "The Good Lord made so many more of them."

In truth, Kemmons would always think of himself as one of them. Though he has been a multimillionaire for decades now, he still lives in the same home he did the day he opened that first Holiday Inn. He still drives automobiles that are comfortable but far from extravagant. He would rather eat a hot dog than caviar. He wears nothing fancier than a dark business suit, and he wears that almost every day.

Because it wasn't ever really for the money that Kemmons worked like a man possessed all those years. He did it for his family. He did it because he just liked doing it. But more than anything, he did it for Doll.

"She sacrificed so much for him in his childhood, raising him by herself," says Kemmons' longtime engineer, Bob McCaskill. "It became his ambition to succeed for his mother's sake. And once it was part of him, it went on all his life."

So to know the whole story of Kemmons Wilson, business pioneer and American original, you have to go back into another era. Back to the flat bottomlands of the Arkansas Delta and the year 1913.

That was the time and place that an 18-year-old widow with barely a nickel to her name made up her mind: No hardship could keep her from raising a son who would leave his mark on the world.

CHAPTER ONE

— DOLL —

"Eliminate from your vocabulary the words, 'I don't think I can,' and substitute, 'I know I can.' "

Kemmons Wilson

$\mathscr{I}$n 1919, author Sinclair Lewis, America's first Nobel laureate for literature, took a four-month tour of the American West in a Model T. He returned with the idea for his classic novel, *Main Street*.

But he also wrote an article the next year titled "Adventures in Automobumming" for the *Saturday Evening Post*. In it, he bemoaned the scarcity of decent accommodations on the nation's highways. And he made a stunningly accurate prediction:

> Somewhere in these United States there is a young man who is going to become rich. He may be washing bottles in a dairy lunch. He is going to start a chain of small, clean, pleasant hotels, standardized and nationally advertised, along every important motor route in the country. He is not going to waste money on gilt and onyx, but he is going to have agreeable clerks, good coffee, endurable mattresses and good lighting.

Needless to say, Lewis did not know Kemmons Wilson at the time. And at that point, the 7-year-old Kemmons could not have known he would be the young man who would fulfill that prophecy in the form of Holiday Inn.

But Doll Wilson just *knew* that her son was destined for great things. It didn't matter to her where he had come from, or what his

Doll (Ruby Lloyd Hall) Wilson came from a very poor family in Memphis, where she was born August 9, 1895. Her father, a bookkeeper, died when Doll was about 10. Her mother began taking in boarders to support her children. Doll was the oldest of five sisters and had two brothers older than she. As a teenager, she worked as a dry-goods clerk.

On June 28, 1911, Doll married Charles Kemmons Wilson, a fellow Memphian. He had served in the U.S. Navy and worked as a fireman and a clerk. His mother, Lila, gave him the name Kemmons after the doctor who delivered him.

By the time he married, however, the young groom was off to a good start selling insurance for National Life and Accident Insurance Company. He had demonstrated a natural salesmanship, something he would pass on to his son. Because Wilson had done so well, National Life sent him with his new bride over to Osceola, Arkansas, to open an office there in 1912.

The little Mississippi River town of Osceola, about 50 miles northwest of Memphis, had a population of around 1,500. But it was the business center of Mississippi County, a region rich in cotton production in an age when cotton was king in the South. Osceola looked like a growing market where the insurance company could extend its business.

The future looked bright for the ambitious young insurance agent and his bride when their baby boy arrived on Jan. 5, 1913. They named him Charles Kemmons Wilson Jr.

But just nine months later, tragedy struck. At 29 years of age, Kemmons Sr. fell gravely ill with what was probably Lou Gehrig's Disease, a painful, degenerative disease of the nerve cells that control muscular movement. He died October 4, 1913, before seeing his son's first birthday. It left Doll Wilson a widow and single mother at 18.

Kemmons Sr. had had the foresight to buy a $2,000 insurance policy, payable to Doll. That represented a substantial amount in 1913. But an unscrupulous salesman with the funeral home who buried Kemmons Sr. took advantage of the grieving young widow. She was talked into giving her late husband a grand funeral that ended up costing all the money from the insurance policy. Kemmons Sr. was buried in style, but Doll was left penniless when it was over. Ironically, he was laid to rest in Memphis in Forest Hill Cemetery, of which many years later his son would become half owner.

Doll took her infant son and returned to Memphis, moving into her mother's house at 336 North Watkins. In those days before government assistance, Doll had little choice but to go to work. While Kemmons' grandmother took care of him during the day, Doll set out to make a living for herself and her young son.

"My mother got a job as a dentist's assistant that paid $11 a week. Later she became a bookkeeper. But she never made more than $125 a month. Can you imagine that? That's how bad times really were back then," Kemmons says.

When Doll and Kemmons arrived in Memphis, it was a relatively prosperous town, a bustling cotton and timber market on the Mississippi River. It was also a tough town, with hundreds of saloons and honky-tonks. About the time Doll and Kemmons made Memphis their home, the man who would dominate local politics for half a century was beginning to crack down on vice. As Mayor E.H. "Boss" Crump established his political machine, he made Memphis a place where the streets were clean and safe, where boys like Kemmons could play in the neighborhoods and mothers like Doll could breathe more easily.

However, as Kemmons grew older, one of the grimmest eras of American history was building momentum toward a brutal culmination. Though the worst began in late 1920s, when the stock-market collapse signaled the beginning of the Great Depression, the hard times actually began shaping up many years before that. As early as 1923, American banks were already failing at a rate of about two a day. In the worst years, a third of the nation's workers would be unable to find jobs. It became common to see people waiting in long soup lines in Memphis and other towns and cities across the country.

"We were always scuffling to have enough money. I can remember not having enough to eat in those days," Kemmons recalls.

"Streetcar fare was 7 cents, but I would always walk to town because I didn't have the 7 cents. One time my mother and I rented a duplex at 42 South Cox for $25 a month. We rented out one side for $15 a month, and on the side we lived in, we rented out one of the duplex at 42 South Cox for $25 a month. We rented out one side for $15 a month, and on the side we lived in, we rented out one of the rooms for $8 a month. This made our total rent $2 a month, and even that was really hard to get."

Still, it's not the hard times that characterize those days for Kemmons, but rather memories of his mother's devotion to him. "I had the most loving mother anyone ever had. I was her only child and she thought I was the best thing since sliced bread. I really was her life," he says.

In Kemmons' mind, he received more love from one parent than many children do from two: "I do regret that I never knew my father, but I had a very loving mother. When I got old enough, I would always walk down to the corner to meet her at the streetcar when she got off work. She took me to church every Sunday of the world, starting out at First Methodist Church at Second and Poplar.

"She was just the sweetest, most wonderful woman who ever lived. And if anybody ever loved a son, there is no doubt she loved me. She was a good-looking woman, but she never remarried. She hardly ever dated. I used to hear her tell people that she would never marry, because no man was good enough to be the father of her son."

Even after Kemmons married and had his own family, Doll always lived with them in the same house. "Dorothy was an angel. It's hard to have two families in one house. But I wouldn't have it any other way. I always told my mother I never would get married because she had been so good to me. And I was just 34 days shy of my 29th birthday before I did get married."

In later years, Doll would take as much interest in her son's adult endeavors as she had taken in his childhood interests. "When Kemmons built the first Holiday Inn, people said he was crazy," she once told a reporter. "No one had opened a motel here with 120 units before. But I knew that he could do whatever he wanted to do."

Kemmons credits his mother for her valuable input during the launch of Holiday Inn. She worked with him in many of his businesses. "She decorated the first one hundred Holiday Inns. Everything was yellow and green. She loved yellow and green. She picked plain, natural furniture, because she said our rooms should be for the average person who wants a nice, comfortable place to stay," he says.

worked behind the desk. One thing she really enjoyed was the candy sold there, named Doll's Candy, which was eventually sold in Holiday Inns all over the world.

Kemmons made his mother a vice president in the company. She liked to make the rounds of the various departments, visiting with all the employees, no matter what job they did. She toured Holiday Inns in different parts of the country, hugging and kissing the employees wherever she went. For her goodwill tours, Kemmons bought a Cadillac limousine equipped with television and stereo. It was nicknamed "the Doll Buggy."

When she died in 1968, the marquee on one of the Memphis Holiday Inns said, "Doll Wilson ... Known by Many ... Loved by All."

Kemmons' children knew Doll very well because she always lived in the same house when they were growing up. Spence Wilson, Kemmons' oldest son, recalls, "She gave my father the spirit he has of accepting nothing less than the best. I think she was my father's role model."

Kemmons started working at a very young age. He earned his first $5 by posing for an ad for Sunbeam Bread. He doesn't know how his mother got him the job. During World War I, he did his part on the homefront to hasten the Allied victory.

"I used to ride on the back of a truck and sing songs to raise money for war bonds. They had a piano on the truck. I don't know if I sang well or not, but I remember singing the song *Over There*. I was about 5," he says.

Steady jobs began soon after. When he was 6 years old, he began selling the *Saturday Evening Post* for a nickel a copy. After a few months, he discovered the *Ladies Home Journal* sold for a dime and would allow him to be the district manager and have other children sell copies for him. Kemmons soon had more than a dozen neighborhood children working for him. Each magazine sold produced 3 cents profit for the youthful enterprise, with Kemmons getting 1 cent and his workers getting 2 cents. Even at so young an age, he could instill enthusiasm for his projects in the people working for him.

Another early money-raising venture was building rocking chairs in an uncle's basement at night. He sold the rocking chairs for 75 cents. When neighbors went to court to complain about the racket, Kemmons explained he worked at night because he had to go to school in the day. The judge commended him for his industriousness, but settled the matter by outlining a chair-building schedule that would allow the neighbors some sleep.

"I did every odd job you could think of. I was the worst student in the world because I was always tired from working all the time. I had to work; I was hungry. I would go to school and go to sleep," Kemmons says.

"I sacked groceries. One of the stores where I worked was owned by Clarence Saunders, the Memphis entrepreneur who started Piggly Wiggly, the first self-service grocery stores. I had newspaper routes both in the morning and in the afternoon. We had two papers in Memphis then, *The Commercial Appeal* in the morning and *The News Scimitar* [later *The Press Scimitar*] in the afternoon. I had routes of about 160 customers. I got up about 4 in the morning and delivered the morning paper, and then I delivered the other route in the afternoon after I got out of school."

Kemmons' cousin, V.O. Sneed, a Memphis builder, agrees Kemmons lived the life of a workaholic even as a boy. "Kemmons worked all the time and kept himself busy," Sneed says. Since Sneed worked all the time too, the boys never really got a chance to know each other.

At about 14, Kemmons got a job at Wagner's Drug Store at the corner of Madison and Belvedere as a delivery boy and a soda jerk. In between deliveries, Kemmons would work the soda fountain, which allowed him to give pretty girls an extra scoop of ice cream. Another fringe benefit was being able to eat all the ice cream he wanted. Then, as now, "A day without ice cream is like a day without love" to Kemmons.

One evening while Kemmons was on the job at the drug store, an order came in for a delivery to Bill Terry, the Hall of Fame first baseman of the New York Giants. Terry lived on Willett Avenue, several blocks south of the drug store. Kemmons hopped on his bicycle and headed down Belvedere Avenue.

He had just started across the busy intersection with Union Avenue when he felt a crushing force knock him flat in the middle of the street. The boy lay there helpless, his left leg horribly mangled.

"All of a sudden, that car appeared from nowhere and ran over me. I never saw it. The next thing I knew I was lying in the street, and the ambulance was coming to get me. My leg was broken in five places and my kneecap was crushed," Kemmons recalls.

"I was 14 years old and the doctors who saw me first told me I would never walk again."

But then he was examined by Dr. Willis Campbell, a talented orthopedic surgeon after whom the respected Campbell Clinic in Memphis is named. He said, "Kemmons, I'm going to make you walk again." He proved true to his word.

"I was scared, but his confidence made me get over being scared. I owe a lot to Willis Campbell. I stayed in Baptist Hospital for four months, and I was in a body cast for 11 months. My left leg was in a cast all the way down to my knee, and my right leg was in a cast down to my foot, with a big board in between them so you couldn't move them at all," Kemmons says.

"It was the worst thing that happened to me as a boy. All I could do was lie in a hospital on my back. I did some reading and learned some magic tricks, played a little gin rummy, I guess. I tried to keep up with my school work, which I did not enjoy."

Doll took a leave of absence from her job at a meat-packing plant and moved into her son's hospital room to help care for him and tutor him. Between her loving attention and constant prayers, and Dr. Campbell's skillful treatment, Kemmons finally got back on his feet. Though one leg healed two inches shorter than the other, he returned to school a little over a year after the accident.

Kemmons believes he emerged from that trying experience more serious about life. His near-death may well have helped the boy steel himself for the gauntlet of lean years that lay ahead for countless Americans. The greatest peace-time crisis in U.S. history was about to devastate the land. However, in surviving it, Kemmons would demonstrate the intuitive savvy and untiring dedication of a born entrepreneur.

CHAPTER TWO

—POPCORN AND PINBALL—

"A successful person realizes his personal responsibility for self-motivation. He starts himself because he possesses the key to his own ignition switch."

Kemmons Wilson

In the early months of 1930, catastrophe was spreading across America. The stock-market crash in the fall of 1929 had wiped out financial holdings worth billions of dollars and set off a terrifying chain of bank and business failures. The worst years of the Great Depression were unfolding with jarring impact. Those who lived through that time remember it was not uncommon to see once wealthy men sweeping leaves just to get by. Millions upon millions of working people suddenly found there were no jobs to be had at any wage.

Doll Wilson joined the swelling ranks of the unemployed. In 1930, at a time she was not in the best of health anyway, Doll lost her bookkeeping job. Then in his last year at Central High School, Kemmons concluded it was up to him to shoulder the load of supporting the family.

"I decided I had to quit school to try and make us a living. My mother thought I should stay in school, but she couldn't stop me from dropping out. At the time, it was more important to me to eat than it was to get an education."

At the age of 17 Kemmons made up his mind he would never be poor again. "I didn't know what I was going to do. I just knew that we were poor, and I didn't want to be poor. I knew I had to make money."

Necessity forced Kemmons from the classroom. But his instincts were probably pulling him in that direction anyway. Kemmons simply was never one for the world of classroom theory and discourse. He was geared for action from the start. Decades after he had made his fortune, he would continue to work as obsessively as he had as an impoverished teenager.

It would be half a century before he returned to Central High School to be presented with an honorary diploma. Speaking at graduation ceremonies for the Class of 1981, Wilson told them he wouldn't recommend dropping out to anyone. But he explained how he made the best of the hand fate dealt him.

"I told them, 'When you don't have an education, you have to use your brain. An opportunist is a man who meets the wolf at the door and the next day appears in a fur coat.'"

It didn't take the young Kemmons very long in 1930 to decide he wasn't going to turn a wolf into a fur coat by working for someone else. After he left school, he took a job writing the latest stock prices on the board at a brokerage firm for $12 a week. When everyone else went home for the day, Kemmons stayed behind and made friends with the bookkeeper.

"I got him to show me how to do it, and when he left he recommended me to succeed him. They gave me the job, but after three weeks I was still making $12 a week. The other bookkeeper had made $35 a week. I asked for a raise, but they only gave me another $3 a week. So I quit, and that was the first and last full-time job I ever had working for someone else," he says.

If Kemmons wasn't going to work for someone else, he was going to have to think creatively. He had always loved the movies, and often did odd jobs at the Memphian Theater in return for admission to see the feature films. But in 1930, his thoughts moved beyond what was happening up on the screen. Realizing that the theater offered no snacks for moviegoers to munch on, he saw the opportunity to create a market for himself.

"I got to thinking that I could sell some popcorn there. So I talked to the manager, and he talked to his boss, and they finally decided I could put a popcorn machine out front. Then I went down to see Tom O'Brien at United Fixture and Scale Company. I told him I wanted to buy a popcorn machine and he showed me one he had for $50."

"How are you going to pay for it?" O'Brien asked.

"Well, I'd have to buy it on credit," Kemmons answered.

"How much you gonna pay down?"

"I don't have any money, Tom, but I would pay you a dollar a week until I've paid it off."

O'Brien put his arm around Kemmons and said, "Son, you look like an honest young man. I'm gonna sell it to you."

Finding a way to acquire a popcorn machine on credit set the pattern for a lifetime of deals for Kemmons Wilson. As a young man with no money to his name, he knew he would have to convince other people to loan him theirs. In doing that, he learned nothing is more crucial than making friends and establishing trust.

"Young people need to know how important it is to have a good reputation, to keep faith with everybody, to do what you said you would," Kemmons explains. "And you can't do it by yourself. I've really been blessed by a lot of people having faith in me, and that's what it takes."

His hunch about the untapped potential in theater concessions proved correct — so much so in fact that his profits soon far outstripped the theater manager's income," Kemmons recalls. "I started selling popcorn for a nickel a bag, and I did real well. But I got to where I was making $40-$50 a week, while the theater manager was only making $25. He kept counting the sacks I was selling. Finally he came to me and said he was taking the job away from me,"

"I remember telling my mother then that I was going to get myself a movie theater, and nobody else was ever going to take my popcorn machine away from me."

Several years later, Kemmons did just that.

In another concessions venture in his early days, Kemmons rented a cigar stand at the 81 Madison Building. He bought day-old bread for 5 cents a loaf and had Doll make homemade pimento cheese. Then he made pimento-cheese sandwiches, toasted them and sold them at the cigar stand for 10 cents apiece. Kemmons remembers selling as many as 1,000 sandwiches a day.

But the first business he got into after popcorn was pinball. When the theater manager bought him out, Kemmons took the money and bought five used pinball machines for $10 each. He placed them in drugstores and hotel lobbies and anywhere else that would attract pinball players. He split the take from each machine with the owner of the business where it was located, and moved the machines frequently in search of busier sites.

"I hustled like mad. I'd get $10 ahead and I'd buy another machine and find another location. I didn't like the machines myself, I just liked the money they made," Kemmons says.

Ewing Carruthers, a longtime friend of Kemmons, recalls how he witnessed the young supersalesman at work on the day they met in the early 1930s. Carruthers was a teen-ager then, running the hamburger stand at East End swimming pool in Memphis. One night, a young man pulled up in a small Austin automobile with a pinball machine tied on the back with rope.

"Fellow, I've got a great deal for you," said the young man — who turned out to be Kemmons — striding up with a big smile on his face.

"That's fine, but I don't have any money," replied Carruthers, who was earning $7.50 a week and two hamburgers a day at the time.

"That doesn't make any difference. I've got a deal you can't turn down," the young man shot back.

"I can't turn it down and I can't pick it up, because I don't have any money, I told you," Carruthers said.

"You don't need any money. I'm making you a deal like this: You see that pinball machine? I'll put it here in your stand, and all we have to do is plug it in. We'll split the money as it comes in."

"I don't have any money to invest in a pinball machine, and I don't know how to operate one anyway. And who's going to maintain it when it gets out of whack?"

"Listen to me very carefully. All you have to invest is a little electricity, and let me put my pinball machine in your stand. I'll come by three nights a week and we will split the nickels.

"And if you have any trouble," Kemmons continued, "just give me a call and my mother will answer the phone, and I'll come over and fix whatever is wrong with it. If it doesn't work, I'll bring you another one, because I have ten of them. They're my first investment in business, and I'm going to make a lot of money."

Ewing finally consented, and Kemmons unloaded his pinball machine and plugged it in.

"It turned out to be a lot of fun that summer and the next," Carruthers recalls, "because about three nights a week, Kemmons would come by and take the nickels out of the machine and put them all on the glass top. Then he would take two of his big fingers and start dividing them up: 'Two for you, two for me. Two for you, two for me.'

"I have tried to tell Kemmons since then, that because I was responsible for one tenth of his first investment being successful, it seemed to me he owes me a tenth of his assets today. But he is a little blind about things like that, and he just doesn't see the logic in it."

The location of another of Kemmons' early pinball machines brought someone into his life more precious to him than any investment he ever made.

The machine was located in the William Len Hotel in downtown Memphis at the corner of Monroe and Main, where a young woman named Sarah Boswell ran the cigar stand. Kemmons would stop by about twice a week to check his pinball machine. While he was there, he would always buy Sarah a Coca-Cola, which cost a nickel at the time.

"She finally told me one day, 'Kemmons, I know how tight you are with your money, but if you will spend an extra nickel, I will introduce you to one of the cutest girls you ever saw,' " Kemmons recalls.

"I said, 'All right, I'll spend the nickel.' And she introduced me to Dorothy Lee, who is now my wife. She was working as an assistant bookkeeper on the third floor of the hotel at that time. That was the best nickel I ever spent in my life."

Dorothy Lee was more than cute. She was a striking brunette with a light-up-the-room smile. Kemmons likes to brag that he was so handsome Dorothy could not resist him. However, she says the truth is she was not immediately impressed with the busy young man, so full of himself and his big dreams.

"Oh, I thought he was conceited. I really didn't particularly like him. But I changed my mind," Dorothy remembers.

"As I got to know him, I saw he was ambitious and that Kemmons is actually not a conceited person at all. He is a very warm person."

Dorothy had grown up in the Cooper-Young area of Midtown Memphis, with one brother and three sisters. One sister, Rose, died of an illness at the age of 21, but all the others still live in Memphis. Her father worked at the International Harvester plant, then one of the largest employers in town. As a girl, Dorothy attended Peabody Elementary and Central High School, but Kemmons had dropped out long before she started her high school days.

After graduation, Dorothy attended the Miller Hawkins business school, then got a job as assistant bookkeeper for the William Len Hotel. She would work there until the night she married Kemmons. Their relationship, however, began rather slowly.

"I remember the day I met him," she recalls, "but it didn't matter at the time. It wasn't anything I was concerned about. Oh, he was OK, but I think I was in love with someone else when we met."

"It was probably six months before we started dating, and I never really did stop dating other boys until we married. I almost married somebody else."

In fact, Dorothy almost didn't show up for their first date. "I thought he was kidding when he said he wanted to come by. He had said, 'How about me coming by?' and I said, 'Oh sure,' and didn't even give it a second thought. I had gone off, and I wasn't even at home when he got there," she remembers.

"And he brought another guy with him! I said, 'Are you scared of me?' They sat out in front of the house in a car and waited for me. When I got there, I was surprised to see him. I thought, 'My gosh, what have I gotten into?'"

Kemmons liked Dorothy all along. But he felt he had to hold back on a serious commitment in order to honor the vow he had made to his mother long before. "I kept resisting marriage because I had told my mother I would never marry. She didn't think any girl was good enough for me."

So Kemmons and Dorothy dated for four years, and Dorothy

almost married someone else a couple of times. But she obviously had a sincere interest in Kemmons from the beginning. On many of their early dates, she showed she was more willing than many girls would have been to pitch in and help Kemmons with his business chores.

"She used to help me move my pinball machines. I had an Austin, a little bitty car, with a steel rack on the back where you could set the pinball machine. But you had to have two people to lift it up there," Kemmons says. "On a lot of our dates, I would carry Dorothy with me and we would take the machines and move them around. She had to lift one half of the pinball machine, so she had to be pretty strong."

It was a pinball machine that also played a role in getting Kemmons involved with one of the other great passions of his life. About 1933, he had one of his machines in the Linden Circle Drug Store, which was owned by Jack Embry. Whenever Kemmons stopped by to check the machine, he would have a Coca-Cola. The two men soon became good friends.

One day Embry said, "Kemmons, would you like to learn to fly?"

"Yeah, I've always said I wanted to learn to fly," Kemmons answered.

"Well, let's buy an airplane."

"All right, let's do."

Just like that, Kemmons set off into the world of aviation. In the years to come, being a pilot would play a major role in Kemmons' success in business, particularly in the rapid development of Holiday Inn.

After first deciding to acquire a flying machine, the two men looked around a bit and then settled on an Aeronica-C3, a small plane with a 38-horsepower, two-cylinder engine. "Any oldtime pilot knows that airplane," Kemmons says. The owner agreed to sell it for $800, flying lessons included. The two aspiring flyboys put up $400 apiece.

"I learned to fly just real quick. I liked it, loved it," Kemmons recalls. "As it turned out, Jack never learned to fly. But I was using that machine. I flew it nearly every day."

He liked to show off his newly acquired flying skills. One afternoon, he learned that several young women he knew were going out on a boat on the Mississippi River. So Kemmons quit work early and flew out in his plane to the river to find the girls.

"I found them, and I dived down in that 38-horsepower airplane three or four times. The last time, as I dove down and pulled back up, the engine quit," Kemmons remembers.

"Well, there was a sandbar nearby and I was able to glide to it. But those girls never came back! I guess they thought I was still just playing. Well, I was out there until about 11:30 that night before somebody finally came looking for me. The mosquitos about ate me alive."

Often on Saturday or Sunday afternoons, Kemmons would take Dorothy on a flight out to a small town in the area. Dorothy would sell tickets for $1 to anyone who wanted to take a flight in the plane.

However, one day Embry complained, "Kemmons, don't you think it's kind of unfair that you are flying that airplane all the time and I own half of it?"

"Well, I guess it is," Kemmons replied. "What do you want to do?"

Embry said, "Let's sell it," and Kemmons agreed.

They had no luck selling the plane for a time. Then a man contacted Kemmons and explained he had a house on which he owed $3,100 and was about to lose it to the bank. He offered to trade his equity in the house for the airplane. When Kemmons discovered the house was located at 811 Cypress Drive in Hein Park, a very nice neighborhood to this day, he made the trade. The next day he took Embry a check for $400.

"What's that for?" Embry asked.

"Why, it's for your half of the airplane," Kemmons said.

"Well, what did you do with it?"

"I made a trade."

"I ain't gonna take the money. I want half of whatever you traded for."

"Well, that's all right too, but I traded for a house. You sure you want a house?"

Embry said he did, so on the deed, the new owners became Jack Embry and Kemmons Wilson. A little time went by, and the two men found themselves enjoying a Saturday evening of dancing with their dates at The Peabody Hotel in downtown Memphis. They liked to share a bottle of champagne and make a big night of it.

"Well, Jack had met a little girl and he had fallen in love and he had bought her a diamond. I guess it had to be four or five carats, one of the biggest diamonds I ever saw. So one night he was up there with her, and I was with Dorothy, when we were still dating."

Embry said, "Kemmons, you know we ought to make a deal. Don't you think the first man who gets married ought to get the other man's half of that house?"

"Jack, you don't think I'm an imbecile, do you? Here you are, you've already bought a ring, you're engaged and getting ready to marry. Why, you've already set a date even. No sir," Kemmons said.

So they had another bottle of champagne and Embry said, "Kemmons, you would give me a nice present if I got married, wouldn't you?"

Kemmons said, "Well, I'm sure I would, Jack. You're my friend."

"Well, why don't you just say the first man who gets married gets the other man's half of the house?"

Kemmons was feeling so good he finally shook on the deal, fully expecting to lose the race to the altar. As things turned out, however, Embry broke up with his fiancee, and Kemmons married Dorothy — which made the house his after all. A few years later, when Kemmons was away during World War II, Dorothy moved into the house on Cypress Drive with their two children and Doll.

Ironically, Embry later bought the house back from Kemmons. After Kemmons returned from the war and began building another house for his family, Embry told Kemmons he would like to buy the house on Cypress Drive. He offered $3,000 to cover the mortgage and an additional $400 for Kemmons' original share of the airplane. Kemmons accepted — though the offer was far below market value, he says. Embry moved in, and as this book was being written almost 50 years later, was still residing in the house on Cypress Drive that played such a memorable role in his friendship with Kemmons.

CHAPTER THREE

——BUILDING MATERIALS——

"There is nothing more exciting in the world than to create something, to dig a foundation, to build a building on it."

Kemmons Wilson

*K*emmons finally got his own movie theater by using his fast-developing creativity and persuasiveness to finance the deal. He heard there was a little theater for sale in Fort Pickering, a small community along the Mississippi on the outskirts of Memphis. The DeSoto Theater had been closed for years, but after making a trip out to look it over, Kemmons went to the man who owned it. He offered to pay the $2,000 asking price — if he could pay it out at $25 a week after he got the theater open.

When the theater owner agreed, Kemmons went to National Theater Supply Company. It was run by Bob Bostick, a man who would become a close friend and provide invaluable assistance as Kemmons learned the movie business. Bostick sold Kemmons some $4,000 worth of equipment that day, with nothing down, and helped him get the theater open. Once again, Kemmons had managed to get into a new business without so much as a down payment.

He did well enough with his first theater to build a new one at the corner of Airways and Lamar in Memphis, again with much assistance from Bob Bostick. That theater also succeeded, and with the help of associates like Louie Weaver, Kemmons kept expanding over the next several years until he owned 11 movie theaters.

In those early ventures, Kemmons invested in things he loved —

popcorn and movies. However, another business in his beginning years as an entrepreneur involved a product even closer to his heart.

"There was an ice-cream store at Madison and Cooper. A fellow named Mack Lewis owned it, and I helped him out for 35 cents an hour and became friends with him. After about six months, he says, 'Kemmons, you are ambitious; you ought to get into the ice-cream business.' I said, 'Mack, I don't have any money. How can I get into the ice-cream business?' " Kemmons recalls.

"He said, 'I can fix it up. I work for the Tuthill Company that manufactures countertop ice-cream machines.' They sold for approximately $3,000, and Mack got 40 percent commission. He told me he would lend me the entire $1,200 commission he would make, and I could take $750 of that and make a 25 percent down payment and use the other $450 to pay the freight and get the machine installed. I gave him a note for $1,200, paying it off at $600 a year for two years. So I bought the machine with nothing down."

After considering various locations, Kemmons rented space in the old Hamby Hotel in Helena, Arkansas. He hired a man to run it, then drove over each week, spending three or four days there before returning to Memphis to be with his mother and take care of his other business interests.

"I had the ice-cream store about two years, and we were fairly successful. I finally sold the business and made about $1,200. I was always blessed with people helping me, like Mack. I think they could see how ambitious I was and how hard I would work," Kemmons says.

In the early '30s, Kemmons was working at least 15 hours a day, "running my pinball machines and my movie theaters and everything else I could get into," he recalls. Then he once again used creative financing to land one of the most profitable of his early businesses.

During this time, he had gotten to know Cy Lynch, a Dallas businessman. Lynch had the Texas and Tennessee distributorships for a line of phonographs called Seeburg. Kemmons first met Lynch when Kemmons became the Seeburg dealer for Memphis, working under

Lynch. Seeburg was a strong number two in the phonograph industry behind Wurlitzer, a brand Kemmons would begin selling later.

Lynch was also involved in cigarette sales. One day in 1933, he called Kemmons and said it was no longer worthwhile for him to operate the 110 cigarette machines he had in Memphis, because he couldn't keep an eye on the operation. He asked Kemmons if he was interested in buying the machines. Kemmons said he was, except that he didn't have the money to pay for them. Lynch offered to sell the machines on credit, and Kemmons said he would be in Dallas in the morning.

Kemmons drove all night and was sitting in Lynch's office by 9 a.m. They quickly agreed on the price of $110 each for the machines.

Then Lynch said, "Well, how are you going to pay for the cigarettes?"

"What do you mean, how am I going to pay? I told you I didn't have any money," Kemmons replied.

"Well, this is different. Cigarettes are just like money," Lynch said. "There are $8,000 worth of cigarettes in those machines, and I have got to have the cash for them."

A disappointed Kemmons said, "Mr. Lynch, I'm sorry I wasted your time and mine, but I don't have any way in the world to get $8,000."

He started the long drive back to Memphis, "just thinking all the time." About 15 miles out of Dallas, it occurred to him to find a pay phone and call Toots Loeb, a friend of his who owned the Memphis Tobacco Company. After feeding $4.75 worth of change into the phone, Kemmons reached his friend.

"Toots, I think I'm going to be a big customer of yours. I'm talking about buying 110 cigarette machines, and I'd like to do business with you," Kemmons said.

"Boy, I'd like to do business with you," Loeb said.

"I've got an idea. Will you give me 10 days credit?"

"Yes sir, I will."

"I'll be in to see you tomorrow."

Turning the car around, Kemmons raced back to save the deal with Cy Lynch, and was in his office again within an hour of the time he had left.

"Mr. Lynch, I thought of something I can do. I talked to my friend at Memphis Tobacco Company and he said he will give me 10 days credit. So I will give you 10 checks, dated one day apart, for $800 apiece. Now, the money is not in my bank account, but I will check those machines two and three times a day to make the checks good," Kemmons said, recounting his unconventional pitch. By giving Lynch the 10 checks for $800 each, he had paid him all the $8,000 due for the cigarettes. Kemmons explained to Lynch that the Memphis Tobacco Company would give him 10 days credit. With the 10-day terms given to Kemmons, he now owed the money he had given Lynch to Loeb.

"He said he would do it, so I sat down and wrote those 10 checks. And I went back and bought my cigarettes from Toots. And I paid off every one of those $800 checks. Not a one of them ever came back.

"So, again with no money, I had another new business."

Very soon, Kemmons would make his most significant discovery about financing — through an embarrassing mistake. And this would lead him into what would become the core of his empire: the construction business.

"There is nothing more exciting in the world than to create something, to dig a foundation, to build a building on it," he says.

"Nothing ever gave me more satisfaction than to go out and buy a piece of land, put the streets in, build the houses, see families move in and children be born. That's really something. Nobody who makes money out of the stock market can ever get that thrill."

Kemmons' mother had always told him how much she would like a home of her own. By 1933, at the age of 20, he had saved enough money to build Doll a house at 6241 Poplar Avenue. Kemmons paid cash, $1,000 for the lot and $1,700 for the house. His 1,000 feet of frontage on Poplar was then so undeveloped it was practically rural. Today, the area is one of the busiest and most densely developed business corridors in Memphis. Kemmons owns a bank located on the very same property he originally bought for his mother's house, though he no longer owns the real estate. He rents from the current owners of the property, which also features Poplar Towers, a 10-story office building, and several other buildings.

About three years after he built Doll's house, Kemmons had a chance to land the regional dealership for Wurlitzer jukeboxes, which required him to stock $6,500 worth of jukeboxes up front. He called his friend, Bayard Boyle of Boyle Investment Company, and said he wanted to see if he could borrow $6,500 on the house on Poplar. Bayard came by early the next morning with his tape measure in hand to check out the house.

He said, "Kemmons, this is a nice little house. I think I can get you a loan for $6,500 on it. But you will have to get a survey."

"I said, 'Survey? What's a survey?' " Kemmons recalls, chuckling at the memory.

Bayard told him a survey was required to legally establish where the property was situated. So Kemmons got a surveyor out to take care of the matter, only to make an even more mortifying discovery. He had built his mother's house on a different lot from the one he had purchased.

Fortunately, Charles G. Smith, who had sold Kemmons his lot, was "the nicest old gentleman you ever knew" and lived across the street.

"I went over to his house and asked him if he would come out and show me again where my lot was. We walked across Poplar, which had no traffic at all back then. He stepped off the lot for me and said my house was right in the middle of my lot. But I explained that somehow I had actually gotten the deed for another lot," Kemmons remembers.

"And he just said, 'Well that's no problem. We'll just switch deeds.' "

So they did and Kemmons got the $6,500 loan and bought the Wurlitzer distributorship. It turned out to be one of the best of his early investments. In almost no time, Kemmons won a $10,000 prize for selling more Wurlitzers than anyone in the United States, on a per-capita basis. The company sent Lawrence Welk to Memphis to present him with the check.

But arranging that loan had given Kemmons Wilson something much greater than a jukebox business. A realization had come to him that would change the course of his business interests as much as any other insight of his career.

"I said, 'If you can buy a lot for $1,000, build a house for $1,700, and then borrow $6,500 on it, that's the business I want to be in,' "

Kemmons remembers vividly. "So that day I became a homebuilder."

He knew he had discovered a formula that could be used to finance almost any deal, no matter how big. With enough debt leverage, you could make every dollar work like 10. "Leverage is everything, and you can only make money if you use other people's money. You never have to be afraid of going into debt," he explains.

So it did not worry Kemmons for a minute that he knew almost nothing about building houses. "No job is too hard as long as you are smart enough to find someone else to do it for you. You find a fellow who can frame a house, another fellow who can do the plumbing. You just sub everything out," he says.

The man Kemmons credits most with helping him in the homebuilding business is Raymond Williams, who served as his general superintendent for many years. Kemmons calls Williams "a great carpenter and a great human being." Some years, they built hundreds and hundreds of houses. Kemmons bought a lumberyard so he could purchase all the materials wholesale.

Even though Kemmons was no homebuilding expert, he soon made a discovery that sounds obvious in retrospect, but which gave him a solid edge in the business for many years.

"I always sold my houses easier than anybody else because I found one secret. I think most everybody knows it now. The space in the middle doesn't cost anywhere near as much as the space around the outside of the house. Back in those days, it was costing something in the neighborhood of probably $4 a square foot to build a house. But you could increase the size of the house and get extra footage in there for maybe $2 a square foot. When you take a 1,000-square-foot house and simply make all the rooms larger, so that the house is 1,500 square feet, you do not change the cost of the plumbing, wiring, doors, windows and other things. That is why the cost of each additional square foot comes down," he explains.

"So I always built a house that was larger than anybody else's and sold it for about the same price. That was what I did. Anybody who had any common sense would know that would be true. I think the Lord blessed me with better common sense than most anybody in the world."

Kemmons' earlier discovery about leverage from the collateral value of real estate also led him to begin buying up property as fast as he could find good deals. In the 1930s, there were plenty to be found.

"It was so bad back then in the Depression, the insurance companies and the banks had repossessed all these houses and apartments. Well, I found out they really wanted to sell those things and get them off their books. They weren't making any money off them without someone living in them," he recounts.

"They would sell them for 10 percent down. I cut that in half by becoming a real-estate agent and getting a 5 percent commission on the sale. So actually I only had to pay 5 percent down. I bought many a good apartment building for $1,500 or $2,000 per unit."

By the end of that decade, Kemmons had bought up more than $4 million worth of property in Memphis. He was no longer a poor boy with a popcorn machine.

Before turning 30, he had transformed himself into one of the city's most resolute young businessmen on the rise, with an empire that included real estate, cigarette and pinball machines, jukebox sales and movie theaters. The sight of Kemmons Wilson hustling around town in his Chevy pickup, day and night, to keep up with all his enterprises had become a familiar one.

Amidst all the wheeling and dealing, Kemmons finally found time — but just barely — to get married. He was in too big a hurry to begin wedded life with a real vacation, so he combined business with pleasure on his honeymoon.

"When he proposed, Kemmons said if I wanted a honeymoon, I'd have to go along to New Orleans with him," Dorothy recalls. "He had to go to a Wurlitzer convention there and he couldn't take time off to go anywhere else."

So on the evening of December 2, 1941, Dorothy and Kemmons married in the parsonage at Galloway Methodist Church at Cooper and Walker, where Dorothy was a member. However, she almost didn't make it to her own wedding. An error at her bookkeeping job at the William Len Hotel kept her working long past quitting time.

"There was a discrepancy in our total that evening, and we had to have all our books balanced before we left. We had to find the mistake. So I worked almost up until time for the wedding. I just barely had time to go home and shower and get to the minister's home," she remembers.

After the wedding, they headed for a party at The Peabody until about 11 that night. Then it was time to depart for New Orleans and the Wurlitzer convention. The newlyweds went down to Central Station and caught the Panama Limited heading south at midnight.

In New Orleans, they checked into the Roosevelt Hotel. The next day the convention started, and Kemmons jumped into it with his trademark enthusiasm, shaking hands, making pals, working the room tirelessly.

"Saturday night, December 6, they had a big party for everyone. I took my new bride and we danced and had a big time," Kemmons relates.

Early the next morning, the Wilsons were awakened by the ringing phone. Kemmons picked it up and heard the voice of a fellow convention-goer he had lived it up with the night before.

"Kemmons, we are at war," he said.

"For crying out loud! I'm on my honeymoon," replied an irate Kemmons before he slammed the phone down.

A few moments later, the phone rang again. This time, his friend simply said, "Turn on your radio."

"So I turned the radio on," Kemmons remembers. "And that's when I found out about Pearl Harbor."

CHAPTER FOUR

——FLYING THE HUMP——

"A person has to take risks to achieve."

Kemmons Wilson

$\mathcal{A}$fter the Japanese attack on the U.S. naval fleet at Pearl Harbor, America went to war with Japan and its Axis partners, Germany and Italy. World War II would soon change the lives of every American.

Kemmons knew he would answer the call of duty. But in the meantime, he had business to tend to around Memphis. One of the first things he did after his honeymoon was to return home and open the new movie theater he had built on Airways Avenue. He made it a true family operation, installing Dorothy behind the ticket window and Doll at the candy counter. Kemmons took up the tickets himself. "Low overhead," he recalls with a grin. Dorothy worked there until a few weeks before their first child, Spence, arrived in late 1942.

By then, Kemmons had logged around 200 hours of flying time, so he wanted to get into the Air Force as a pilot. The military desperately needed flyers, and it needed them fast. So the requirements to qualify for a set of wings were somewhat less elaborate than in today's Air Force, to say the least.

"I had some vending machines out at the Fourth Ferrying Group [a base for the Air Force's Air Transport Command] in Memphis, and I had met all the people out there. There was a Lt. Col. Earl Johnson, who was the head of the base. He said, 'Kemmons if you will go on and enlist and go to Fort Oglethorpe, Georgia, I can get you pulled back in here. If you can pass the test, you can become a flight officer in the Air Transport Command.' "

Passing the written part of the test proved no problem. But then came the check flight.

"I had never flown anything except that old plane Jack and I had, with its little 38-horsepower engine. And here I had to go out and fly an AT6 trainer now, which had 650 horsepower," says Kemmons, shaking his head at the memory.

"Capt. Bud Baron was designated to give me my flight check. I'll never forget him if I live a million years. We took it up and went through some maneuvers. Then he said, 'All right, let's see how you can land it.'

"So I gave it a try, and I must have bounced that thing 20 feet in the air. He grabbed the stick and took over til he got us back on track. The second time I landed it, I did a fairly decent job. The third time, I guess it was passable.

"Baron said, 'Well, you're sure not much of a pilot, but I don't believe you will kill yourself.' So he signed my form and I became a flight officer in the U.S. Air Transport Command."

For a couple of years, Kemmons was stationed in Memphis with the Fourth Ferrying Group, piloting different types of planes to various stateside destinations. Soon though, he knew he would be assigned to more distant duty in the war. So before he could depart Memphis, Kemmons faced some hard decisions about his business holdings. He had built an impressive and valuable array of enterprises and real estate, especially for someone who started with absolutely nothing barely a decade before. One of the poorest boys in town had become a wealthy man. But he was also leveraged to the hilt, carrying some $3 million in debt.

As long as he was around to stay on top of things, the debt never worried Kemmons for a second. However, now that the war was about to take him to the other side of the world, he grew anxious at the thought of leaving so many loose ends behind. A second son, Bob, would arrive in 1944, and Kemmons knew Dorothy and Doll would have their hands full taking care of two young children. He didn't want them burdened with managing the numerous properties and businesses he had accumulated.

"I was afraid of all the debt I was carrying. That's a lot of debt to leave on a young bride and a mother. So I sold everything I had and wound up with about $250,000 cash, free and clear, which I invested in war bonds. It was the worst mistake I ever made. If I had just held onto it all, the equity would have doubled or tripled by the time I got back," Kemmons says.

In 1944, at the age of 31, Kemmons left everything behind and went off to join the war. Before being sent abroad, he had to put in a few months at Rosecrans Field in St. Joseph, Missouri, to get instrument training.

While there, Kemmons, and his young family shared a house with the young family of Stuart Tribble, whom Kemmons had met waiting in line to find off-base housing. The couples began a lifelong friendship. Then his orders came through. In 1944, the Air Force sent Kemmons halfway around the planet to participate in one of the most-crucial but lesser-known air operations of World War II.

It was called "The Hump Airlift." It has been described as "a military miracle ... that saved one-fifth of the world's people" in *Flying the Hump*, a history of the operation written by Otha C. Spencer. The airlift was designed to keep China in the war on the side of the U.S. and its Allies against Japan. However, the Japanese had captured enough of China to control virtually all access to it. The only way into China consisted of a few barely-negotiable air routes from India's British-held Upper Assam Valley, across the Himalayan Mountains, over the jungles of Burma and into Southeast China. The corridors became known as The Hump, "the most dangerous routes in all of the operations of the Allied Air Forces," according to Spencer.

Without the airlift, China could never have stayed in the war, a crucial element in the Allied strategy to defeat Japan. At a reunion of Hump pilots some 40 years after the war, Chinese General Y.T. Loh recounted in somewhat broken English the dire situation confronting China's forces:

> The Japanese took all our ports. We can't do anything.
> ... We have nothing, not even a drop of gasoline. Later
> comes the Hump pilots. ... the U.S. have its big army,

yes, very good ... but the most important factor was you have some young, wonderful Hump pilots to bring supplies over there. Otherwise, we wouldn't make it.

Kemmons was one of those pilots. He shared a tent with a couple of buddies he met back in the States, the late Leo W. "Mitch" Mitchell and Elton F. Duncan Jr., who now lives in Rock Hill, South Carolina.

"Kemmons was a real good pilot," recalls Duncan. "He was very likable, a really unusual personality. He was always happy and well-met. I was single, but Kemmons and Mitch were married. I was a young fellow on the loose, so they kept me out of trouble. We would go out on the town together all the time, but neither one of them ever chased the girls. I have seen Kemmons take a drink, but I have never seen him drunk."

The similarities in the three men were remarkable. Elton says all three men wore the same sizes, except that his pants were a little longer. So whenever the laundry came back, whoever got to it first would just grab what he needed and stamp his name on it. After the war, Dorothy would laugh about clothes Kemmons brought home that had each of the three men's names stamped on it.

Mitchell was also married to a woman named Dorothy, and later, Duncan married a woman named Dorothy as well. As the three couples stayed in touch over the years, they kept the three women straight by calling Kemmons' wife Dorothy, Mitchell's wife Dot and Duncan's wife Dottie.

Flying the C-47 "Gooney Bird" and the C-46 "Old Dumbo" — so nicknamed for their bulk and lack of speed — over The Hump was "the most dangerous, terrifying, barbarous aerial transport run in the world," wrote authors Theodore White and Annalee Jacoby in *Thunder Out of China*. Herbert F. Feis in *The China Tangle* called the operation "the greatest effort of its kind in the war."

Every flight was an exercise in peril. With their slow, clumsy, unarmed aircraft always overloaded with barrels of fuel or other cargo on the long flights, the crews negotiated the brutal, unpredictable weather of the mighty Himalayas and the remote, steamy jungles. It meant flying regularly through violent rain squalls of monsoon season, crippling ice storms, the lash of hundred-mile-an-hour crosswinds and the turbulence of crushing downdrafts and updrafts. So many planes went down into the snowy peaks and dense jungles below, the string of wreckage became known as The Aluminum Trail. More than 600 transport planes and 1,000 crewmen were lost before the war ended.

"You didn't come back on your own. The good Lord brought you back," Duncan says.

But those who made it through established nothing less than a modern branch of military science. "Air crews of The Hump perfected a new idea in warfare: airlifting supplies and men on a grand scale," Spencer writes. What those crews learned "later saved Berlin with its airlift and taught the army how to move troops and evacuate the wounded by air in the Korean and Vietnam wars."

While Kemmons was stationed in that part of India, he flew C-47s along the leg of the route that stretched from an airfield called Dum Dum near Calcutta to another air field at Chabua. He has never forgotten the nerve-wracking route.

"We flew through a mountain pass where the mountain ranges were only eight miles apart. The Himalayas on one side were about 17,000 feet high, and the Naga Hills were about 10,000 feet high on the other," Kemmons recalls.

"It was scary as hell, believe me. Only the lucky came home. When you are flying a pass eight miles wide, you only have to be off course two minutes and you are dead. If you turn the wrong direction, it doesn't take long to cover four miles. It was wild."

Not even the trials of wartime stopped Kemmons from keeping an eye out for promising new business deals back home. While in that remote corner of the world, he kept making his plans for the minute he returned to Memphis.

A fellow airman whom Kemmons got to know in India owned the Georgia franchise for a new soft drink called Orange Crush. Every time one of his monthly franchise statements arrived in the mail, he would show it to Kemmons, who was astounded by the profits. Every statement seemed more spectacular than the last. Orange Crush,

Kemmons determined, would be the first new venture he got into after the war

"That guy was making money hand over fist. I told him when I left India, the first thing I was going to do when I got home was get an Orange Crush franchise in Memphis," Kemmons recalls.

After his discharge, he arrived back in Memphis on a Friday in November of 1945. The following Monday morning, he was sitting in the Chicago offices for Orange Crush, still in uniform. He insisted the company should take the franchise for Memphis back from the present owners and sell it to him. He argued that the present distributors also held the Pepsi franchise for Memphis, and thus were dividing their loyalties. Kemmons promised to devote all his attention to Orange Crush. He persuaded the company to see things his way, and he returned to Memphis and spent $150,000 building a bottling plant in Memphis.

Despite his best efforts, Orange Crush turned out to be one of the worst investments Kemmons ever made. In time, he learned the reason his Air Force acquaintance made all that money during the war: His firm had managed to land a huge sugar allotment from the government, at a time when sugar was being tightly rationed on the homefront.

"I don't remember that guy's name, but I wish I had never seen him. He didn't tell me he had an almost unlimited supply of sugar," Kemmons says.

"During the war, people would drink anything they could get that had sugar in it. But a year and a half after I got my franchise, I couldn't even get my wife and children to drink Orange Crush. After the war, everyone just wanted to drink Coca-Cola. I lost a ton of money on that."

Despite the disastrous Orange Crush deal, Kemmons was soon making good money again building houses. As the postwar boom returned America to a consumer economy, and the Baby Boom spawned an insatiable market for family housing, Kemmons was soon selling houses as fast as he could build them.

At first, many were simple, neat, three-bedroom houses in the $7,000-$12,000 range, aimed at a working-class market. A buyer could get into an $11,000 home, for example, for $700 down and $69 a month. However, as postwar prosperity expanded, Kemmons got more into the mid-range of the market, and sometimes the high end. He was one of the first homebuilders in Memphis to equip his houses with air-conditioning. He also built warehouses, commercial buildings and apartment buildings during this period. And as usual, Kemmons found every angle to expand his profits. He started an insurance firm, for instance, because he discovered he could insure his houses and buildings at a discount that way. It soon became quite successful on its own.

Kemmons always likes to say he remembers the first million dollars he owed better than the first million he owned. Nonetheless, with his construction operation at the heart of his business empire, he made himself into a millionaire before Holiday Inn ever entered his mind. He could have enjoyed considerable affluence for himself and his family if he had just kept putting up houses and other structures around Memphis for the rest of his life. A newspaper article published in the summer before the first Holiday Inn opened called him "one of the most spectacular builders in this city." Another alluded to his "meteoric up-by-the-bootstraps rise in the building field."

And Kemmons' family grew as rapidly as his fortune. Kem arrived in 1946, Betty in 1948, and Carole in 1949. That gave Kemmons and Dorothy five rambunctious young children, all blue-eyed like their parents.

Before they got married, Kemmons had always told Dorothy he wanted a houseful of children. And not long after returning from the war, he realized he was going to need a bigger house.

CHAPTER FIVE

——EVEN THE MISTAKES PAY OFF——

"Mental attitude plays a far more important role in a person's success or failure than mental capacity."

Kemmons Wilson

*T*he first home Kemmons built for his family after the war was a white-brick, three-bedroom house on Galloway Drive in what was then known as the Red Acres Subdivision. It was a pleasant, wooded area located in what were then the eastern suburbs of Memphis, in the direction where the city was growing. When the house was completed in 1947, it was the young family's nicest home to date.

Kemmons' house sat on one of three adjacent lots he had bought from former City Judge Albert Carruthers. The judge also owned a fourth lot in the same parcel, and six months earlier had sold it to another man.

A few months after the Wilsons moved in, Wallace Johnson happened to be doing some business at city hall. Wallace was a fellow homebuilder and a friend of Kemmons', who would become his partner in Holiday Inn several years later. While at city hall, he overheard a conversation between a clerk in the tax assessor's office and a man who was demanding to know why his taxes had gone up so much.

"Well, it's very simple," the clerk said after he had checked the records. "You built a house on that lot of yours."

"I didn't build any house," the man replied. "I pass that lot every day on my way to work, and I can guarantee you there is no house on my lot."

Wallace did not enter the conversation, but he heard enough to figure out what had happened. Later, he called Kemmons with some unwelcome news.

"Kemmons, you have built your house on the wrong lot," he said.

"Wallace, I built one house on the wrong lot out on Poplar. I sure wouldn't do it again."

"Well, you have anyway," Wallace replied.

The property in question had been recorded with the city as Lots 1, 2, 3, 4, beginning at the west end. But when Judge Carruthers sold the lots, he mistakenly numbered them from the east end. Thus, when Kemmons thought he bought lots 2, 3, 4 he actually got 1, 2, 3. The other man owned the real Lot 4. But that was the one where Kemmons chose to build his house. And as with most everything he did, he built it in a hurry.

"Now, I knew what a survey was by this time," Kemmons recalls. "But I called every surveyor in Memphis, and they were all too busy. Nobody could get out there for about eight weeks. I said 'Why, I can build a house in eight weeks.' So I went ahead without the survey."

He tried to straighten out the matter the same way he had the first time he built a house on someone else's property, by simply swapping deeds. This time, however, the landowners were not quite so agreeable.

"The guy said, 'Well, that's fine, we'll just switch deeds and that will solve the problem.' But he went home and his wife said, 'No sir, you're not going to switch any deed. That's our house. It's built on our lot,' " Kemmons remembers.

"I think he was a good man, but his wife really thought she had something. I had my lawyer, John Martin, talk to him, and the man finally said, 'I tell you what I'll do. I paid $1,500 for that lot. If you will give me $2,250, I'll take it.' So I paid him for his lot and then I owned all four of them. So I'm awfully happy I made that mistake, or I never would have gotten that other lot.

"But I ought to be in the Guinness Book of Records for building my own house on the wrong lot two different times."

Three years after moving into that house, the family had outgrown it. So Kemmons decided to use the other three lots next to it to build a house the family would never outgrow.

But it would not be a mansion. Neither Dorothy nor Kemmons ever wanted one. Mainly they just wanted big, open rooms, with all the space ever needed for five growing children — and many years later, for the frequent visits of 14 grandchildren. Their vision took shape: a marbled-brick, six-bedroom, ranch-style house with ivy framing the white shutters, a sweeping, circular driveway and, later, a swimming pool. Kemmons and Dorothy have lived there ever since, and he insists they will never live anywhere else.

As for the smaller house next door, originally built on another man's lot, Kemmons as usual found a shrewd angle on selling it.

"My accountant, Roy Scott, a CPA, was also a lawyer and one of the smartest guys I ever met. He could answer any question I wanted to ask. I was building this house we live in now, and he came over to see me one night," Kemmons recalls.

"You know I'm getting ready to move into my new house and I want to sell you this one, Roy," Kemmons told him.

"Oh no, Kemmons, I couldn't afford a house like this," Scott quickly said.

"You can sure afford this one. I tell you what I am going to do. I'll sell it to you for $12,500, and you can pay me for it any way you want to."

"You've got to be kidding. Why would you do such a thing as that?"

"Because I want you next door," Kemmons responded, "so I can come over and ask you questions every night. I'll get way more out of the house that way."

Today Kemmons reflects, "So Roy bought the house and lived there until he died. He willed the house to his daughter, Shirley Philyaw, who lived there until she died. In 1994 the estate sold the house to a couple for $225,000, who then tore it down. They are now building a new house there next to my current home."

In Memphis in the early 1950s, the unique strains of diverse regional music were percolating together into a new sound that would soon shake the world.

For many years, blues musicians had moved up to Memphis from the Mississippi River Delta where the music first took form. However by the '50s, they were beginning to be heard beyond the juke joints of Beale Street. When younger musicians learned to rev up blues chords with electric guitars and to work in rhythms from other musical styles such as country and bluegrass, something brand new and revolutionary was born in Memphis. Rock and roll was here to stay.

During that time, Kemmons got to know another hustling young Memphis entrepreneur who would play a pivotal role in that definitive musical era. Many young entrepreneurs came to him for money, because Kemmons was becoming known as a guy who would finance anything if they could convince him of the merit in the deal. So Sam Phillips came to see Kemmons one day and told him he had an idea for a unique new radio station, if he could raise $25,000. Kemmons decided it was worth a try and put up the $25,000 for Phillips, with the agreement that when Phillips paid the money back, they would each become half-owners of the station.

"The station turned out to be real successful. It was a novelty called WHER. Sam had girl engineers, girl announcers, girl everything," Kemmons recalls.

Later, it also gave Kemmons the idea to hire Dotty Abbott, one of the announcers at WHER, for another radio venture of his.

"I decided I wanted to have a show I called *Music to Make Love By*. Pretty good name, isn't it? I went to WMC, which closed at midnight at that time, and made a deal to lease their station from midnight to 6 in the morning for $1,000 a month. I told Dotty the music I wanted her to play had to be a woman singing to a man or a man singing to a woman, real sweet and soft romantic music," he says.

"Boy, she really did a fantastic job. We used to get mail by the sackloads. All these truckers driving all night long would write her love letters, and tell her they wanted to marry her. She got letters from as far away as California and Massachusetts."

However, it was Kemmons' assessment of another personality associated with Sam Phillips that showed Kemmons could be wrong in as big a way as he could be right. Phillips, of course, has gone down in history as the man who first recorded Elvis Presley. At his now legendary Sun Records Studio on Union Avenue in the 1950s, Phillips also launched the careers of stars like Carl Perkins, Jerry Lee Lewis, Roy Orbison and Johnny Cash.

For many years though, Sun was only a struggling, shoestring operation for Phillips, in an age when rock was more of a budding novelty than the multi-billion-dollar industry it would later become. To help pay the bills, Phillips operated the Memphis Recording Service in the same small storefront space as Sun. Anyone who wanted to hear what they sounded like on a phonograph record could walk in, plunk down four bucks and have a professional recording made.

In the summer of 1953, Presley — then a shy, 18-year-old truck driver — stopped by to record a couple of ballads for his mother, as the story goes. It led to Phillips recording Elvis' first single, *That's All Right*, a year later, and 18 more songs. Many fans consider the Sun recordings Presley's best work.

But he was still best known as an unconventional regional performer, not the King of Rock and Roll, when RCA offered to buy the rights to Elvis from Phillips for $35,000 in 1955. At the time, Phillips needed the money. He had a half-dozen or so other young rockers with star potential he wanted to promote, but lacked the finances to do so. Should he hang onto Elvis, or take the money?

Late on the night he had to decide, Phillips called Kemmons and got him out of bed. He told Kemmons he really needed his opinion on the matter. Without hesitating, Kemmons said that Elvis was a nice young man, but there was no doubt what Sam should do.

"$35,000 for a performer who is not even a professional? I'd sell that contract!" Kemmons exclaimed.

Elvis would go on to become the most successful recording artist in history. And ever since, Kemmons has had to live down what must have been the worst advice he ever gave.

However, the absurdity of that advice became apparent mostly with hindsight. At the time, Kemmons' advice made a lot more sense. The $35,000 figure was actually the asking price Phillips had set, thinking it far too high for anyone to meet. Phillips recalls that the contract for Frankie Lane, then a much bigger star than Elvis, had just been sold by Mercury Records to Columbia Records for only $25,000. In fact,

$35,000 was the highest amount ever paid for an entertainer at that time, and RCA considered its acquisition of Elvis a huge gamble.

And as Phillips has often reminded people, he *really* needed the cash. He had completed the recording of Carl Perkins' new single, *Blue Suede Shoes*, and believed it could become a big hit. The only problem was Sun did not have the resources to get it manufactured and on the market nationally, an expensive proposition for a tiny record label. The money Phillips got for selling Elvis not only enabled him to release *Blue Suede Shoes* and have a huge, classic hit with it, it also provided the seed money for him to launch many of the other performers who got their start at Sun.

Nor did it sour Phillips' and Kemmons' relationship. They have remained close friends and occasional business partners. For a time in the late '60s, they even operated a recording studio and label together called Holiday Inn Records. "I have always felt very close to Kemmons, almost like a brother," Phillips says. "We are both hardheaded and we have had some pretty damn good discussions and differences. But we have never had a personal fight on anything. He's still an incredible guy to pick his brain."

Before his untimely death in 1977, Elvis enjoyed ribbing Kemmons about his advice. The two men did not really know each other when Elvis was with Sun. But in later years, they became acquainted and ran into each other from time to time.

"Every time Elvis saw me, he put his arm around me and said, 'Boss, you made a big mistake, didn't you?' " Kemmons recalls. "And I always said, 'I sure did.' "

Kemmons remains the first to laugh about his fiascos, and probably tells such stories on himself as often as anyone. He never worries about yesterday's mistakes, mainly because he always knows he will have a new idea to look forward to tomorrow.

And as the summer of 1951 approached, Kemmons Wilson was about to come upon the biggest idea of his life.

CHAPTER SIX

–THE VACATION THAT CHANGED THE WORLD–

**"I like to think that I'm so normal that anything I like,
everybody else is going to like too."**

Kemmons Wilson

$\mathscr{P}$erhaps the ultimate irony of the Kemmons Wilson story is that a man who almost never takes a holiday or a vacation got the idea for Holiday Inn while on a vacation.

Even today, nearly two decades after his official retirement, he can barely stand to take anything resembling a vacation — unless it includes the opportunity for real-estate or other business dealings. But in 1951, it was even more difficult to pry him away from all the work he had going in Memphis. He was still very much the driven young man who considered 16-hour workdays routine and could only squeeze in time for his honeymoon during a business convention.

His son, Bob, recalls, "One of the first things I can remember from growing up is that on vacations, Pop was always working. We had fun, but he wasn't there much. When he was, he was always working on something, trying to figure out some deal or looking at some land."

But somehow, in the summer of 1951, Dorothy persuaded Kemmons to load up their five youngsters and Doll in their big Oldsmobile and motor off to see the sights of Washington D.C.

"Dorothy had been bugging me about how she wanted to take our children to Washington. She wanted them to see the places where our government was. She kept on until I said, 'Well, I'll do it.' So we took off about 10 days, drove up there and saw all the sights in

Washington," Kemmons recalls.

"We had so much luggage we couldn't get it all in the car, so we put a rack up on top and strapped the luggage on it. We looked like a bunch of gypsies going down the road. We had just started out, and Bob said he needed to tell his mother something. She said, 'No, no, just sit back there right now and be quiet.' Finally a car pulled up beside us and told us we had lost a suitcase off the top. Bob said, 'I was trying to tell you, but you wouldn't listen.' So we had to go back and gather up all the clothes, which had tar all over them from lying in the road."

Today, the Wilson children have few specific memories of the '51 vacation, other than having a fun time. They were, after all, still very young; the oldest was eight — the youngest, two. For them, it was an adventurous outing, not a week that would change the world. Dorothy mainly remembers taking care of all those children. And Kemmons, as always, was in too much of a hurry to keep track of the details.

"I remember Dad usually drove faster than he should," Spence, the oldest, recalls. "But it always impressed me that he could usually talk his way out of a speeding ticket when he got stopped. It was very rare for Dad to get a ticket."

While in Washington, the Wilsons stayed with the family of Frank Perper, a longtime friend who lived there. In what would add a twist of a footnote to the story years later, Perper became a Holiday Inn franchisee.

However, the part of that vacation that turned out to be so immensely significant had nothing to do with the friends and sights the Wilsons saw that summer. What did lead to revelation had a lot to do with the workaholic disposition that shaped Kemmons' way of thinking. Quite possibly, if he had been like most 38-year-old family men at the time, he would already have endured enough vacations to take for granted the realities of such trips. He might well have regarded shoddy accommodations and extra charges for children as inevitable circumstances — not the opportunity of a lifetime.

But for a man who had spent his life in constant labor and relentless pursuit of any angle in sight, the preposterous cost and inconvenience of lodging a family stood out like, well, just like a 50-foot-tall, green-and-yellow, flashing-neon road sign.

"When you had five children, it got very expensive," Dorothy recalls. "Kemmons looked at me and said, 'Dorothy, you know, the average person just can't afford a vacation, especially with a big family. I'm going to do something about it.' "

The Wilsons were a close family, and Kemmons was always looking to save a dollar, Spence says. When they stopped at a motel for the night, they would all share one room, with the boys bedding down on the floor in sleeping bags. And since they were all in the same room, to Kemmons' mind, they should only have to pay the standard charge for one room.

"But everywhere we stopped, they charged an extra $2 for each child who stayed in the room. A room was only about $6-8 in those days. I had five children, so my $6 room became $16, or my $8 room became $18. I told Dorothy that wasn't fair."

Again, Kemmons certainly couldn't have been the first father of that era to grow aggravated at the way he was gouged by such practices. But with most families, such a tempest would simply play itself out as one more round of the usual vacation routine: Dad blows his stack again over something no one can change, and after a while, all is forgotten and life goes on the same.

However, on this vacation, Dad was a man who interpreted the entire spectrum of life in terms of its business potential. He didn't just get mad. He figured lots of other fathers were getting mad too. And he figured he could solve the problem for them, and make a lot of money off the deal. This time, the moment did not pass in the rush of daily family chaos. The wheels started turning in Kemmon's head. Before he was done, the modern American motel chain was born.

"I don't take many vacations, but as I took this one I realized how many families there were taking vacations, and how they needed a nice place they could stay," Kemmons says.

"I told Dorothy, 'I'm going to go home and build a chain of motels that will never charge for children as long as they stay in the same room as their parents.' "

It's not hard to understand Dorothy failing to jump up and down in response to Kemmons' grand announcement. Consider that she was riding along in the August heat in an un-airconditioned automobile with five young children and two other adults. At that moment, she had just a few other demands on her attention.

"Well, how many are you going to build?" she asked.

After a moment's thought, he replied, "Oh, about 400 ought to do it."

Kemmons has claimed ever since that Dorothy made light of him for considering such an outlandish scheme.

"She laughed at me, and that's what made me mad and made me do it, I think," Kemmons insists.

"I think he exaggerates," Dorothy counters. "I probably questioned him. I couldn't imagine 400, I admit that. But I don't think I really laughed."

Whatever the case, Kemmons had not just plucked the figure of 400 out of thin air. He had made an instant calculation of how many motels he really thought it would take to blanket the nation, if he built one every day's drive apart.

"I thought it was about 3,500 miles across the country east to west, and about 2,500 miles north to south. I figured there were maybe 10 major roads in each direction. And I divided the length of each of those roads by 150 miles, thinking if you wanted to drive 150 miles in a day, or 300 or 450, it wouldn't matter," Kemmons says.

"So that was how I got the 400 figure. It was just a snap judgment I made in the car, driving and talking."

Dorothy's skepticism was certainly justified. There wasn't anything remotely close to a 400-motel lodging chain in the world at that time. In an article published not long before the Wilson's 1951 vacation, *The Wall Street Journal* estimated there were only about 20,000 roadside lodging accommodations of any kind in the entire United States at the time. And a great many of those were little more than "unappetizing roadside camps."

But in Kemmons' mind, that shortcoming was very quickly shaping up as the real opportunity in the whole situation. The motels of the day (as opposed to the upscale hotels located in downtown areas) were not only too expensive for families, they were too often hot, dirty, noisy and cramped. Much of the plumbing was lousy. Few motels had restaurants on the premises, and those that did tended to serve lousy food.

"There really weren't any motels that amounted to anything at that time. They were all 10-, 20-room, mom-and-pop deals. Back in those days, nobody would think about renting a room without going in first to check if it was all right," Kemmons says.

"I told Dorothy I was going to start a chain with a brand name you could trust."

So Kemmons knew from the start exactly what he would put in his motels: the comforts and conveniences that he found lacking. "I like to think that I'm so normal that anything I like, everybody else is going to like too. The idea that my instincts are out of line just doesn't occur to me."

At the same time, the big Wilson vacation of '51 also drove home to him another powerful marketing element of the motel business: the amenities that appealed to children.

He recognized that their happiness was the key to satisfied parents, Dorothy recalls. "He noticed how our kids always wanted to stop where they had a pool. And those were the places we usually did end up stopping."

Kemmons also realized on that trip that at most motels, when the family got hungry they had to pile the kids back in the car and head off somewhere else in search of a place to eat. He knew parents who were already tired from driving all day hated getting back into a hot, cramped car. So, he decided, all his motels would have a family restaurant right on the premises.

While he was doing all this conceptualizing of his dream motel, Kemmons was also doing a lot of measuring. Many years before, he had begun a lifetime habit of carrying a tape measure in his pocket everywhere he went. So for the rest of the vacation trip, Kemmons methodically measured every cranny of every room where he and his family stayed. By the time he got back to Memphis, he had sized up the ideal dimensions for efficiency and comfort so accurately, his formula remains the most widely used more than four decades later.

The perfect motel room, he concluded, should be 12 feet by 18 feet, not counting the the bathroom. That would provide space for two double beds and the chairs and other furniture, and still have open area to move about the room easily.

"And that is still the standard for the world. Nearly everybody in the industry builds most of their rooms like that, even today," Kemmons points out.

Whenever Kemmons builds anything, he first sketches out the floor plans himself. Although he has never had any drafting lessons, he likes to get a rough sketch on paper before he talks to engineers or architects. Once the Wilsons were home again in Memphis after the vacation, Dorothy recalls him sitting in their dining room, sometimes until 2 in the morning, working on the drawings of the motel he had in his head. Then he took them to Eddie Bluestein, a draftsman who did a lot of work for Kemmons.

"I told Eddie exactly what I wanted. I had everything drawn out, in my crude way, with a pencil, but not to scale," Kemmons says.

Eddie Bluestein was a consummate professional. But his greatest contribution on that job did not come from his drafting. It resulted from his happening to turn his television to a channel that was airing *Holiday Inn* on the evening he finished Kemmons' motel plans. The 1942 film didn't have much of a plot, but with Bing Crosby crooning and Fred Astaire dancing, no one cared. And what a name.

Holiday Inn ... hmm ... has a nice ring to it, Bluestein mused. Well, why not? He scribbled the name across the plans and took them to Kemmons the next day. Kemmons asked where he got the name. When Eddie explained, Kemmons went for it immediately.

Obviously, those were simpler times. One can imagine how fast the copyright lawyers would swoop in today if an entrepreneur had a whim to name his new motel chain, say, Jurassic Park Inn. No makers of any recent hit movie would ever allow such a thing, not without extracting hefty licensing fees first. But Kemmons never heard a word from the makers of *Holiday Inn*.

"No one with the movie ever contacted us about us using the name, and we didn't have sense enough to check with them," Kemmons recalls.

"But we had a lot of other people sue us over it later. When we got to be big, everybody figured it was a gravy train. I guess we spent several million dollars to clear them up. You can imagine how many little Holiday Motels and Holiday Houses and places like that there must have been. It was a good name."

CHAPTER SEVEN

──ON HISTORY'S THRESHOLD──

**"Opportunity comes often. It knocks as often as you have
an ear trained to hear it, an eye trained to see it, a hand
trained to grasp it, and a head trained to use it."**

Kemmons Wilson

*A*s for where to build his first motel, Kemmons decided on the
land he owned in front of his lumberyard at 4941 Summer Avenue.

Years later, when Holiday Inn was entering its heyday, Kemmons
would warn a young franchisee never to build on land "just because
you own it." But in Kemmons' case, the land he happened to own on
Summer Avenue was prime real estate for his purposes.

Summer was also Highway 70, the highway from Nashville to
Memphis and the main route into Memphis from the east at that time.
At the time, it was often called "the Broadway of America," because it
was such an important east-west motor route.

Today that stretch of Summer is a six-lane thoroughfare running
through a busy retail and commercial district. But in 1952 when
Kemmons opened his motel there, out on a two-lane highway, it barely
seemed like a part of Memphis.

"That was just way out," says Sam Phillips, who would become one
of the first investors in Holiday Inn when it went public a few years
later. "Everything in Memphis at that time was centered right
downtown. But Kemmons had the vision to say, 'Hey, I'll get them on
the way in.' To me, that was the visionary thing. Most people would
have thought they had to build closer to town, to get the businessman
where he does business."

Kemmons never worried about building so far from the center of town. He believed travelers were already beginning to avoid the old downtown hotels because they were expensive and more difficult to reach at the end of a long day. He believed most people would choose the convenience of a roadside motel, where they only had to pull off the highway and park near their room. A motel chain that not only offered such convenience but also the same quality anywhere you went would hit the jackpot, Kemmons was sure.

He began telling people that the motel business was "the greatest untouched industry in America." Just about everyone, Kemmons figured, had a car and a family and a desire to travel. The modern tourism industry was just coming into existence, centered on the family automobile. Trains were in decline, and planes were still too expensive for most travelers, certainly for young, working families on a budget.

Automobile tourism would be given a huge boost in 1956 with federal approval for construction of the $76 billion interstate-highway network. It would guarantee not only that Americans would travel more, but with its cloverleafs and bypasses, that they would increasingly drive past cities entirely and occupy overnight lodging far from city centers.

Still, in the early '50s, even a 40-room motel was considered pretty large. For Kemmons to get financing for three times that many rooms, he had to sell the idea there was a market for such a thing. In doing so, he emphasized that Memphis was growing faster than the local lodging industry. His research showed that not a single hotel room had been built in the city since 1929. Most importantly, Kemmons promised that a Holiday Inn would not only be a stop along the way, but a destination in itself.

Ultimately, Kemmons utilized for the first time a finance technique called a "takeout commitment," which he would employ countless times in the years to come. Duke Poindexter, a Memphis loan broker, helped Kemmons arrange the financing.

"Duke came to me and said, 'Kemmons, I think I can get you a loan.' He knew I needed money to build my Holiday Inn. That was his business, helping arrange loans in return for a 1 percent commission. So he went to Galveston, Texas, to meet with Mr. Moody, the owner of National General Life, an insurance company there. He took my plans and sold them on the idea this was going to be a good deal. They agreed to loan me $325,000 when the hotel was completed. That is what you call a 'takeout commitment' from them," Kemmons explains.

"With that, I went to Allen Morgan at First Tennessee Bank to borrow $325,000 from the bank. The bank knew it would get its money back because I had the takeout commitment. A bank never wanted to lend money out for any length of time. They didn't mind putting it out for a year or two, but then they wanted it back. Insurance companies made long-term loans. I think my loan with them was for 15 or 20 years at 4 percent.

"That was the first loan of that size I did that way. When I built houses, I borrowed money, but I always had the money to pay it off as soon as I sold the house. But at that point, the loan to build the first Holiday Inn was by far the biggest single loan I had ever had."

He borrowed $325,000 to build the first Holiday Inn, but was able to complete it for $280,000. Over the years, the story has often appeared that it was completed in 90 days. But even though he always worked fast, Kemmons says it wasn't that fast.

"It was closer to six or eight months. I got back off that trip in the summer of '51, and by the time I got the financing, it was early the next year. Raymond Williams, my building superintendent on my houses, built it pretty fast though. When we decided to go into the Holiday Inn business, he built the first four for me in Memphis, and then about another ten," Kemmons recalls.

As much as any element in the construction of that first Holiday Inn, the sign that would stand out front may have been the most crucial to Kemmons. From his years in the movie-theater business, he knew the value of a sign that caught the eye and presented a marquee. He wanted a sign no one could miss, even from a great distance, and from either direction on the highway.

"I called Harold Balton, a friend of mine in the sign business. He came out with George Roberts and I told him I wanted a sign that was at least 50 feet tall. And I wanted a marquee with changeable letters on it so I could welcome different people and groups to the hotel. When he got back with me, he had four or five sketches on there, and one was just a great sign. I said, 'That's it, just like that. Don't change a thing,' " Kemmons says.

"That sign cost $13,000 back then. That was a lot of money to spend on a sign. But I thought it was really necessary. That was about all the advertising I had then."

That first sign read Holiday Inn Hotel Courts. Within a few years, the wording would evolve to Holiday Inn of America. As more and more Holiday Inns opened, the sign would become one of the best known symbols in America, recognizable to any eye long before motorists got close enough to read the lettering. Even children who could not read at all learned to associate the sign with a fun place to stop. To kids, the big green-and-yellow sign translated as: a swimming pool, vending machines, a free ice machine, children's menus in the restaurant and plenty of room to run around. The Wilson children even had their own rhyme:

> I see the sign, the sign sees me
> God bless the sign, and God bless me

The Holiday Inn sign would become known in the company as The Great Sign, its image reproduced on Holiday Inn napkins, placemats, coasters, matchbooks, plastic bags, postcards, clocks and even laundry bags. By 1960, Holiday Inn would establish a department devoted specifically to the care and promotion of the Great Sign, assigned to supervise and maintain rigid standards for all uses of its image.

As the manager for his first Holiday Inn, Kemmons hired Helmut Vogel, who had immigrated to the United States from Germany 14 years before. Trained in Europe in the art of French pastries, Vogel had been the respected head of the pastry department at The Peabody Hotel for several years. But as he learned of Kemmons' plans for Holiday Inn, he grew so enthusiastic about it that he left The Peabody to work for Kemmons.

"He was really a fantastic guy. He read in the paper that I was building a hotel and he came to see me and told me he was the one guy who could run it. I listened to him, and he convinced me, so I hired him," Kemmons remembers.

Vogel's wife, a high-school biology teacher, had died suddenly the year before. He saw the job of Holiday Inn manager as one "where I could lose myself in my work," he told a newspaper reporter shortly after it opened.

Work, he did. Vogel's job performance defined the standard for Holiday Inn managers. When the second Holiday Inn opened, he was promoted to general manager for both. When the third opened, he was given the title of vice president for the company.

To build chairs for the first Holiday Inn, Kemmons hired Ben Gaines, a Memphis upholsterer who had re-covered some furniture for Kemmons' home. At the Holiday Inn, Kemmons furnished the fabric, and Gaines and his wife, Ludie, a seamstress, covered the chairs. "When it came time to determine who owed who how much money, we had no idea," Gaines recalls, "so we decided to become 50-50 partners," beginning a long business relationship and family friendship. Gaines Manufacturing Company grew rapidly and was eventually traded for $8 million worth of stock in United Inns, which was owned by Dr. William B. Cockroft, one of the largest franchise holders of Holiday Inn.

The Holiday Inn on Summer Avenue opened almost exactly a year after Kemmons returned from the vacation to Washington. The official opening date is placed at August 1, 1952. However, Vogel actually started allowing guests to stay in rooms weeks before that.

The giant yellow-and-green sign had gone up out front while construction was still in progress. In no time, people began stopping and asking for rooms. To start building good will with the public, Vogel accommodated them as best he could. If he had a room available with at least carpet and running water in it, he would let guests stay in it for free. If the room also had a mattress and box springs on the floor, he charged them 50 cents. So by the time the first Holiday Inn was completed, it already had developed something of a clientele.

The new hotel's lobby had walls of hunter green, with chartreuse draperies and furniture upholstered in Chinese red. In guest rooms, some 30 different color schemes were employed, meaning no one look would be duplicated in more than four or five rooms.

Once officially open, the motel's original prices were $4 for a single room, $6 for a double. And, as Kemmons had promised, there was no extra charge for children who stayed in the same room with their parents.

"If I never did anything else in the world, I changed everybody on that. At every motel today, children stay free," Kemmons says.

The day of the grand opening made some lasting impressions on Kem Wilson, Kemmons' youngest son. "I was only 6 years old and can remember getting all dressed up but not fully comprehending what the festivities and fanfare were about. I also recall the motel seemed like a gigantic place compared to the ones we had stayed in before. I do vividly remember they said to cut the ribbon on the count of three, but I jumped the gun and cut on two."

Carole, the youngest Wilson child, says, "If you look at the picture, you notice I wasn't paying attention. I was looking back. Mom was probably telling me to quit fidgeting and look at the camera. But we don't really remember much."

Her sister Betty concurs: "Most of what we know about that story is hearsay. I guess mother must have been frantic, getting us all dressed and polishing all the white shoes that day."

The first Holiday Inn was barely open for business before Kemmons was moving on to build more. In the September 1952 full-page newspaper ad in which he announced the open house for the first Holiday Inn, he listed the sites for his next three: Highway 51 South, promised to open the next month; and Highway 61 South and Highway 51 North, both scheduled to open in 1953. True to form, Kemmons managed to defray some of the cost of the ad by selling about a third of the page to other businesses, with a page-width headline thanking them "for their excellent work and cooperation."

Kemmons' schedule of openings proved a bit too ambitious, but not by much. Within a span of less than two years, Kemmons had 448 rooms operating in Memphis, making him a major player in the local lodging market. "A one-man motor court boom began in Memphis," said Hotel World-Review, a weekly publication for the industry.

Kemmons had a strategy to literally corner the local market: "I went out and built three more Holiday Inns in Memphis, one on each corner of the city. So you couldn't come into town without passing one of my places."

When the third Holiday Inn opened, *The Commercial Appeal,* Memphis' morning newspaper, took advantage of the occasion to publish a special 16-page section. The cover featured an aerial photograph doctored to portray a gigantic Holiday Inn sign looming into the clouds over the Memphis skyline. Inside, the section was filled with stories about Kemmons' new motels and ads sold to various companies congratulating Holiday Inn or promoting their business connections with it.

Kemmons wasted no time finding ways to garner business and attract attention. He made a deal with the airlines in Memphis to send guests over to his Holiday Inn South, near the airport, whenever a flight was delayed by weather — a more common occurrence in 1953 than today. It was the first of many such reciprocal business arrangements he would engineer in the years to come.

To publicize the furnishings he chose for his motels, Kemmons told newspaper reporters how he took home a large selection of mattresses and had his family take turns sleeping on each of them until they selected the very best one for the Holiday Inn rooms. He developed a knack for finding such angles to grab free ink in the local papers.

But once he got the four Holiday Inns built in Memphis, Kemmons ran into a dead end. He had borrowed all the money he could on his own, and he was still 396 motels short of the grand total he had so confidently announced to Dorothy.

"I realized I was out of capital and I had to do something else. I decided I was crazy. There was no way I could get enough money to build 400 hotels this way," Kemmons recalls.

"So I got to thinking about how I could do it. And finally I thought about my friend, Wallace Johnson."

CHAPTER EIGHT

-THE ABSOLUTE DEFINITION OF A PARTNERSHIP-

"If Wallace gets to heaven before I do, I'm going to go to the Pearly Gates and ask St. Peter to give me Wallace as my partner for eternity in heaven."

Kemmons Wilson

If there is any word Kemmons Wilson likes better than *work*, it would have to be *now*. Past and future have always been relatively minor considerations for him, when compared with the unlimited potential of now. The best time to do absolutely, positively, just about anything — if you are Kemmons Wilson — is now.

In early 1953, Wallace Johnson was an acquaintance of Kemmons, but not a close friend. At that point, the two had never done any business together. Still, when Kemmons reached the conclusion that Wallace just might hold the key to making Holiday Inn the biggest motel chain in the world, Kemmons acted immediately. He didn't deliberate at great length on the matter. He didn't see if he and Wallace might get together sometime soon. Not even tomorrow would do. The time to take Holiday Inn national was, of course, now.

"I have been accused of many things in my life," Kemmons says, "but never of indecision."

Wallace's account of the historic, late-winter night in 1953 when Kemmons first called is preserved in his autobiography, *Together We Build*. Wallace was going over financial figures and work schedules for his homebuilding operation, when the phone rang. The interruption in his evening irritated him, as he always made himself very accessible during office hours.

"I've got a business idea that I think might interest you," said Kemmons, whom Wallace knew only as an up-and-coming businessman and a fellow builder. "Are you busy?"

"You mean tonight?" asked Wallace, who thought well of Kemmons but had never been involved with him in any deal or project.

"Yes, I'd like to come over." *Now.*

Wallace hesitated, because his desk already was covered with work that really needed to be finished that evening. But the enthusiasm in Kemmons' voice was infectious, and Wallace gave in.

It would be 2 o'clock the next morning before Kemmons left. But when the two men shook hands goodbye, they had created a partnership that would last until Wallace's death 35 years later. Just like that, Holiday Inn was on its way to the rest of the world.

"It was my closest partnership, by far," Kemmons says. His son, Bob, says it was even more: "Pop and Wallace Johnson were the absolute definition of a partnership. Never once was there something that one didn't do for the other when he needed it. Absolutely never."

Years later, after Holiday Inn had succeeded beyond all expectations, Kemmons and Wallace were interviewed separately for a newspaper article. During the interviews, each was asked, "What do you consider your biggest piece of luck as a businessman?"

Wallace said, "I think my luckiest break came when Kemmons Wilson asked me to be his partner in developing Holiday Inns."

Kemmons, who did not know Wallace's answer at the time, told the reporter, "My biggest piece of luck was that Wallace Johnson agreed to come in with me."

The two men first met just after World War II. Kemmons had returned to Memphis from his overseas duty to find that a new homebuilder seemed to have taken over the real-estate market.

"As I drove around town, I saw signs everywhere that said, 'Let Wallace E. Johnson build a home for you on this lot.' I don't believe I exaggerate to say he must have had 500 signs like that scattered all over town. I said, man, that must be the richest fellow in Memphis. I want to meet him," Kemmons says.

"So I called him one day and told him who I was. He said, 'Oh, I know your name.' I said, 'I'd like to come by and see you.' And he said,

'I'd love for you to come by.' "

When they met, Kemmons said, "Wallace, you must be the richest man in town. Where did you get all those lots where you have all those signs?"

Wallace just laughed. "Oh, Kemmons, I don't own a single one of those lots. They all belong to somebody else. I just put the signs out there, and if somebody comes along and wants to build a house, I go see if I can buy the lot."

Wallace had in fact had about 5,000 cheap pasteboard signs printed up with that message on them and then posted them on practically every vacant lot in town. He landed deals to build quite a few houses in this manner before lot owners began to catch on and started raising their prices when he called. It was exactly the audacious kind of move Kemmons wished he had thought of himself.

Wallace was 12 years older than Kemmons, but the two men had much in common. Wallace could have been the brother Kemmons never had. He had a rags-to-riches story almost as poignant as Kemmons'. Wallace liked to say he was "just a po' little peckerwood boy from Mis'sippi." He had grown up on a farm near Kosciusko, Mississippi, the son of a blacksmith. Wallace earned his first dollar picking cotton at 7, and had contracted to build his first house at 18. Like Kemmons, Wallace had quit high school in his teens to earn a living, but he returned to finish and get his degree at the age of 22.

Both men loved work so much, they considered it play. Both had started with nothing and built successful construction operations on little more than endless hours of work and a sharp eye for squeezing the most out of every nickel. "He had a lumberyard, I had a lumberyard. He was just like me. He knew if you were going to build right and make money, you had to have your lumberyard so you could get everything wholesale," Kemmons said.

And both men had a well-known willingness to borrow any amount of money they could get their hands on. A banker who knew them, Jimmy Ross of National Bank of Commerce in Memphis, joked that instead of joining their assets, as most partners did, Kemmons and Wallace joined their liabilities. "For a non-banker, Wallace has more friends among the banking fraternity than any man I know," Kemmons once said.

Wallace considered his building and borrowing a calling from on high. A magazine once noted how he routinely prayed out loud: "Oh, Lord, let me this week start an office building that we have ready to go in Indianapolis. Let me start the building at Sam Houston Hospital in Texas, too. ... and let me pay the bank the $800,000 that I owe. Amen."

Another published prayer went: "Make me, Oh Lord, one of the leading Baptists ... Oh, God, please, oh, please, let us build 2,000 dwelling units this year ... and if it be Thy will, let me be a vice president of the National Association of Home Builders."

Wallace had almost as much faith in his mortal business partner. Not long after they agreed to join up on Holiday Inn, Kemmons was in Florida. Kemmons recalls flying to Miami with Dorothy for a meeting there of the Young Presidents Association (a business organization of company heads), then renting a car and driving up the coast to see Marineland, which had recently opened near St. Augustine.

One day at lunch a restless Kemmons finished eating and went over to chat with the cashier. Not surprisingly, the conversation focused on one of Kemmons' favorite subjects: What was land worth around there? The man told him that beachfront land not far from the restaurant had sold recently for $20 a front foot, and that there was an auction of similar land beginning shortly that very afternoon. Kemmons lost all interest in visiting Marineland and hurried off to the auction.

Once there, Kemmons discovered that anyone who bought one lot could buy as many more as they wanted adjacent to it. More than 3,200 feet of ocean frontage was up for auction. The first sale concluded as Kemmons arrived, and sold for the same $20 a-front-foot price that the cashier had mentioned. Even though all land prices were much cheaper then, Kemmons realized this was a real bargain: each lot had 100 feet of ocean frontage and extended back 1,240-1,780 feet. Through the middle ran U.S. Highway A1A. That meant there was 3,200 feet of frontage on the ocean, 6,400 on the two sides of U.S. A1A, and 3,200 on the Inland Waterway.

When the bidding on the next lot began, someone bid $8, someone else bid $10, and Kemmons bid $20.

"Sold to this gentleman over here," the auctioneer announced. "Now, which lot do you want, sir?"

"I want all of them," Kemmons replied, invoking the clause allowing him to buy lots adjacent to his.

"Do you know how much that is?" the somewhat flustered auctioneer asked.

"Yeah, that's about $68,000," Kemmons said.

"Do you have that much money with you?"

"No, but if you will go with me and we get hold of my banker, he will tell you I am good for it."

After calming protests from the other bidders who had been shut out, Kemmons and the auctioneer went to a nearby bank.

"I called Lou Wittenberg at National Bank of Commerce in Memphis. I said, 'Lou, I know I don't have $68,000 in the bank. But will you tell this man my check will be good and I will get it covered. He said, 'Oh sure, let me talk to him,' " Kemmons recalls.

Then Kemmons called Wallace and told him, "I just bought some ground here for myself, but I guess you can have half if you are interested."

"Anything you bought, I want half of it," Wallace immediately replied, without laying eyes on the Florida land.

Kemmons and Wallace initiated plans to build a Holiday Inn there, along with a shopping center and a complex of rental duplexes to be called Holiday House. They even built two models of the duplexes back in Memphis, which Kemmons still owns today. But in the end, that project never got off the ground.

"We were going to build a resort, but we never did it. I guess we got too busy with all this other stuff. I think we finally sold it for a million dollars, but we never should have sold it. It's got to be worth $20 million today," Kemmons says.

Over the course of their long and usually profitable relationship, the two men established the habit of always considering every decision they reached as "our decision," with neither ever blaming the other for a bad one. Over the years, they developed a general working relationship in which Kemmons tended to be the innovator and promoter, while Wallace handled financing and kept an eye on day-to-day operations. Over nearly four decades, they launched millions and millions of dollars worth of deals — over and beyond Holiday Inn — without any contract between them other than a handshake. They just split every deal down the middle.

About 20 years into their partnership, Kemmons said, "If Wallace gets to heaven before I do, I'm going to go to the Pearly Gates and ask St. Peter to give me Wallace as my partner for eternity in heaven."

When Kemmons turned 75, Wallace expressed reciprocal feelings. On a framed photograph of himself, he wrote: "To Kemmons Wilson on his 75th birthday, from your partner in person for 35 years and one in heaven for an eternity." The photograph still hangs in the hallway of Kemmons' home.

However, when Kemmons first sought out Wallace in 1953, it was in quest of more earthly connections. Wallace was vice president of the National Home Builders Association, and Kemmons saw that as the route to take Holiday Inn national.

"I realized I had made a big mistake in telling my wife I could build 400 Holiday Inns. Then it dawned on me, if I could get all the big homebuilders that were members of the Homebuilders Association to build one in their hometown, I could get 400 real quick. So I called Wallace and told him I had an idea and wanted to come over and see him. I told him my plan, and I told him he could have half of Holiday Inn if he would help me. He was a very enthusiastic guy. He said, 'Man, let's do this.' "

The idea was that by getting hundreds of hotels in operation quickly, Holiday Inn could then introduce a national reservation system and marketing program for all the hotels. By selling other homebuilders the plans and license to build Holiday Inns, Kemmons and Wallace were launching one of the first business franchise systems in the country.

"I didn't know what the word franchising meant, but I needed money," Kemmons says. "So Wallace and I started approaching builders. We wrote letters to builders all over the country, inviting them to come to Memphis to hear about the deal we were offering. Wallace wrote the letter and put my name on it with his. They didn't know who I was, but they knew who he was."

Of that initial mailing, Wallace would later recall, "It was a rather mysterious letter, a teaser, for we invited them to come to Memphis, at their own expense, to see something we had to show them. We didn't tell them what it was, but said it was important to them and their future."

More than 60 homebuilders accepted the invitation and met with Wallace and Kemmons in Memphis in March of 1953. The Memphians agreed to sell the visiting builders franchises for $500 down and a nickel a night royalties for each room. The franchisees would pay their own construction costs. Most of the builders agreed to take a set of plans home and to build a Holiday Inn.

It took more than a year, but on June 14, 1954, the first Holiday Inn franchise opened in Clarksdale, Mississippi, built there by William Holcomb of that city. On August 12, 1954, Holcomb sent in the first franchise fee ever received by the company, a check for $115.60

It was a start, but not quite what Kemmons had envisioned. He had hoped that a year after the meeting with the builders, there would be a Holiday Inn in every major city and at every important highway junction. The largest motel chain in the country would be up and running overnight. Kemmons and Wallace told *Business Week* magazine they envisioned a 100,000-room network of Holiday Inns stretching from Florida to Oregon within three years.

As it turned out, only three of the builders who visited Memphis followed through and put up a Holiday Inn. Kemmons began to accept the reality that his colleagues were just not adventurous enough to move as fast as he wanted. They were satisfied with their construction businesses, and saw no reason to stick their neck out and try a completely different business. But to Kemmons, they didn't see the opportunity offered by a changing world.

"They were just too busy doing other things, or didn't get around to it," he says. "A lot of people have good ideas but don't carry them through."

Looking on the bright side, Kemmons also decided that he was fortunate so few builders had held Holiday Inn to the original franchise offer. "$500 and nickel a night per room," he laughs at the memory. "Lucky, we didn't sell too many at that price, or we never could have done it. Even if they built a 120-room hotel, that would only be $6 a night in royalties."

Later franchise arrangements would provide for a healthier return. Giving up on the homebuilders, Kemmons and Wallace decided "to find people with capital — doctors, lawyers, people looking for investments — and talk them into buying franchises. We helped get people to build the Inns, and in some cases we built the Inns for them. I spent a lot of my time then helping them. I worked as much at night as I did in the daytime. I'd go til 11 or 12 at night if there was anybody to tell about Holiday Inn."

Kemmons liked to assure potential franchisees that getting into the motel business was a snap, "nothing but bricks and sticks." Holiday Inn began offering franchisees a turn-key package in which their new inn could be completely furnished and provided with a trained manager as part of the franchise deal. Eventually, the company would offer a package that included sending out specialists to survey the site and recommend the best location and the type of inn best suited for it; to design and build the inn; to assist with the mortgage; to completely furnish the inn; to hire and train the personnel; and to provide projections of costs and profits.

Among the earliest Holiday Inns to open outside Memphis were franchises in Birmingham, Alabama; Oklahoma City; Abilene and Amarillo, Texas; Kansas City, Missouri; and Wichita, Kansas. At the end of 1954, there were 11 Holiday Inns. As the decade progressed, the big green-and-yellow sign began popping up farther and farther from Memphis, in a diverse cross-section of American cities such as Charleston, South Carolina; Las Vegas, Nevada; Dauphin Island, Alabama; Topeka, Kansas; Indianapolis and Kokomo, Indiana; Destin, Florida; Lynchburg, Virginia; Hot Springs, Arkansas; Allentown, Pennsylvania; Columbus, Georgia; and Tucson, Arizona.

Most succeeded almost immediately. Offering bargains for weary families, the room rates represented "luxury accommodations at budget prices," Kemmons liked to say. Weary parents could find respite from the heat of the road in the air-conditioned rooms. Their kids could cut loose in the swimming pool after being cooped up in the car all day. With soft-drink and ice machines placed in the hallways, guests were spared the cost of room service. Porters were available, but instructed not to force themselves on guests at every turn with their hands outstretched for tips. Because the inns were located on the edge of town, parents could relax outside their rooms on pleasant evenings and enjoy the peace and quiet.

Not long after Kemmons and Wallace joined forces, they hired their first salesmen: Elmer "Jack" Ladd and Ernest "Barney" McCool, Wallace's brother-in-law. Ladd, who always dressed and spoke with style, had sold men's clothing in Miami Beach before World War II. A Memphis reporter once called Ladd "an all-time supersalesman." One of the first Holiday Inn sales he made was to a Kentucky builder who finally said he would give Ladd $1,000 (the franchise fee at that time) just to get rid of him.

"I met Jack Ladd in the Ferry Command in World War II," Kemmons says. "He was a pilot and I was a pilot, and we got to be friends. He wasn't from Memphis, but he liked it and he decided to come live here after the war. I put up the money and helped him build some houses for me. I guess we built 30 or 40 houses before we started Holiday Inn. Then he decided he wanted to get involved in that. He was an awful good salesman."

He certainly must have believed in his product. In those days, Ladd and McCool had to make their road trips in the first Holiday Inn company car, an old station wagon that had once been used to haul manure on a farm of Wallace's. They cleaned it up as best they could, and painted it in the company colors of green and yellow. But a long, hot day on the road brought out the unmistakable fragrance of the vehicle's previous duty.

"That station wagon stunk. I still remember that. I don't see how they could ride in that thing," Kemmons says.

It took more than a strong nose to make it with Holiday Inn in the early years. It took a strong stomach to hang in with a company that had far more debt than revenue, almost no cash, and a couple of high-rollers running the show who seemed oblivious to the risks they were taking.

John Cleghorn, who would later join the company to manage its public-relations department, recalls, "Jack Ladd said when they went out to sell franchises in those days, at the end of a hard day, Kemmons would go to sleep and Wallace would read his Bible. So there was no one left to worry about things except Jack, and that is why he got an ulcer."

Wallace used to say that money was so tight in the beginning that Ladd and McCool would hide any franchise checks they received by taping them to the bottom of their desk drawers. They knew if Kemmons and Wallace saw them, they would spend them before the salesmen could get to the bank and take their commissions. When the first Holiday Inn annual report — a typewritten document — was released, it listed "Cash on Hand" as $50.

Bill Branim, an accountant who became a partner with Roy Scott and formed the firm Scott-Branim Co. and has done a lot of work for Kemmons over the years, recalls that in the early days of Holiday Inn, Kemmons always said that his two ambitions were to be able to pay his taxes on time and to give his employees a cash bonus. For years, he handed out promissory notes instead.

"We gave many a note for Christmas bonuses, notes that we would pay $100 or $500 later. We didn't have the money then, but we picked them all up later. But Holiday Inn really had the spirit. All those people were really working. They thought it was going to go, and they made it go," Kemmons says.

At one point, Kemmons and Wallace gave 10 percent of the company stock to Memphis attorney John Martin. He had done legal work for both of them for years. But when they told him how they were taking Holiday Inn national, he warned them they were in great danger of violating federal interstate-commerce laws. They had rushed into the expansion so quickly that they had not taken time to formalize exactly what they were selling. They were calling it a franchise, but in the eyes of the law, it was little more than a name, a set of plans and a dream. That fell considerably short of the federal requirements to sell franchises in interstate commerce.

"I can remember John said we had what you call a 'naked franchise.' That was the term he used. We didn't have it all bundled up in the right way. That's when we said we would give him 10 percent of the company to get all that straightened out. But he only kept it for three or four months. We scared him to death when he found how much money we were getting obligated for," Kemmons says.

"Wallace would go off one way and I would go off another way. The next time we had a meeting we had signed demand notes for around $3.5 million altogether, from the banks in the towns where we were going to build the Holiday Inns. And when we told John he said, 'You mean you have signed all those notes that they could come to you tomorrow and demand their money? That could bankrupt this company!'

"I would tell him, 'John, they are not going to demand that money. They want that Holiday Inn in their town. They think it will be good for business.' But he kept saying, 'I just can't live like this.' "

Or as Wallace put it, "John thought Kemmons and I were off our rockers." So they asked Martin what he would have charged them for the legal work. After considering the matter, he said about $25,000.

"Would you be happy if I gave you $25,000 for that stock then?" Kemmons asked.

"I sure would. I can't stand this pressure," Martin said.

With that, Kemmons and Wallace just headed for the bank again. "We went to Jimmy Ross at National Bank of Commerce, told him we needed to borrow another $25,000 and told him what it was for. He said, 'Well, I'm going to get your ox out of the ditch once again.' So we paid John the $25,000 and got the stock back," Kemmons says.

About 30 years later, Kemmons would estimate what that decision cost Martin. In 1982, there were 37 million shares of Holiday Inn stock outstanding. If Martin still owned 10 percent of the company, he would then own 3.7 million shares, which at the price at that time of $30 a share would be worth $111 million.

"But we still were always the best of friends. I loved him almost like he was my brother. He never regretted it. He just said we were too big a gamblers for him."

As Martin once said, when Wallace was ribbing him for not sticking with his share of Holiday Inn: "Wallace, if I had stuck with you and Kemmons, and kept up the pace we were going, I'd be dead already."

However, none of the debts and pressure ever worried Kemmons much. "I can remember people saying, 'Aren't you afraid to get out and do all this stuff?' " he recounts. "I said, 'No, I started off broke. I can't ever be any worse off.' "

As his longtime friend Sam Phillips observes, "The road was not paved with gold in the beginning. Kemmons paved it with gold with his genius and persistence and totally untiring effort. I've never seen anybody with his energy. He has the ability to just work all the time and still enjoy himself.

"But Kemmons Wilson has not been driven by the almighty dollar. He had to have money to make money, sure. But there was just something in his nature, like a chemist at his bench who says, 'Man, I'm onto something here. I'm going to find what it is.' That was Kemmons. He had an insatiable appetite to win, one of the most insatiable I have seen in my life, and I have dealt with a lot of people."

CHAPTER NINE

—THE HOLIDAY INN WAY—

**"There are two ways to get to the top of an oak tree.
One way is to sit on an acorn and wait;
the other way is to climb it."**

Kemmons Wilson

*K*emmons became acquainted with the abilities of Bill Walton, the third member of the triumvirate that would make Holiday Inn a corporate reality, in 1954. That year, Kemmons was elected president of the Memphis Home Builders Association.

"I was so busy I knew I couldn't do a good job, and I didn't want to do it," Kemmons recalls. "But my friend Jack Rich, who had been president the year before, said, 'No, you have to be the president, but I have found you a young guy who can run it for you.' So Jack hired Bill Walton, and he did such a good job for me. I was a hell of a good president, but it was all because of Bill Walton."

Walton was already a successful lawyer who had been retained as legal counsel and acting administrator for the Home Builders Association. During that time, builder Bill Clark, a client and friend of Walton's, recommended that Walton hear out Kemmons on his motel-chain idea.

Kemmons and Wallace sat under a tree with Bill, drinking lemonade, at a Home Builders Association picnic in 1955. It was there they persuaded him to leave his established law practice and become Holiday Inn's chief operating officer.

Not long after that, Kemmons had Walton over for dinner. After dinner, Walton recalls, Kemmons said, "Let me tell you about this idea. First of all, it's going to make a lot of people a lot of money — I mean a lot of money. You can probably make as much money as you want to make.

"Our lawyer, John Martin, tells us if we are going to sell these franchises, what we have right now is a 'naked franchise.' And if we don't put some meat on the bones of this naked franchise, we could get in some real trouble selling it in interstate commerce. We want to protect the name Holiday Inn. We want to set up a franchise system. And we want a corporation that can go public. Do you think you can do all that for us?"

Walton thought it over a moment, then told Kemmons he could. In truth, he was far from certain. Later, he would pray for guidance.

"I said, 'Lord, You and I both know I don't know the first thing about franchising, protecting the name of a company, or putting together a corporation that can go public. If this is something you want me to do, you will have to show me the way,' " Walton remembers.

"In each of those areas, I doubt there was another lawyer in the city of Memphis who had any idea about those things. All that was a specialty in the legal profession that was pretty well confined to New York, Chicago, Boston, Los Angeles and San Francisco at that time. For one of those lawyers to even talk to you about it, his retainer fee would probably be $100,000."

On top of that, Walton was asking himself if he was out of his mind to consider leaving his law practice for a $500-a-month job and a dream. Maybe the stock options Kemmons promised would indeed be lucrative someday. But at the moment, $500 a month was barely enough to meet his mortgage and support his young family. And yet, as it had with Wallace Johnson two years before, something about the way Kemmons practically glowed with enthusiasm made Bill Walton want to be a part of Holiday Inn. He told Kemmons he had a deal.

Kemmons outlined his hands-off style. "You can do most anything you are big enough to do. You have sense enough to know what I need to know about. You just bother me with what you think I need to know. Otherwise, you can do whatever you want to," Kemmons said.

"I know what people say about me and my ideas. But this is a good idea and it is going to work."

Walton recalls that people did call him and ask him if he knew what he was doing — leaving a respectable law practice to join up with Kemmons. The first time Walton saw his Holiday Inn office, he asked himself the same question.

The Holiday Inn headquarters at that time were set up in a former plumbing shed at Wallace's lumberyard at 875 Rayner. It had corrugated-metal siding, a wooden screen door, a dirt parking lot, weeds growing through the narrow sidewalk out front and a flat roof. One of the back rooms still had a dirt floor. Doors had to be laid across packing crates for desks. The windows offered a view of a coal yard.

"I just looked around and I thought to myself, 'Man, have I made a mistake.' At the law firm, we owned our own office building downtown, a half a block from the courthouse. I had walked away from that. I thought, 'I have lost my mind. How are we ever going to make this work?' " Walton remembers.

"Well, that was 1956. And 15 years later, we were the largest hotel system in the world. We were larger than Hilton, Sheraton, Marriott, all of our near competitors combined. We had close to 300,000 rooms and more than 1,700 inns. Our total revenue was about a billion dollars. And we had a total of 150,000 employees," marvels Walton.

But back in 1956, that was unimaginable. Walton recalls how Jimmy Ross, president of National Bank of Commerce, would call him at the Holiday Inn offices. He would say, "Bill, if you are going to keep taking money out of this bank over there, it sure would be nice if you would put some money in sometime."

More quickly than he expected, Walton found the guidance he had prayed for. He took a chance and called the president of Coca-Cola for advice. After spending time with the specialist in charge of protecting the Coca-Cola name from infringement, Walton realized he had a blessing in disguise.

When Kemmons had begun building his Holiday Inns, the many new features he always offered — such as children staying free, a swimming pool, an 80-inch-long bed, free advance reservations, etc. — he had also unwittingly established Holiday Inn as a unique service. That Holiday Inn service could be protected from imitators, just as Coca-Cola protected its unique product.

Those standardized, special services became "the meat on the bones of that 'naked franchise' that John Martin was talking about," Walton says.

To further institutionalize the name Holiday Inn and the unique services it represented, the big green-and-yellow sign and slogans like "The Nation's Innkeeper" were copyrighted. Walton emphasized always using the word *inn* rather than *motel* or *hotel*. Franchise agreements were written so tightly that no deviation could be allowed from the original services and specifications that established Holiday Inn as "a brand name you could count on."

Walton established an operating manual that specified all the requirements that every franchisee had to meet. Then he set up a training program so that franchisees would be trained to operate in what became known as The Holiday Inn Way.

"I used to say, 'There's the motel way and the hotel way and The Holiday Inn Way.' When someone tried to impress me in the training school that they had already been in the hotel business for years, it was not uncommon for me to say, 'I'd just as soon not have you in this Holiday Inn system then. Because if you are going to try and tell us how you did it in the hotel business, I don't want to know. You are going to have to do it The Holiday Inn Way, or get out,' " Walton says.

Kemmons would later say the company preferred to call its units "inns" because "They are not complete hotels nor complete motels, but offer services of both ... for more comfort and convenience than what you would find in a hotel or motel alone."

Terms like *lavish, luxurious, finest, plush, spacious, gracious, ultra swank* and *ultra modern* became common in Holiday Inn promotional materials. *No Vacancy* signs were forbidden. If all rooms were filled, clerks were instructed to find the guest a room in the nearest acceptable lodging.

"When someone came in for a room, we would tell them we were sorry that we were full, but we would call and confirm a room for them not too far away," Kemmons says. "It was Holiday Inn's thinking that this made two friends - the traveler who was looking for a room, and the innkeeper who needed to sell a room. It worked wonders."

Kemmons' oldest son, Spence, discovered as a teen-ager just how seriously that policy was enforced. He was working as desk clerk at the Holiday Inn in Midtown Memphis one night when Kemmons stopped by to drop off a group of people he had taken to dinner and who were guests at the Holiday Inn. While Kemmons was telling his party goodnight, a man arrived at the hotel and asked Spence for a room. The Holiday Inn was full, however, and Spence had already tried earlier without success to find accommodations elsewhere for previous customers.

Spence explained that to the man, who said he understood perfectly and was about to leave when Kemmons intervened. He introduced himself to the man and explained Holiday Inn's policy about always finding a room for guests if one was not available at the Holiday Inn. Kemmons told the man that the desk clerk was his son, and promised that Spence would find another room somewhere.

"Well, it embarrassed the heck out of me," Spence recalls. "But I made no telling how many calls that night, and I finally did find that man a room at another hotel in Memphis."

Holiday Inn employees were encouraged to learn the names of guests and to smile and speak to them often. Employees, especially managers and front-desk clerks, were required to become "animated encyclopedias of information," as Wallace Johnson once put it.

By 1954, the signs were changed from Holiday Inn Hotel Courts to Holiday Inn Hotel of America. By 1957, the signs began to read simply Holiday Inn of America. The installation of The Great Sign became an event in many communities. When the new Holiday Inn in Wichita, Kansas, erected its 59-foot-tall sign, it was proclaimed the largest self-supported neon sign in the Midwest. A Holiday Inn sign indeed represented a substantial mass of architecture on any landscape. Standing 16 feet wide, four feet thick, weighing five tons and containing 1,500 feet of neon tubing and 500 light bulbs, each sign contained more electrical wiring than seven typical homes of the period.

The owners of the Holiday Inn in Wichita were two young entrepreneurs named Bob Frock and Ed "Swede" Linquist. "They had only been opened about a year," Kemmons remembers, "when they called me to tell me what they had done. Most of the Holiday Inns had been built in a 'U' shape and Bob Brock asked me to fly down to see the improvements they had made to their hotel. He sounded so enthusuastic that I made plans to fly down early the next morning. When I arrived I saw, for the first time, what we later named 'The Holidome'. Brock and Linquist had covered the space between the two story buildings and, by doing this, created an indoor swimming pool and 20,000 square feet more space which really made the hotel outstanding. I turned to Bob and Ed and said, 'This is really great. I can assure you we will copy this "near miracle" many times,' and from then on nearly every Holiday Inn had a holidome."

The marquees on The Great Sign were employed on a daily basis as part of the distinctive Holiday Inn marketing mix. The marquees were changed every day or two to spell out a welcome to individuals or groups. "People love to see their names on a billboard," Kemmons reminded his managers. The signs also were used to advertise meetings being held at that Holiday Inn, promote special dishes served in the restaurant, arouse interest in new features or just offer a line from the company's book of snappy sayings designed to catch the traveler's eye. A typical offering: "Kilroy was here. Why don't you stop too?"

Another of the key early Holiday Inn employees was Clyde Dixon. He went to work for the company in 1956, at a time when Kemmons' mother still considered Holiday Inn very much hers and Kemmons' baby.

"Personally it was frustrating for me the first two years I was there, because Doll was very, very protective of Kemmons," Dixon recalls. "She felt that new people like me were outsiders, that we were coming in and taking over jobs that she felt she had the ability and the capacity to do. And so, frankly, she made my life pretty miserable the first two years. But Kemmons was always reassuring."

Dixon ultimately became a senior vice president with Holiday Inn. He founded the Innkeepers Supply Company and became president of the products division, which supplied hotels with all the products needed for their operations. Dixon's top assistant was Warren Andrews, president of Holiday Inn's restaurant-supply operation (Merchants Supply Company). "He was really something special," Kemmons recalls. "He was probably one of the best restaurant-supply experts in the United States."

Dixon says people who started with Kemmons in the early days took a big chance, and those who stayed for the long haul tended to have the same entrepreneurial, can-do spirit as Kemmons.

Dixon says Kemmons never liked titles. Holiday Inn was a hands-on company, and everybody did everything. Kemmons believed in an open-door policy and would talk to anybody in the company and pay no attention to protocol. Holiday Inn was run like a family organization, in the sense that everyone counted.

"We were one family," Dixon remembers. "The people that stayed there did have that warm feeling. And the inn people felt they were part of that family too."

Among the earliest Holiday Inn franchisees were John Q. Hammons and Roy Winegardner, two men who would play influential roles in the Holiday Inn story for many years to come. Both were businessmen in Springfield, Missouri, who saw the untapped potential in a quality motel chain early on. In the early '50s, Hammons recalls that a small chain caught his eye, a string of about 15-20 motels built along old Route 66 called Del Webb's Highway Houses. The chain never grew a lot larger, but its potential impressed Hammons.

In 1959, Hammons and Winegardner put together $100,000 and bought 10 Holiday Inn franchises. "We headed out and were given 90 days to select the locations, which we did in Kentucky, Ohio, West Virginia, New York and Tennessee. We started building Holiday Inns, and in our first 10 years we developed 31," Hammons says.

"Those Holiday Inns were successful because there was a need. A void existed of a recognized chain image, and that began to be sold to the public. They could have dependability on what they were going to get when they went from city to city, and it began to grow and became one hell of a chain. Then others started to copy the idea, but they were too late. They weren't in the race because Holiday Inn was the firstest with the mostest in that period."

Hammons believes that many franchisees became strong leaders and influenced the development of Holiday Inn. Several, like himself and Winegardner, developed so many franchises that their Inns became like chains within the larger chain.

"Holiday Inn was a success story because the players that were in it were making money. And when they made money on one Holiday Inn, they said, 'Well, hell, we'll go for two and three and four.' And then it got to be a challenge to see what was the best location you could get and what was the best market you could get," he recounts.

"There was a determination by the company to grow and to steady the quality level ... the quality of the hotel operation, the quality of the hotel. And they were pretty careful to get the right franchisees in too. They didn't just pile anybody in who paid $10,000."

Winegardner would go on to be named first vice chairman by Kemmons in 1974, and after Kemmons retired in 1979, Winegardner was named chairman and chief executive officer. Hammons became the largest franchisee of Holiday Inns in the '70s and '80s, as well as one of the major developers of other hotels as well, such as Embassy Suites. In 1995 he began construction on the 100th hotel he has been involved in, and he has plans for dozens more. His company, John Q. Hammons Hotels, is listed on the New York Stock Exchange, and he still develops Holiday Inns.

Hammons' association with Holiday Inn enabled him to know Kemmons well, from the early days of the company through today. "Kemmons was a dreamer," Hammons recalls. "He was a doer; he always had fantastic ideas and always had a positive attitude. At the same time, if he had to sit back and examine and listen to all the different playbacks, he could do that too. He was a par excellence promoter and an innovator, and he was always thinking on how you might accomplish something.

"He didn't win them all, but he won most of them."

Many of Kemmons' employees displayed as much commitment to winning as he did, and he is quick to credit their efforts.

One of Kemmons' favorite stories from the early days involved The Great Sign and an employee who truly understood The Holiday Inn Way. In the late 1950s and early '60s, the Cocoa Beach Holiday Inn near Cape Canaveral, Florida, was managed by Henri Landwirth, a Polish immigrant who had survived a Nazi concentration camp in World War II. In 1962, Landwirth sent a request to his boss at headquarters in Memphis for $600 to purchase 99 flags representing the countries of the United Nations, to be displayed in front of the Cocoa Beach Holiday Inn.

Landwirth thought it would provide a distinctive flourish at a time when thousands of reporters and other visitors were guests at the Cocoa Beach Holiday Inn during the early space launches at Cape Canaveral (later named Cape Kennedy). The Holiday Inn grounds, just a few miles from the launch site, offered an excellent view of the early rocket blastoffs. In addition, CBS news anchor Walter Cronkite — then the best-known broadcaster on television — would soon be visiting to cover astronaut John Glenn's '62 trip into space in the *Friendship 7* capsule.

"Well, my boss turned the request down, because the $600 was not in the annual budget. With that, I told him I would go to the chairman of the board for the money," Landwirth recalls.

"So he called me," Kemmons says, "and I said, 'Hell yes, go on out and buy 'em.' But I said, 'Be sure that when Walter Cronkite is going to be on television that you stand him in front of that Holiday Inn sign. No matter what you have to do, put him in front of that sign.' "

So Landwirth got his flags. And he went to the producer for the *CBS Evening News* and persuaded him to set up Cronkite's 15-minute, national-television broadcast of Glenn's launch right in front of the Cocoa Beach Holiday Inn. Viewers across America and in many other countries that Sunday night saw Cronkite with the big Holiday Inn sign looming over his shoulder. The marquee read: *Hopes and Prayers of Free World Are With John Glenn.*

"That was the best national publicity we ever had," Kemmons says.

"The beauty of it," Landwirth notes, "was that it didn't cost a dime. I doubt that Kemmons would have ever paid for 30 seconds of air time, let alone 15 minutes."

Kemmons took notice of Landwirth's drive and initiative, and one evening when Landwirth was in Memphis, had him over for dinner with the family at the Wilson home. In their conversation, Landwirth realized Kemmons assumed he was a franchise owner by that time, because he was involved with five Holiday Inns.

"I told him that I was only an innkeeper and owned no financial interest in any of the Holiday Inns. Kemmons was very surprised to hear this, and told me that if I would ever like to have a franchise, he would do everything in his power to make it happen," Landwirth says.

"Years later, when Disney announced they were coming to Central Florida, opening up a new market for Holiday Inn, I went to Kemmons. He immediately recalled what he had promised, and told me to apply for any franchise that I wanted. I did receive two franchises that subsequently made my partners and myself very financially secure. After all those years, with nothing in writing, he kept his word."

CHAPTER TEN

—HOLIDAY INN BLASTS OFF—

**"Remember that we all climb the ladder of success
one step at a time."**

Kemmons Wilson

$\mathcal{A}$s the young company went about establishing The Holiday Inn Way, it was also determinedly courting the business customer. This meant urging traveling businessmen to book their entire travel itinerary at Holiday Inns through the company's reservation network, promoting Holiday Inns as ideal sites for meetings and conventions, and welcoming civic and business groups by announcing their meetings on the big Holiday Inn signs.

In 1961, Kemmons told *The Wall Street Journal*, "The traveling man is the biggest part of our business in every part of the country except a few resort areas." The same year, a Holiday Inn ad was headlined "192 Ways to Bring Meetings to Your Men Instead of Men to Your Meetings." At that time, the company had 192 inns. Other ads of the period declared, "Build Business With Holiday Inn Meetings" and "End Your Sales Day the Profitable Way at a Holiday Inn."

At the same time, Holiday Inn was becoming more and more familiar to readers of the business pages. On August 19, 1957, the company went public, trading stock for the first time in the over-the-counter market. On the first day, buyers snapped up all 120,000 shares offered at $9.75 a share, providing the company with a little over $1 million in cash. It also brought another future Holiday Inn executive to Kemmons' attention.

"That's why I hired Lem Clymer. He out-traded me on the offering. He was a vice president of Equitable Securities Co., an investment banking firm with offices in Nashville, which did the underwriting. They were the second largest capitalized investment company at that time, second only to Merrill Lynch. I kept trying to get Lem to give us $15 a share. And then I was trying to get $10.75. So finally I said, 'OK, $9.75.' That's what he wanted and he never budged. I told him later, 'Boy, you are too good a trader for me. I have to have you on my team,' " Kemmons says.

Clymer joined the Holiday Inn board in 1957, and was named senior vice president of mergers and acquisitions in 1968. He would play a leading role in the phenomenal string of mergers and acquisitions Kemmons negotiated for Holiday Inn in the '60s and '70s, and also become president of the company.

After Holiday Inn went public, its momentum accelerated more rapidly every year, quickly building to juggernaut proportions. In 1958, the 50th Holiday Inn opened, in Dyersburg, Tennessee. The next year, the 100th opened, in Tallahassee, Florida. Two years later, the 200th opened, in Palm Springs, California. In 1960, the company was opening an average of one new Holiday Inn every week. By 1962, the average was two a week.

And in December 1962, in Vincennes, Indiana, Holiday Inn Number 400 opened its doors. Kemmons had fulfilled the outrageous prediction he made to Dorothy just over a decade before. "Well, that was probably one of the biggest kicks I ever got, to tell Dorothy about that 400th Holiday Inn."

But by the time he achieved that once-impossible dream, Kemmons had no time to gloat. The same year, Holiday Inn built its first hotel in New York City, and *The Wall Street Journal* devoted a lengthy front-page article to analyzing the secret of the company's explosive development. *The Journal* said demand for franchises was so great Holiday Inn was no longer selling franchises so much as it was selling knowledge of how to make money with a Holiday Inn. A thorough screening process weeded out the less promising for reasons such as poor locations, irregular financing and cutting into the business of Holiday Inns already operating in the franchisee's proposed area.

Once an application was approved, detailed cost forecasts were prepared for the franchisee. Inn operators were allowed leeway in architectural matters as long as the result was in compliance with "the Holiday Inn look." Jack Ladd, by then senior vice president and marketing director, defined it as a look that "suggests spaciousness and enjoyment without arousing fears of excessive charges." Some plans that diverged too radically from that look were vetoed, such as those from owners in Western states who wanted to build log-style inns. But with Holiday Inn's phenomenal track record, most franchisees were only too happy to comply, therefore individual Holiday Inns tended to vary little architecturally. Most early Inns were one- or two-story, concrete-block and brick structures, built in a square or U-shape around the pool.

Memphis architect Bill Bond began working with Kemmons on the Jackson, Tennessee, Holiday Inn in 1954. Kemmons soon had him working on other Holiday Inns almost constantly.

"Everybody who worked for Kemmons always had to work virtually 24 hours a day," says Bob McCaskill, the Memphis engineer who has done work for Kemmons for more than 30 years, "especially back in those early years of Holiday Inn. There was one time that Bill Bond had really been working long hours for Kemmons for several days. And finally, when they finished up one day, he knew he just had to take a break.

"When he got home, there was a note on the refrigerator from his wife that she had taken their younger son to watch their older son play basketball. Well, no sooner had Bill sat down than the phone rang, and it was Kemmons. He said, 'Bill, I just got something figured out and I need to you to come back over.' Bill said, 'Well, I would, Kemmons, but I can't right now because I am baby-sitting.' Kemmons said, 'That's OK, I'll just come over to your house,' and hung up.

"So Bill goes racing over to the gym, snatches his baby son, Matthew, from his wife and tells her, 'I need to borrow him for a few minutes.' Then he races home, and just as Kemmons was pulling up to the front door, Bill and Matthew were coming in the back door."

Another key player in shaping the distinctive look of Holiday Inns joined the company in the late '50s. After Kemmons saw the work that Montgomery, Alabama, interior-designer Tom Wells had done on a franchisee's Holiday Inn in that city, Kemmons offered Wells the job of chief interior decorator for Holiday Inn. To this day, Kemmons calls the late Wells "the greatest interior decorator ever. He decorated close to 500 Holiday Inns for us, I'd say."

Wells had studied at the University of Alabama and Parsons School of Design in New York. Shortly after he was hired by Kemmons, a Memphis reporter wrote that Wells "mixes all styles and periods and colors ... using one or two predominant colors and then bringing in all the jewel tones." Wells told the reporter, "There's too much matching in decorating. We never match anything."

Kemmons' son, Bob, recalls Wells as "a prince of a fellow — the only decorator I've ever known who could work for Pop."

Wells' widow, Mary Wells, remembers her husband had the same drive to succeed as Kemmons. It was common for Kemmons to call Wells at 6 o'clock on a Saturday morning, and the two men would then set right off in their excitement to look into one new project or another.

"Once Kemmons honed in on something, that was it and everything else went out the window. He doesn't go around the bush to get what he wants. He just goes right straight through it," Mary says.

"Kemmons never gets tired of finding out about new things or starting something. He's always wanting to do something different. Once he gets it, then somebody else has got to handle it. He's not really interested in running it."

She remembers how Kemmons brought Tom ice cream when he was dying of cancer, and how Kemmons helped Mary after Tom died.

"Tom adored Kemmons, absolutely loved him to pieces," Mary says. "Kemmons is generous in a time of need. ... I guess he figures if you don't need it, why give it to you? But if you do, he will go out of his way to help you and will do it creatively."

Many designers might have bridled at Kemmons perpetual insistence on squeezing every nickel. However, McCaskill still marvels at Wells' deft diplomacy with Kemmons, which even enabled Wells to turn Kemmons' tightfistedness to advantage on occasion.

"Tom Wells got to be close friends with Kemmons and really knew him very well. One time we were going over to Arkansas on business

— Tom, Kemmons, myself and a couple other men. Now, Kemmons always likes to use the old bridge over the Mississippi because it is the quickest way to get to Arkansas. But he was not paying attention, and we ended up heading for the new bridge," recalls McCaskill.

"When he realized it, he pitched a fit. 'I want to go on the old bridge! Why are we going on the new bridge?' he kept saying. Finally, Tom, who had a very dry wit, said, 'Kemmons, it's because it's cheaper to use the new bridge.' And Kemmons just said, 'Oh.' And that was the end of it."

With so many different franchisees operating individual Holiday Inns, quality control required constant, exhaustive efforts to make sure every inn kept the bathrooms clean, the shrubbery trimmed, the desk clerk courteous and everything else consistent with Holiday Inn standards. A team of investigators was established to make regular, surprise calls on every Holiday Inn at least four times a year to check on things. Managers who failed inspection and failed to correct problems could be fired. In serious cases, the franchise could be revoked.

Before a new motel ever opened its doors, the innkeepers were brought to Memphis for a five-week training course. In 1959, the Holiday Inn Innkeeping School was launched in Memphis. *The New York Times* once called Holiday Inn's method "The Hospitality Crusade." Trainees would work under simulated, on-the-job conditions. Training-film strips were distributed to inns to teach waitresses how to serve meals most pleasantly and to show maids how to make a bed in less than three minutes. Manuals were provided for every subject imaginable, even a 32-page booklet on how to clean a bathroom The Holiday Inn Way. Signs on the walls exhorted the participants: "Sell Sell Sell" and "Sell-Serve-Succeed."

Rigorous training and national advertising were now considered to be at the heart of Holiday Inn's success. By the early '60s, each inn was required to contribute 8 cents a room daily to the national advertising campaign, which included buying prominent space regularly in national magazines such as *Time* and *Look*, in national newspapers such as *The Wall Street Journal*, and on television, radio and billboards.

One innovative series of ads on the theme of "Sooner or Later Nearly Everyone Stays at A Holiday Inn" paired the company with a series of other widely-known major brands such as Levis and Dutch Master Cigars, reinforcing the household-name image. In a reciprocal deal with Pan-Am, the airline referred passengers at its some 550 airline counters to Holiday Inn, while every Inn provided guests with information on Pan-Am flights. Similar arrangements were made with the Continental and Greyhound bus lines.

As the number of inns multiplied, the company began to adjust its policy of only building on the outskirts of town. Studies determined that building at least one downtown Holiday Inn in major cities could be profitable. That also meant building more highrises, such as a 33-story hotel in Chicago and an 18-story hotel in New York. Some highrises, including those in Denver and Austin, were built in a circular shape, providing a wide-angle view from the balcony of each room. Several highrises were built with revolving restaurants on top, inspired by the revolving Space Needle restaurant at the Seattle World's Fair.

Also in the early '60s, Holiday Inn began buying back more and more of its inns from franchisees. The chain had grown large enough that its overhead was spread over so many hotels the parent company could operate the inns at a greater profit than it could franchise them, in many cases. And with more capital to invest, direct ownership by the company had become more feasible. By the late '60s, Holiday Inn owned about a fifth of its inns, with the rest operated under franchise agreements.

In 1964, Holiday Inn paid stockholders a cash dividend — 20 cents — for the first time. In 1968, the 1,000th Holiday Inn opened, in San Antonio in the middle of HemisFair, the world's fair hosted by the city that year.

As Holiday Inn skyrocketed through the '60s, it became a darling of Wall Street. The stock went on the New York Stock Exchange September 30, 1963, and opened at $24.50. Kemmons took Dorothy and Doll to New York for the opening of trading, and Doll bought the first 100 shares.

"Time and again, we were the most active and popular stock trading on the New York Stock Exchange," Bill Walton says.

"We started over the counter, and usually it takes eight to ten years until the stock is seasoned by enough trading to justify being listed on the New York Stock Exchange. But Kemmons is like a bulldog when he gets an idea. That was his original idea, to be traded on the New York Stock Exchange. And sure enough, they accepted Holiday Inn about three or four years earlier than normal."

Holiday Inn further solidified its dominance in the lodging market when it formed an alliance with Gulf Oil in the early '60s. It involved Gulf purchasing a large block of Holiday Inn stock, and extending millions more in credit and financing. But most valuable to Holiday Inn was a pioneering arrangement that allowed the hotel chain to accept Gulf credit cards for food and lodging. That sounds commonplace today, but at the time was unheard of. The credit-card industry was almost nonexistent, except for the oil-company cards. One Holiday Inn marquee proclaimed: *Go Gulf — We Did.*

"Nobody had credit cards back then, except the oil companies. So Wallace and I were talking and one of us commented on how great it would be if we could get a credit card. So we decided we needed to make a deal with an oil company. So we got biographies of all the heads of the big oil companies and researched them. And the one we decided we liked best was Bill Whiteford, chairman of Gulf. We called and made an appointment with him, and Wallace and I met with him and Del Brockett, their president," Kemmons recalls.

"We told them we wanted to use their credit cards, and in return we would get them locations next to all the Holiday Inns we built, whenever possible. We also told them we wanted to borrow some money from them. Well, we worked out a deal where they agreed to loan us $15 million on the signature of Holiday Inn and to guarantee $40 million of additional loans, and for us to use their credit cards. It really gave us a big boost. This made us the first chain in the United States that had a credit card good at any Holiday Inn location."

The executive staffs of Holiday Inn and Gulf began meeting once a year. The staffs were gathered in the dining room at one of their annual meetings at Ligonier Lodge when Brockett was called from the room. When he returned, he announced the shocking news that Whiteford had been killed in an automobile accident driving to the meeting. Brockett was later named the new chairman.

The single most crucial development of the '60s in catapulting Holiday Inn to truly stratospheric growth came in 1964. At that time, computers were a brand-new technology, just beginning to move into the business market. But Kemmons had a hunch that they could give Holiday Inn a big edge. So he reached an agreement with IBM to install a system that would allow travelers to instantly make reservations or find out what rooms were available at any Holiday Inn anywhere.

"The only way we could make a reservation back then was to make a long-distance call, and phones were a lot more expensive than they are now. I thought that there ought to be some way to establish a better connection between the Holiday Inns. I hired Jack Connolly, an electronics expert who was working for IBM, to find us some way to make up a system to connect all of them," Kemmons recalls.

At first, negotiations were stormy. "IBM didn't want to do a custom system for Holiday Inn," Walton says. "They said they had never done that for anyone. So Kemmons walked out. He said, 'We'll get somebody else to do it.' IBM had asked $10 million at first, but after that they came back with a better price."

IBM developed a system customized to Holiday Inn's needs for a price tag of only about $8 million. It would become known as Holidex.

"Tom Watson, the chairman of IBM, came down here to Memphis and requested a meeting with Wallace and me. He told us IBM really wanted to do the deal, and he thought it was something that would really spread to the other hotels. But they hated to tell us Holiday Inn's credit wasn't good enough. Our credit wasn't bad; the company just wasn't big enough yet to sign a note for $8 million. So he said if Wallace and I would endorse the note ourselves, they would do it. And without any hesitation at all, we agreed."

It represented a huge gamble on an unproven technological gambit. "Podner, this deal is either going to make this company or break it," Kemmons said to Wallace as they signed the contract.

"But I thought it would make us. And from the day we got that, it was no longer a matter of selling franchises, it was a matter of taking orders for them. They stood in line waiting to get a Holiday Inn franchise. It gave us a huge edge over our competitors, because nobody else had anything like it."

Talking with a reporter a few years later, Holiday Inn Senior Vice President for Administration Dick Ashman marveled at Kemmons' utter confidence, even when gambling megabucks on high-stakes moves like Holidex. "Kemmons buys something, gives it to Bill Walton and forgets about it. He assumes it's going to work. ... I had been with the company three years, and they gave me the whole Holidex project and left me alone."

Ashman was just one of the many intensely ambitious young men Holiday Inn began employing and vaulting rapidly up the ladder as the company's growth kicked into high gear. Ashman was hired in 1961 as a field auditor, then 90 days later was made head of the accounting department. Such stories were repeated throughout the company. Jeff Mann became a desk clerk at 25. A week later, he was promoted to innkeeper. Six months later he was moved into franchise sales, where he soon became president of the division.

"You get more responsibility in this company in such a short period of time — it's absolutely unbelievable," Ashman observed.

Ray Schultz, who later became chief executive officer of the Promus Hotel Corporation, left IBM to join Holiday Inn in 1968. He had first become acquainted with Kemmons as one of the IBM team members who worked the Holiday Inn account in the development of Holidex in the early '60s. "I recall Kemmons was a tough negotiator and established a price of $5,000 for the reservation terminal to be used in what became the Holidex system. At that time, IBM was unaccustomed to having customers set prices. But you guessed it, we built a $5,000 terminal for Holiday Inn," Schultz says.

In 1968, Kemmons interviewed Schultz for the position of vice president of information systems. "He wanted to know if I wanted the job. I told him I did, and his next question was, 'What are we going to pay you?' I said, '$25,000 a year.' He said, 'You're crazy. I don't pay my president that much.' I said, 'You'll have to pay me that much.' He shook his head and said OK," Schultz remembers.

Schultz also recalls a Holiday Inn board meeting in which the vote did not go the way Kemmons wanted it to, prompting Kemmons to say, "We'll just have to vote again until we get it right."

Another of Schultz's favorite memories is the time he had dinner with Kemmons and George Waters, executive vice president of American Express. "Kemmons said he didn't believe that anyone needed more than $40,000 a year. In fact, he didn't think anyone could even spend more than that. George Waters responded that if everyone flew a company jet, borrowed money from his employees to use pay phones, and stayed free and ate free in hotels all over the world, then Kemmons was probably right," Schultz says.

It wasn't just young men who made their mark at Holiday Inn. Les Price had retired from General Outdoor Advertising Company and was 65 years old when Kemmons talked him into coming to work as head of the Holiday Inn advertising department.

"He was a big help to us," Kemmons says. "He just did a fantastic job."

The bustling, ever-growing nerve center of the vast Holiday Inn network was Holiday City, the company headquarters on Lamar Avenue in Memphis. The company liked to call it "the capitol complex of the innkeeping capital of the world." A magazine reporter wrote, "There is no metropolitan center in the country — and almost none in the world — that is not doing business with a miniature 'city within a city' covering 80 acres on the southeast edge of Memphis, Tennessee. ... It is Holiday City, the hometown of Holiday Inns, Inc."

In 1970, Holiday Inn became the first lodging and food-service chain to top a billion dollars in gross sales. The next year, with the opening of a Holiday Inn in Anchorage, Alaska, the company became the first lodging chain to have facilities operating in all 50 states.

In 1972, the $5 million Holiday Inn University was dedicated on an 88-acre campus with library, dormitories, study halls and 175,000 square feet of classroom space in Olive Branch, Mississippi. It taught not only innkeeping but business management.

Bill Walton was the driving force behind the university. He saw it as a place to train the next generation to carry on the ideas that built Holiday Inn, "to teach a thorough, balanced approach to administration in the service industry." He says he welcomed every incoming class, congratulated every graduating class, and preached The Holiday Inn Way at every opportunity. He liked to joke that the campus grounds included a man-made lake so trainees could practice walking on it.

Walton had Tom Wells locate massive pieces of antique English furniture for Holiday Inn University, because "I wanted it to have the dignity and the solid appearance of Oxford University. And it did. It looked like a university. It was impressive. And everybody who wanted to operate a Holiday Inn had to go through it."

Within a span of two decades, a company started by a man who never finished high school had turned innkeeping into an enterprise of higher education.

CHAPTER ELEVEN

—THE TIME IS NOW—

**"Work only half a day. It makes no difference which half —
it can be either the first 12 hours or the last 12 hours."**

Kemmons Wilson

*A*ll the while that Holiday Inn was steamrolling its way into the annals of modern American business phenomena, Kemmons kept blazing his own legendary trail. Working and traveling at a pace few other humans could tolerate, he generated a reputation in those years that would reach near-mythical proportion.

"Mr. Wilson drove the car," says architect Bill Bond. "Everybody else was in for the ride."

In countless media accounts, Kemmons became famous as the man who ordered apple pie as soon as he sat down in a restaurant, so he could have dessert out of the way by the time his steak was cooked. By the early '60s, Madison Avenue was helping cultivate Kemmons' mercuric image. A national-magazine campaign for National Car Rentals, headlined "For Men Who Hate to Wait," featured Kemmons on the advantages of always having a rental car waiting at the airport. A spot for Aero Commander planes presented Kemmons under the headline "Constantly on the Go."

In 1967, *Memphis Press-Scimitar* columnist Robert Johnson reported on a day with Kemmons. It begins with a 7 a.m. flight out of Memphis in the Holiday Inn Lear Jet, a "luxury hotrod ... a six-passenger skyrocket" that jumps off the runway "like a striped owl." Kemmons has barely taken his seat before he begins reviewing "20

— 89 —

pounds of blueprints" with Charlie Bland, his vice president for construction. Next he confers with other department heads on plans for his mother's goodwill tours, on booking entertainers for Holiday Inn lounges and other matters.

At 8:20, the jet lands in Chicago. A real-estate associate of Kemmons picks up the group in his Lincoln Continental. After breakfast at a Holiday Inn on Lakeshore Drive, Kemmons is interviewed by a Chicago newspaper financial editor. Next they join another real-estate developer to head for the groundbreaking for an urban-renewal project in which Kemmons and Wallace will be involved in the construction work. There, Kemmons poses for photographs with Mayor Richard Daley.

Next Kemmons inspects a huge new cafeteria recently opened in the city, which feeds 6,500 daily. Then he drives about town looking at real estate and discussing plans for a shopping center. He spots a piece of land he likes, and after a few minutes dickering, buys five acres for $400,000. After a quick flight to Dayton, Ohio, where Kemmons goes over plans for a Holiday Inn there, the group returns to Memphis. The reporter calls it a day. Kemmons keeps working.

In 1965, *Look* magazine reported: "Kemmons Wilson sells hard in a soft drawl, rises at 5:30 a.m. and revels in his 19-hour days." For one of the shots in the accompanying photo spread, *Look* had Kemmons pose in a Holiday Inn swimming pool full of floating dollar bills. He was joined in the water by Union Planters National Bank Chairman John Brown and First National Bank Chairman Allen Morgan. It was Morgan who inspired the shot when he told a *Look* reporter, "We've all been in the Holiday pool up to our necks in floating loans."

However, when the magazine's editors realized that real currency had been used in the photograph, they feared it would violate federal counterfeiting laws and asked Kemmons if he could get the bankers in the pool again with fake money. "Sure," Kemmons replied, "I owe them so much money, they'll do anything for me."

In an editor's note to the issue featuring Kemmons, *Look* observed: "T. George Harris - one of *Look's* top word men - and photographer Jim Hansen arrived in 'Kemmons-town' to be welcomed by 'himself.'

When the *Look* team visited Memphis in August 1965, it was a 7.5-million circulation magazine. Hansen recalls how Kemmons was described in an editorial briefing at *Look* as "the undisputed point man of the world lodging revolution." Managing Editor Bill Arthur told the staffers working on the story, "We've got to pull out all the stops on this one, because mounds of research tells us Kemmons Wilson is a man on top of his game — a classic rags-to-riches story."

The first day's interviews began the minute the *Look* crew stepped off their plane in Memphis and continued past midnight. Work resumed at 5:30 the next morning, with a photo shoot of Kemmons riding a golf cart about a six-lane stretch of highway covered with Holiday Inn carpeting — all set up as part of a Holiday Inn promotion of its high-quality carpets.

The relentless pace continued for a week, "exploring activity in every corner of the Holiday Inn World headquarters," Hansen says. During the team's visit, Kemmons flew them with him to Hot Springs and Little Rock for several meetings, including a working lunch with then-Arkansas Governor Winthrop Rockefeller, as well as to Freeport, Bahamas, to inspect a new Holiday Inn.

"It was a wonder to complete our seven-day mission scrutinizing every waking aspect of the nation's hottest business wizard," Hansen says.

Kemmons' mother was included in the interviews, after Harris asked if it would be too tiring for the 70-year-old Doll to be involved in the story. "No," Kemmons replied, "your greatest problem will be trying to keep her out of it."

Dorothy was also interviewed. She told the *Look* Magazine crew that she and Kemmons usually discussed their children and disagreements they might have in special talks before bedtime. "The agenda is always spontaneous, but business discussions are rare," Dorothy said. "Pillow talks have always been a way to keep our heads on straight — but they are sometimes pre-empted when Kemmons includes a bowl or two of ice cream in the conference arrangements."

The last day of shooting did not wrap up until 2 a.m. At the conclusion, Kemmons turned to Hansen and said, "I've done everything but turn handsprings to pose for your camera and prove how hard I work. Now I have a question for you: What is the secret of taking great photos?" Without hesitating, Hansen replied, "Use lots of film," and noted he was leaving Memphis with 1,283 rolls of film shot that week.

Clyde Dixon, who retired at Holiday Inn as a senior vice president in 1977, still marvels at the driving force Kemmons generated in Holiday Inn's boom years. "Kemmons needed 100 guys standing outside his office to go check out things for him," Dixon recalls. "He had this absolute belief that he could do anything, anytime, better than anybody who worked for him."

Ultimately, Dixon says, Kemmons learned to accept that other people might never do things as well as he believed he could, but that he had to live with the best they could do.

"If he could have done everything himself, he would have done it," Dixon remembers. "He used to say, 'How could you guys be sick? Nobody gets sick.' He had a bad cold or something, and he would go, go, go."

According to Dixon, Kemmons had three major loves in business. He loved to buy land and imagine what he could do with it. He loved to develop and build things differently from anyone else. And he loved to buy things cheaper than anybody else. "His favorite expression was, 'How can you guys be so stupid? Nothing costs that much,'" Dixon says.

Undoubtedly, the activity that kept Kemmons burning up the road more than any other was selecting sites for new Holiday Inns. He enjoyed it more than any aspect of the business, and he picked hundreds of sites himself. He usually recognized what he wanted immediately, routinely buying land on the spot. He liked locations that were highly visible, situated on the right-hand side of the road as drivers were heading into a city, and came with extra acreage in case he wanted to expand.

It was not uncommon for Kemmons to buy a piece of land, then immediately recoup a fourth or more of the price by selling a corner to Gulf Oil for a gas station. Hundreds of Gulf stations were opened adjacent to Holiday Inns in this manner.

For many years, Kemmons also routinely passed judgment on the sites franchisees selected for their inns. Mississippian Mike

Sturdivant, who would later become a candidate for governor of that state, landed a franchise as a young man just out of college in his hometown of Meridian. Kemmons flew down to take a look at the site Sturdivant selected.

But once Kemmons took a look at it, he said, "Mike, that's not the place to build a Holiday Inn. Why would you want that place?"

"Well, I already own it," Sturdivant responded.

"Well, you remember this: The worst thing you can ever do is build a hotel on a location just because you own it," Kemmons counseled. "You have got to find the right location." Kemmons then helped find another location for the young man's Holiday Inn, which proved very successful.

Part of what made land-buying so much fun for Kemmons was doing it in an era of relatively cheap land. "Nobody ever heard about price per-square-foot back in those days. It was all by the acre. If it was more than $1,000 an acre in the early days, I wouldn't even look at it. And $1,000 an acre was about 3 cents a square foot. Now you pay $10 and $15 a square foot for almost anything."

He figured a piece of land should cost no more than 10 percent of the total cost of the hotel to be built on it. Other considerations in the Holiday Inn site-selection process were traffic flow, surrounding road systems, distance to airports, average income in the area around the site, potential for business development and the strength of any motels in competition nearby.

Kemmons became known as the best site-picker in the business. Even his industry colleagues readily acknowledged him as the undisputed master.

In 1962, Kemmons was invited to join fellow hotel-chain heads Marion Isbell of Ramada Inns, Bill Marriott of Marriott Inns and Howard Johnson of Howard Johnson Motor Inns on a panel at a convention in New York. After each had spoken, they took questions from the audience.

"Mr. Isbell," came the first question, "I would like to know how you find a good location for a Ramada Inn?"

"It's the most simple thing in the world," Isbell replied, with a wink to Kemmons. "I just find out where Kemmons Wilson has a location for a Holiday Inn, and I build across the street."

When Kemmons really wanted a piece of land for a Holiday Inn, virtually nothing could deter him. His son Spence recalls traveling in North Carolina in 1970 with Kemmons as he searched for a Holiday Inn site in the area. Near an interstate highway, he found some land he considered ideal. There was no For Sale sign, but Kemmons managed to find out that the owner lived in a small house on the property.

"We go up and knock on the door. We had seen someone in the back," Spence recalls. "But nobody answers. Dad says, 'Hey, is anybody home? I want to talk to you about some land.' Still, nobody answers. But he is persistent and keeps knocking and asking if anyone is home. Finally a voice from inside shouts, 'Go away!' "

So Kemmons is standing on a porch far from home, and he has no idea who or what is inside the house. But they have quite clearly ordered him to leave. He is the chairman of the largest lodging corporation in the world, with thousands of employees who could pursue the matter for him later. But still, he keeps knocking.

"I wanted to leave," Spence says, "but Dad says he still wants to try and talk to them. I don't know how long it took, but it took a dadgum long time. I was getting embarrassed. I said, 'Look, Dad, they don't want to talk to us, why don't we just leave it alone?' "

"But he just kind of hung in there. And finally someone cracked the door open, and Dad started talking to them. And before long, he was going over a proposition to buy the land and build them a house wherever else they wanted. It's a very lasting memory in my mind. I constantly refer to it whenever I think it would be easier to quit something and find something easier."

One of Kemmons' favorite site-hunting grounds in the '60s and '70s was fast-growing, freeway-lined California. Whenever Kemmons was in the state, Guilford Glazer, a land-developer there who worked with Kemmons, knew he could count on getting no sleep. Kemmons would keep him up til all hours looking at land. One night at 3 a.m., they were stopped by the highway patrol for driving too slowly on a freeway, "because we were poking along looking at real estate," Glazer recalls.

Bill Bone was another Californian who worked with Kemmons

finding hotel sites there. An associate of Glazer's, Bone was once assigned by Kemmons to determine the owners of property at every freeway off-ramp throughout the vast Los Angeles freeway system, and to determine each site's availability, zoning and other details.

"In those days, Holiday Inn was expanding very rapidly in California, and Kemmons spent two or more months every year looking for sites. Whenever Kemmons would come to town, he would typically work all day in Memphis and then arrive in Los Angeles around 9 or 10 p.m. I would pick him up at the airport and we would drive around and look at sites until about 1 a.m. Then I would pick him up for breakfast about 5:30 a.m. to start looking again. We typically had barbecued ribs for breakfast," Bone says.

"He would keep this up for three days before returning to Memphis. On one occasion, after two and a half days at that pace, Guilford was so worn out he got in a taxi in West Covina and $100 later arrived at his home and went directly to bed."

Bone finally figured out how Kemmons managed to pull off those feats of endurance. "The trick was that Kemmons would catnap as we were driving between sites on the freeway. Then when we arrived he would wake up, look over the site, and go back to sleep again as we drove to the next site. Everyone else stayed awake, and as a result always wore out more quickly."

Over the years, Kemmons has proven he can and will nod off almost anywhere — even in the middle of a trial over a business dispute, claims Frank Herbers, a longtime friend and business associate of Kemmons in Memphis. A lawyer for the plaintiff noticed the drowsing Kemmons and announced to the courtroom, "He is either as innocent as a babe, or he has so much money he doesn't give a hoot."

Kemmons' son Bob says ministers around Memphis are accustomed to Kemmons dozing off during services. On the rare occasions that he doesn't nod off, ministers have been known to comment at the conclusion, "Evidently that was a good sermon, because Kemmons stayed awake."

In the early '60s, Kemmons invited his pastor at Christ United Methodist, Dr. Charles Grant, to attend Holiday Inn's annual convention, because Dr. Norman Vincent Peale was the featured speaker. Kemmons and Dorothy took Dr. Grant and his wife, Mary Anna, with them to the Holiday Inn Rivermont. Afterward, Dr. Grant said, "Kemmons, this was one of the most wonderful evenings of my life, but you don't know why."

Kemmons said it must have been because he enjoyed Peale so much, but Dr. Grant replied, "I did. But what made the evening so wonderful was that I saw you nod off while Dr. Peale was speaking. If he can't keep you awake, I'll never feel bad about your falling to sleep during my sermons."

Harry Bainer, a Memphis partner of Kemmons in several ventures, remembers the time Kemmons slept through most of a Broadway production of *The Last of the Red Hot Lovers*. Afterward, however, he was so entertained by the many gadgets in store windows along the street that they ended up walking 20 blocks back to the hotel.

One evening in 1967, Bill Walton had just completed plans for one of the most extensive reorganizations in Holiday Inn history. He invited Kemmons and Wallace to his house for dinner to discuss the overhaul.

"I had the organizational charts all worked out for what the various departments were going to do. After dinner we went in my study upstairs and spread all the paperwork out on the floor. And I was explaining this big, new organization I was proposing and how it would work. Wallace was down on his hands and knees with me, looking everything over. And I looked over and Kemmons was sound asleep," Walton recalls.

"Wallace said to him, 'Podner, wake up.' Kemmons said, 'Huh? What's going on?' Then he said, 'Bill, I don't care what you do. If this is what you think is the right way to do it, go ahead with it.' "

Lee Yeager, who operated Holiday Press for Kemmons, remembers once flying with Kemmons in a twin-engine company plane between Beaumont, Texas, and Houston. Kemmons was asleep in the back seat with his head resting on Yeager's shoulder. About 20 minutes out of the Beaumont airport, the pilot announced they had lost power in the right engine. When Yeager woke Kemmons with the news, Kemmons questioned the pilot briefly, said, "We are lucky we still have one engine," and went right back to sleep.

But when he was awake, Kemmons in action was something to behold — especially at the negotiating table, as anyone who witnessed it can testify. Bill Bone still marvels at one of Kemmons' marathon dickering efforts in 1965. When Holiday Inn acquired the site to build its first mid-rise hotel in California that year, Bone thought he had dickered the contractor down to a bargain price, which worked out to $10,000 per room.

"No one to our knowledge had ever built a mid-rise hotel that inexpensively. But Kemmons was outraged that the price was that high," Bone recalls.

"He came to town and met directly with the plumber, electrician and all the other trades people for five straight days. He asked them how many man-hours it took to do each step in the construction. He knew the plans inside and out, and he showed the subcontractors how they could do everything more economically."

When Kemmons was done, the hotel was contracted out to be built at a cost of $5,700 per room.

"Kemmons can probably get more work done of all sorts — from dealmaking, to letting contracts, to subletting — whatever is necessary," says Sam Phillips.

"He was nothing short of phenomenal. He could get on an airplane and go to sleep for an hour or so, go to the West Coast, cut a deal, come back into Memphis, and many times go somewhere and go on to another deal in the same day."

The ability and willingness to fly anywhere at the drop of a hat was one of the most crucial advantages for Kemmons in building Holiday Inn. From the start, Kemmons used planes like most people use their feet. "Sometimes I think I live in an airplane," he once told a reporter.

In the earliest days of Holiday Inn, Kemmons was not only the chairman of the board, he was also the company pilot. At first, he flew a single-engine Beechcraft Bonanza, calling it the Holiday Inn plane, although it was actually his own aircraft. By 1956, a second plane was acquired. Kemmons flew the new one, and Jack Ladd, then general franchise-sales manager, used the older one.

By 1960, a twin-engine Aero Commander and two single-engine Cessna Skylanes had been added to the Holiday Inn fleet. Kemmons hired a pilot, Harry Galster, and began calling him Commanding Officer of the Holiday Inn Air Force. The next year, Holiday Inn bought a DC-3 airliner to carry large groups. Kemmons wanted the big plane in particular because it was the civilian version of the military C-47 that he had flown in World War II.

Numerous stories about flying comprise some of the richest lore from the Holiday Inn story. Wallace often recalled the many flights he and Kemmons made in the early days in the single-engine Bonanza. Once Kemmons got the plane leveled off in the right direction at the right altitude, he often would turn the controls over to Wallace — who wasn't a pilot — and take a nap. Kemmons says Wallace probably logged at least 500 hours of flying planes this way, without ever becoming a licensed pilot.

Whenever they spotted a prime location for a new Holiday Inn, Kemmons and Wallace would point and shout and get so excited they tended to forget everything else. On one occasion, when Walton was with them, they even forgot about the plane, Wallace wrote in his autobiography. While they were carrying on about the new site they had spotted, the Bonanza went into a spin and headed straight down. It took all Kemmons' skills as a pilot to pull out of the spin.

When he finally did, Walton, his face white as a sheet, asked what had happened.

"Ask Kemmons," Wallace replied. "He was flying the plane."

In astonishment, Kemmons looked at Wallace and said, "I thought *you* were flying it!"

Today, Kemmons just smiles at his partner's tale.

"That's got to be a little exaggerated," he says. "I can tell you I never went into a spin. But he might have thought it was a spin. I mean, I would turn that airplane almost upside down so I could turn around real quick and see the site better."

"But I did used to set the thing on automatic pilot. I would be so tired I didn't know what to do, so I would say to Wallace, 'You just watch and see if any airplane comes along, and wake me if it does.' He would sit there and watch it and I would go to sleep."

Wallace liked to joke that he and Kemmons could fly across America and drop sacks of flour to mark the spots they wanted to build

Holiday Inns. Over the years, the joke began to be repeated by reporters in newspaper articles as fact. In truth, it never happened.

"I buzzed many a place looking for sites, but I never dropped any sacks of flour," Kemmons says. It's the best way in the world to see a site, just get up there in the air and look at it."

Bill Walton says, "I could entertain an audience all night with stories about flying with Kemmons." One of his favorite episodes occurred when a group of Holiday Inn executives were flying back from Allentown, Pennsylvania. Kemmons was flying the plane over Washington D.C., and Charles Collins, Holiday Inn's general counsel, was flying copilot. Collins warned Kemmons that he thought they had veered into the restricted zone over the capital.

"Naw, we're all right," Kemmons said. "There's the Potomac right down there."

"Yes, I know," Collins said. "The Potomac is the boundary on this side of Washington. And we are way over on the other side."

About that time, a voice from the Washington control tower came on the radio: "Will the unidentified aircraft in the restricted zone identify yourself immediately."

Kemmons still refused to change course, insisting they were talking about someone else, until the tower came on the radio again, with more urgency: "If the unidentified aircraft that has entered the restricted zone does not identify itself, you will be intercepted and shot down."

With that, Kemmons had to concede they were off-course, and he hastily proceeded to maneuver the plane out of the restricted area.

The company was fortunate that with so many of its top executives airborne so often, fatal accidents were avoided.

In 1961, Wallace had a very close brush with tragedy when he decided at the last minute not to board a flight on a small plane flying from Hot Springs to Memphis. It crashed near Walls, Mississippi, killing two of the four passengers, one of whom worked for U-Finish Homes, a company owned jointly by Kemmons and Wallace. The other man killed had only just met Wallace at the airport in Hot Springs and had been given Wallace's spot on the flight when Wallace decided not to go. Wallace had flown in the plane from Pine Bluff to Hot Springs, but decided to stay overnight with his wife in a home they owned there, because she was not feeling well.

Kemmons got a second scare that day after he flew down to the site with his son, Bob, then a teen-ager. Kemmons decided to stay and drive back a little later, so Bob, who already had his pilot's license, returned home in the small plane in which they had flown down. But on the flight back, Bob had trouble working the radio and landed at a different field than where Kemmons expected him to land. When Kemmons learned Bob never showed up at his original destination, Kemmons endured several frantic moments before Bob was able to let him know what had happened.

In 1964, Kemmons himself walked away uninjured from a crash in a chartered, twin-engine Cessna. It was attempting to take off from Cincinnati — at an airport known to pilots as Sunken Lunken because it was low-lying — en route to a Holiday Inn groundbreaking in Columbus, Ohio. That airport was then Cincinnati's main airport before a new one was built in nearby Kentucky. After the left engine failed on takeoff, the pilot was supposed to "feather" the failed engine to reduce air resistance. But he instead feathered the right engine, leaving the plane with no engines operating. However, the pilot managed to maneuver the plane onto the grassy, softer ground alongside the runway before impact.

That quick-thinking maneuver was credited with averting fatalities. But Kemmons just shrugged off the incident, telling a reporter, "I flew today, I'll fly tomorrow." In fact, that very evening, Kemmons flew to Vanderbilt University in Nashville to speak to his son Spence's fraternity.

Bob remembers a flight back from North Carolina on which he, Dorothy, Kem and Betty were flying with Kemmons in a Bonanza. Suddenly the engine quit and Kemmons had a difficult time getting it started again. Bob was thrilled at the possibility of a crash landing, but after several tense moments the engine restarted. However, Kemmons later pressed Beechcraft to investigate the problem he had encountered, and the company changed the design of the plane's fuel-indication system.

It was probably inevitable that from the first day Kemmons ever flew, he would one day get into the aviation business. Holiday Inn purchased its first Lear jet in 1966, an eight-seat, twin-jet model, in typical Kemmons fashion.

"We had a company we called HI-Air. We built hangars and went into the aviation business, buying and selling airplanes and providing other services. And I always had to buy everything wholesale. So we bought three Lear Model 23's for $500,000 apiece, brand new. We sold two of them for $550,000 apiece and kept one, so that made ours only cost $400,000," Kemmons says, still proud of the savings.

He did not fly the 600-mph Lear Jet, turning over that job to jet pilots. However, he still liked to take charge of flights. Harry Bainer remembers once traveling with Kemmons in the Lear Jet on a tour of furniture manufacturers. They landed at a small airport in McKenzie, Tennessee, which was not designed for jets. A pilot with the company they were visiting told Kemmons he was worried the runway would be too short for the Lear Jet to take off again. But Kemmons retorted that they would not even use half the runway.

"Kemmons bet him we would be off the runway before we got even with the terminal building," Bainer recounts. "After we taxied to the end of the runway, Kemmons told our pilot to rev the engine but hold the brakes until he couldn't hold them any longer. Well, our pilot had the plane dancing, and when he released the brakes we shot forward and it felt as if we were ascending straight up. I looked back and realized we *were* practically going straight up. Kemmons proved his point."

For all the countless hours Kemmons spent in planes, what had to be his wildest adventure in the air began in a helicopter in New York City in 1965. He had gone there with Dorothy to be a featured speaker at a banquet at the annual New York Hotel Show. The day of the evening banquet at which he was to speak, Kemmons flew by helicopter to look at some possible Holiday Inn sites in Connecticut and upstate New York with George Falls, who was then in charge of the company's New York operations.

They took off in a rented helicopter from a pad near 42nd Street and 12th Avenue on the Hudson River around noon. They flew directly to each site, inspected it and met with city officials at both. As they were heading back for New York City it was beginning to get dark, and the lights in the populated areas below began to come on. They were passing over the Meriden, Connecticut, Holiday Inn, and at the very moment they were looking down at the inn's Great Sign, its lights suddenly went out.

This puzzled Kemmons and Falls, and then they noticed *all* the lights below them had gone out, except for automobile lights on the streets and expressways. The pilot made inquiries on the helicopter radio and learned that the entire Northeast region, including New York City, had lost its electrical power.

It was the great, historic blackout of '65, which would leave the most densely populated region in the U.S. without power through most of the night because of a malfunctioning power station. It was an event that, until then, most Americans had never imagined could happen to the largest city in the most advanced country in the world. The blackout became one of the biggest news stories of the year. Kemmons was right in the middle of it, and appropriately, he was aloft as it unfolded.

In the darkness, the helicopter pilot could not see any landmarks, only the lights of traffic on the expressways below, so he followed them toward New York City. However, Falls recalls, they really did not know exactly *where* they were flying for some time. Finally, he spotted a huge shopping mall that he recognized and exclaimed, "We're in New Jersey!" For some reason, Kemmons cried out in response, "Pull this thing up!" Falls speculates it was a reflex from Kemmons' days of flying the dangerous corridors of The Hump in World War II. In any case, the pilot did pull the helicopter up and at the same time turned back toward the east, in the direction they then knew the New York City skyline lay.

However, when the turn was completed, Falls was stunned to realize nothing of the great metropolis could be seen in the darkness. It staggered him to know they had flown directly over the entire Borough of the Bronx and the giant George Washington Bridge without even knowing it. Fortunately, the pilot was familiar enough with the area though that he was able to navigate along the Hudson

River in the moonlight and reach the helicopter pad from which they had taken off earlier in the day.

Once they were back on the ground, they realized the subways were all shut down because they had no power. And there were no cabs available, because they were swamped with the overflow from the subways. So the helicopter pilot offered to drive Kemmons and Falls to the St. Moritz Hotel, where Kemmons and Dorothy were staying, and where Kemmons was still expecting to speak at the banquet that night. All three of the men squeezed into the pilot's Volkswagen and managed to find their way to the hotel along the eerily darkened streets.

At the St. Moritz, they found Dorothy in the lobby, which she had reached after struggling down 15 flights of stairs. They headed for the hotel bar, where they found many people who had been planning to attend the banquet. "It soon became obvious the event would not take place," Falls says, "and it didn't take long for Kemmons' mind to turn toward the prime rib that he knew was supposed to be served at the banquet. He summoned a waiter and asked him to find the banquet manager. When he arrived, Kemmons and Ernest Henderson, president of Sheraton Inns, talked him into serving them prime-rib sandwiches in a private room off the lobby."

A dozen or so of the intended banquet guests gathered and had begun to eat, when Kemmons asked Falls to go find some of the people he had met in the bar. They soon joined the party, and before long the wine for the banquet also was procured.

"What ensued was more than two hours of fun where different ones would tell stories and jokes," Falls recalls. "Kemmons and Henderson were trying to out-do one another, and the more they drank, the more the jokes flowed. Finally it broke up, the waiters were well tipped, and candles were given to guests to start their slow, dark climb up the stairs to their rooms."

During the '60s, Kemmons flights began routinely taking him far beyond the U.S. borders. "Once he got things going in the United states, then the world was his cup of tea," says Sam Phillips. "He got in to see everyone from maharajas to kings and queens — anyone he needed to."

In 1960, Montreal became the site of the first Holiday Inn built outside the United States. In 1963, the company's first off-continent inn was opened in Puerto Rico. After several years of site-hunting and negotiations, Europe's first Holiday Inn was built in Leiden, Holland, in 1968. The next year, Holiday Inn established a corporate office for Europe in Brussels. Over the course of the next few years, Holiday Inns were opened in Belgium, England, Austria, Italy, Germany, Portugal, Greece and Luxembourg, and soon many more would dot the landscape of Europe.

Also in 1968, Holiday Inn began opening hotels in the Caribbean and South America. In 1969, the first Holiday Inn in Africa was opened, in Marrakech, Morocco. In 1970, a 28-story circular building in Acapulco became the first Holiday Inn in Mexico. Soon after came Holiday Inns in Australia, New Zealand, the Samoas, the Fiji Islands, Indonesia, Taiwan, Hong Kong, India, Tahiti, Lebanon and Israel. In the '70s, Holiday Inn would establish the largest chain of hotels in Asia, including inns in Japan, Singapore, Thailand, Hong Kong, Cambodia, the Philippines, India, Sri Lanka, Pakistan, Malaysia and Tahiti.

In 1969, the increasing international identity of the company was officially acknowledged by changing its corporate name from Holiday Inns of America, Inc., to Holiday Inns, Inc. The slogan, "The Nation's Innkeeper," was replaced with "The World's Innkeeper."

By 1970, Kemmons had visited every continent except Antarctica. The world leaders he met included Pope Paul VI, Prince Rainier of Monaco, Prince Sihanouk of Cambodia, the Shah of Iran and countless governmental leaders around the world. Increasingly, foreign governments were realizing how the presence of a Holiday Inn could expand tourism in their country, so they welcomed Kemmons with open arms.

"I got lots of land free because they wanted to have a Holiday Inn there," Kemmons says. "I probably got at least a dozen pieces of land in Europe for nothing, and they were probably worth a lot of money. Land is a lot higher in Europe than it is in the United States."

No one was giving away land in Europe's major cities like Rome or London. In many smaller cities, however, officials were eager to give

Kemmons a 99-year-lease for a nominal sum — often $1 — in order to secure a Holiday Inn.

Throughout Kemmons' many adventures abroad, he never worried about language barriers. George Falls, who became assistant vice president for international franchise sales in the late '60s, said Kemmons made up for not being able to speak foreign languages by simple friendliness. He would smile, hug people, pull out magic tricks from his pocket, and generate enough good will to overcome the language gap.

"There are hundreds of languages in the world," Kemmons says, "but a smile speaks all of them. A smile never needs an interpreter."

One of Kemmons' favorite stories concerning his encounters with other languages occurred on a site-hunting trip in Germany. He and Dorothy were riding with Charlie Bland, who was then managing director of Holiday Inn International, as they cruised along the autobahn — the German freeway system. After passing several off-ramps marked *Ausfahrt*, Dorothy turned to Kemmons and said, "I've never heard of this place called Ausfahrt."

"I haven't either," replied Kemmons.

"Well, it's got to be one of the biggest cities in Germany."

Later, they learned *Ausfahrt* means *Exit* in German.

In Kuwait, Kemmons discovered that sometimes the familiar can appear in the most exotic of locales. Vawad Bokhartseen, a businessman there had contacted Kemmons about buying a Holiday Inn franchise. Kemmons had a trip coming up to Asia, so he agreed to make a stop in Kuwait.

"I got off the airplane, and he had someone to meet me." Kemmons remembers. "They explained to me he was on his way in from London, or he would have met me himself. So they took me to his mansion — and it was a real mansion, worth millions of dollars, I'm sure. They tried to entertain me, and they explained to me his plane had been delayed."

"Finally he got there. He rushed in and threw his arms around me and apologized. He spoke a little English, but not enough to really understand. We sat down, and I said, 'Well, before we go out to the site, do you have a family?' He said he had a wife and three children.

I said I would like to meet them. He said, 'You would?' And I said 'I really would.' "

"So we walked down a hall in this huge, incredible place and into a room. And there are his wife and three children, sitting on the floor with four boxes of Kentucky Fried Chicken. They had stopped on the way from the airport, and they were on the floor! I wish I had a picture of it."

In Kenya, Kemmons made a deal everyone said was impossible, when he discovered the president's wife had something in common with Dorothy. "Everybody said President Kenyatta would never see anybody. And then when a friend of mine was finally able to get me an appointment, they said he wouldn't see me very long. So I went in, and his wife was sitting over there in the room needlepointing. And I met her and spoke to her," Kemmons recalls.

"Then I said, 'President Kenyatta, your wife is as silly as my wife.' He looked at me like I was crazy and said, 'What do you mean?' I said, 'My wife needlepoints all the time too.' And I thought he would die laughing. So from then on, we were great buddies. I spent about an hour and a half with him, and we finally got a Holiday Inn built there."

Captain J.W. Clark was president of Delta Steamship Lines, which was acquired by Holiday Inn in the late '60s. He recalls traveling in Argentina with Kemmons, who as always was looking for prime Holiday Inn sites.

"He selected the best location in Parque Palermo — a national park! Despite our advice that national parks were simply off limits to commercial development, Kemmons insisted that we arrange meetings with government officials to discuss the opportunities," says Clark.

At a dinner meeting with government representatives and business leaders, Kemmons was finally persuaded to consider commercial sites instead.

Sleeping abroad proved no more of a problem for Kemmons than it had ever been back home. Rudiger Koppen headed Kemmons's operations in Asia during the years Holiday Inn built several hotels there. He recalls the time in the Philippines when he and Kemmons embarked on a site hunt in a military helicopter provided by Ferdinand Marcos, then president of the Philippines.

"Together with an escort of military personnel and artillery, off we flew in the noisiest aircraft I have ever been in," Koppen says. "Ten minutes after takeoff, I spotted a resort location and turned to point it out to Mr. Wilson. He was already fast asleep! He slept the entire flight."

Holiday Inn staffers went to great lengths to accommodate Kemmons when he was abroad. Koppen remembers preparing for Kemmons' first visit to Asia in 1970 and discovering that the soft-drink Tab was not available there. As it was Kemmons' favorite, Rudiger had two cases sent in from the U.S. and then carried them in his luggage throughout the trip so Kemmons would never be without one.

"Subsequently, I was able to persuade a supplier to import Tab into Hong Kong, so I would not have to search for it on Mr. Wilson's future visits. So he should receive some credit for indirectly initiating the marketing of Tab in Asia," Rudiger says.

Eating abroad proved perhaps the greatest challenge for Kemmons, or at least for his aides. Even back in Memphis, Kemmons' reputation as a peculiar eater was well established, particularly with Dorothy. "Most of all, he is nuts on barbecue. Whenever someone asks if we have been to this restaurant or that restaurant, I say, 'If it doesn't have barbecue, we haven't been there.' He's a funny eater. He won't eat anything green. And he won't try anything. I ask him how he knows if he doesn't try it, and he says he just knows," she sighs in resignation.

Bob Wilson remembers how Kemmons always had longtime associate Hugh Chatham make excuses whenever Kemmons considered the food too exotic, which meant virtually all the time when traveling in other countries. "Pop would have Hugh tell them he wasn't feeling well that day, so he wouldn't have to eat stuff and wouldn't offend their host."

In Japan, Holiday Inn's partner in Tokyo hosted a lavish banquet at the Imperial Hotel in honor of Kemmons' visit, Koppen says. Though it was after 10 that night when the banquet concluded, Kemmons insisted on heading off on foot for a McDonald's two miles away. Upon reaching the McDonald's and discovering it had closed, Kemmons marched off to a hotel coffee shop and ordered a hamburger and milkshake.

Kemmons' daughters traveled with him and Dorothy on several business trips abroad as teenagers. "I remember in Japan and Hong

Kong, they were serving all this sushi," says Carole. "Daddy told them he had an ulcer so he wouldn't have to eat it. He didn't want to offend them, but he sure didn't want to eat that raw fish."

Charlie Bland recounts the time Kemmons and a group of Holiday Inn officials were taken to Alfredo's, a fine restaurant in Rome. The group was served an initial course of fettuccine Alfredo, the house specialty. But Kemmons immediately announced that he wanted meat sauce on top of his Alfredo sauce.

Bland remembers the waiters were frozen in place until Kemmons' request "for this abomination" was translated to the proprietor, Alfredo — who was seated next to Kemmons. Finally, Alfredo nodded for the waiters to comply. Though the other Italians at the table declined the meat sauce, all the Holiday Inn employees quickly asked to have the same as Kemmons.

"When it arrived, Kemmons inquired as to how we liked it. In complete unison, the cry of 'Great!' resonated through the room," Bland says.

"Of course, it actually tasted like Alpo."

Chapter Twelve

—At Home With The Wilsons—

**"If you bring somebody home,
they will remember you better."**

Kemmons Wilson

$\mathcal{N}$o matter how much was going on with Holiday Inn, Sunday mornings found Kemmons and his family at Christ United Methodist Church in Memphis. Some of the most important lessons in life for the Wilson children were learned there. "Mom and Dad gave us a tremendous Christian foundation, very definitely," Betty says.

"Dad always insisted that the entire family sit together in church. Even when we were teenagers, and all the other kids went off with their friends — not the Wilson family. We sat together and filled up a whole pew. Dad just insisted we all worship together and worship regularly."

As Holiday Inn grew up in the 1960s, so did Kemmons' family. By the end of the decade, his three sons were married, and both his daughters were in college.

"I was gone more than 50 percent of the time back then. That's the reason I'm so proud of Dorothy and what a great job she did with our children. She's the one who really raised them. I was gone," Kemmons says.

The children agree with their father's assessment. "Pretty much, Mom raised the kids and Pop provided the dollars to do that," Bob says.

There is no counting the number of times Dorothy packed Kemmons' bags for a business trip on a few minute's notice, whipped up dinners for groups of business associates that he brought home by surprise, or watched Kemmons wolf down dinner and rush off again for an evening meeting — with remarkable patience and good humor.

A Memphis newspaper reporter once wrote: "Packing is no problem for Mr. Wilson ... He calls home, tells his wife when he is leaving and how long he expects to be gone, and doesn't worry about it any more. 'I won't know what I've got until I get there, but somehow she always takes real good care of me,' he says."

"Mother was always the woman behind the man," her daughter Betty says. "She loves him, and she loves people like he does, so it was easy for her to move right along with all the entertaining and fanfare that their lives involved."

Dorothy's devotion to her family was recognized nationally in 1970 when she was selected American Mother of the Year. The honor took her and the family to the White House to be congratulated by President and Mrs. Nixon, and to New York for an appearance on the Ed Sullivan Show. John Q. Hammons, who was the largest franchisee of Holiday Inns in the late '70s and '80s, began sending flowers to Dorothy that Mother's Day with a card saying "Mother of the Year Every Year," and he has done so every year since.

In coincidental but poetically appropriate timing, Kemmons received the Horatio Alger Award at the Waldorf Astoria Hotel in New York two days before Dorothy received the Mother of the Year Award at another ceremony in the same hotel. His citation for the honor read:

His spectacular rise to success,
starting with a few cents to buy popcorn, is one of the most extraordinary
feats in the history of American business.

Dorothy accepted her award with modesty, demurring that she didn't need to be honored for doing something she loved. She also said Kemmons actually was more involved in raising their children than he let on: "Every big decision concerning our children was made by both of us. No child should ever be able to play one parent against the other. I don't remember ever saying 'yes' when 'no' was right. Our children respected that and accepted guidance, knowing how much we loved them."

Spence recalls that as busy as Kemmons was, he made it to many of Spence's junior-high and senior-high basketball games. "I didn't shoot much, and he always thought I should take more shots," Spence recalls, noting that it was a good example of how Kemmons always encouraged his children to try harder and be aggressive.

Flying was especially thrilling for the Wilson children, who have many memories of soaring through the skies with their father. Often he would let them sit in his lap and steer the plane. All three of the boys later got their pilot's licenses. Bob says his Dad once took him along at the last minute on a business trip, but in the rush they forgot to bring any clothes for Bob. Once they arrived, Kemmons had to buy him all new ones. Kem remembers Kemmons taking him along to a Holiday Inn opening in Missouri, where Kem got to meet two of his all-time favorite sports heroes, Mickey Mantle and Whitey Ford.

"I remember Daddy teaching Betty and me how to drive when we were about 12, driving up and down Galloway," Carole says of the street they grew up on.

"I remember best the times he would come home from work and prop up in bed to read the newspaper. Carole and I would always take his shoes and socks off, or Doll or Mother would," Betty says.

Kemmons had a special relationship with his daughters. They arrived seven years into his marriage, when Kemmons was beginning to think he would have only sons.

"He was always bragging on his girls. After three boys, he was glad to have girls come along. He used to say he didn't want anything but sons. Then I was born, and Carole shortly thereafter. And after that, he always said, 'You girls have made me eat my words,' " Betty recalls.

"I remember how he was the kingpin at work, and then he would come home and be the kingpin at home," Carole says. "We all were just crazy about him because he showed so much love for us. He wouldn't, you know, necessarily ask you, 'Well, how was your day, today?' But you knew he was glad to be home."

Even if Kemmons was often absent, when necessary he laid down the law after he got home. One summer at Pickwick Lake, Spence accidentally shot another boy with a BB gun. When Kemmons arrived for the weekend, Spence says, "He wore my little fanny out. And I can assure you I didn't ever shoot anyone with a BB gun again. I didn't get many spankings, but when I got them from Dad, I remembered them."

Spence also recalls how the swimming pool in the Wilson's backyard resulted from a promise Kemmons made as he was heading off on a business trip in the early '50s. At that time, Kemmons had placed a giant, inflatable, army-surplus raft in the backyard and filled it with water for the children to splash around in. But, deciding the boys were old enough for a real pool, he promised to build one if all three boys would learn to swim by the time he returned from that trip. When he got back, they could all dog-paddle the length of the big raft.

Later, the permanent pool became the focal point for the children's get-togethers with their friends. That suited Dorothy just fine, because it enabled her to keep an eye on things from a vantage point in the den.

"When the kids would have parties over here around our pool," she says, "I could sit on the sofa in our den and still know everything that was going on. With the windows where they are, I could see who was walking up the driveway, who was around the pool, if the boys were pushing the girls in the pool. They had a jukebox out there so they could dance, and they just had fun."

Dorothy remembers, "One night when they were teenagers, they wanted to have a band. I said, 'OK, but you tell the band there will be no beer, no whiskey, nothing.' I didn't allow it. But I noticed some of them were running around in back of the pool house. I thought, 'That's strange.' So I went back there, and the band had a cooler of beer. I went back around and told the band, 'You stop, you get that cooler and pick up all those cans and you get out.' Oh, the kids thought it was terrible. But they turned on the jukebox and had a good time anyway.

"I have always been very honest with my kids. I still am. I used to tell them, 'I don't care who you bring home, but they have to mind. This is my house, and I have rules.' "

At 14, the children all had to get summer jobs. The girls worked as camp counselors, stenographers and in mail rooms; the boys helped carpenters, roofers, plumbers and other workers at building sites.

"Those construction jobs were tough work. You had to get up early and work a pretty long day, and you really got hot. But because of that, I have never feared any kind of work," Spence says.

"We all worked every summer and grew up knowing the value of hard work and a dollar. The jobs were mostly construction oriented on either Dad's homebuilding operations or Holiday Inns. I did get the opportunity to go down to Grand Bahama my sophomore year in high school and help construct the largest Holiday Inn ever built. We slept in mobile-home trailers and really experienced a fantastic summer," Kem recalls.

The girls often got to work near Kemmons. "Carole and I had summer jobs at Holiday City when we were teenagers. Usually it was sorting mail in the mailroom and things like that. Any time Daddy could break away, we would always go to lunch with the boss. That was fun for us to be out there with him," Betty says.

"He was never too busy. He could be in a meeting with 10 men, and we could still go in and give him a hug and a kiss," Carole remembers.

The summer jobs were part of Kemmons and Dorothy's strategy to keep the children down to earth, despite their father's growing fame and wealth.

When Carole was in college, she remembers everyone in her sorority house and their dates gathering around the television one evening to watch a special on Kemmons and Holiday Inn.

"The program said he was worth $200 million. And I went, 'What!' And I called him and said, 'You're worth $200 million, and all the allowance you give me is $100 a month!' It was funny. But literally, we never knew we had money. We knew we didn't really want for anything, but we didn't feel rich," she says.

Dorothy says Kemmons told Carole the reporter got it mixed up: "Honey, it was a misprint. I don't own that much money, I owe it."

Spence recalls, "Somehow, Mother and Dad instilled something in us that we never felt like we were better than anybody."

When Spence was a junior or senior in high school, on a lark he snuck into Ellis Auditorium with several friends to see a wrestling match. When they were caught, the police asked each boy who his father was. Spence knew they would never believe Kemmons Wilson's son would have to sneak into a wrestling match. So at first he just said his father was "a businessman," but it just made the cops madder. When Spence finally did confess, the officers hit the roof, first chewing him out for making up such a thing and then for someone in his position setting a bad example.

"Most people who don't know that we are Kemmons Wilson's children are impressed when they find out.

But Mom and Dad taught us not to be too impressed with ourselves," Carole says.

Betty recalls, "Mother and Dad always felt the importance of teaching us the value of a dollar. Even when we went off to college, we lived very modestly. Kem and Carole and I were all at the University of Alabama together, when she was a freshman and I was a sophomore and he was a senior. I can remember very vividly one time when I had blown my $100 for the month. But I never even considered calling home for more. I called Carole and Kem and borrowed from them to make ends meet. But it was a very healthy concept they taught us."

"We didn't overextend their allowances," Dorothy says. "We were very conservative about that. It's so foolish to buy children with money. You can't have everything you want. There are things I still would like to have that I don't have."

Another strategy Kemmons and Dorothy employed with great success was offering their children a substantial reward for avoiding alcohol and cigarettes.

"Mom and Dad made a deal with all of us that if we didn't drink or smoke until we were 21, we would get $10,000 — $5,000 for not drinking and $5,000 for not smoking," Carole says.

"I think it really helped us know what to do, especially in college. I know I would probably have tried it, but I couldn't see taking a drink for $5,000. But if Mom and Dad hadn't done that, I guarantee Kem would have. And me too," Betty says.

Kem can't argue with that. "I still, to this day, have never had a drag on a cigarette, but I'm sure I would have experimented if not for the incentive Mom and Dad gave us. This challenge was instilled in us at such an early age that I had already made my mind up long before I was pressured by my peers. Even though I was tempted along the way, I found there were people who respected my decision. I truly felt a great sense of accomplishment on my 21st birthday. I have had friends come up to me 25 years later and say they admired the way I stood up for my convictions.

Consequently, I have made the same challenge to my children," he says.

"I can look back today and say that this test helped shape my character. It gave me an early goal in life, a real prize to strive for. I believe it was this self-discipline and willpower that did more for us than anything else Mom and Dad could ever have thought of. It gives you a pretty clear look at life when you don't smoke or drink at that age and you see how other people behave. When we got to be 21, we had seen enough people make fools of themselves drinking and smoking that whatever we did even then, we did in moderation," Kem said.

The family's most frequent vacations while the children were young were long summer stays at a cabin they owned at Pickwick Lake. Dorothy would take the children and stay for a month or more, and Kemmons would come over for weekends. Bob remembers Kemmons liked to drive the boat and let the children ski behind it. But when the boys began playing summer baseball, Dorothy never wanted to go off on vacation without them, so Kemmons sold the place at Pickwick.

She also tried to minimize traveling with Kemmons on business when the children were young. "He liked me to go. But when I would, the kids would say, 'Momma, you stay home and let Daddy go.' Once they got older, I made quite a few trips. I've been all over the world," Dorothy says.

"Carole and I had more opportunity to travel with Mother and Dad than the boys did," says Betty. "They were in college by the time Holiday Inn was really going international. I remember particularly when we made a trip to the Far East. It was incredible. In Cambodia, we had a private audience with Prince Sihanouk. He gave me a silver lion, and Carole a silver box."

Though Kemmons built his business empire without an education, he made sure all five of his children earned college degrees: Spence at Vanderbilt, Bob at Southern Methodist, and Kem, Betty and Carole at Alabama. All three sons also went to Harvard Business School after finishing their undergraduate work. Spence completed an MBA there, while Bob and Kem both went through the Small Business Management Program, a three-year, part-time curriculum.

Kemmons likes to claim credit for steering Spence to Harvard. In the late '50s, Kemmons had been impressed by Mike Sturdivant, the young man who built a Holiday Inn in Meridian, Mississippi. "He had a partner named Earl Jones. They had been roommates at Harvard Business School. As I got to know them, they were the sharpest young guys I had ever met. So I kept telling them, 'Every time you are around Spence tell him what a great school Harvard is, how he ought to go there,' " Kemmons says.

"So they did, and finally Spence took the bait. He got his bachelor's degree at Vanderbilt, and he came in and said, 'Dad, I want to go to Harvard.' But I said, 'Son, I don't want you to embarrass me. There's no way in the world you could pass the entrance test to Harvard.' I don't think I ever saw Spence so mad in his life. He said, 'I'll show you!' So he did. And he didn't know until after he had been there a while that we had planned this thing. We have all laughed about it a lot.

"But Spence went up there and graduated. And he is about as good as anybody you will find in finance. He is much better than I am, much smarter than I am."

Bob says he wasn't the most devoted student in the world. But he did hustle and negotiate his way through a degree at Southern Methodist, hardly a pushover school academically. Bob recalls that he got to know the dean better than anyone, because he spent so much time in the dean's office getting himself out of trouble.

His final semester in school, he only had to complete one last course to graduate. It was a philosophy course, and he hated it. But he gutted it out, made sure he had satisfactorily completed all the requirements, then headed home for Memphis in relief. However, when his grades arrived, he had been given an Incomplete for the philosophy course, and thus could not graduate. Dorothy and Kemmons were not pleased. But after Bob made one more trip to Dallas and the dean's office, he got it straightened out and brought home an official letter certifying that he had indeed graduated.

Probably the strongest memory that all the Wilson children share is the way their father seemed to bring everyone he knew home to meet them.

"Daddy was constantly bringing people home. Mother never knew how many to prepare dinner for. And it didn't matter if we were asleep.

He would just wake us up. We constantly had the opportunity to meet interesting people," Betty recalls.

"He was always bringing people home that he met through the Holiday Inn years," Kem says. "We probably met some famous people but were too sleepy to know it."

Whether they remember the individuals they met or not, Spence believes it made a lasting impression on the Wilson children. "He was always very proud of us and always wanted us to meet the people he was doing business with. Every now and then, it got kind of tiring or tedious, if you had other things to do. But I think in a subtle way, we got a message about him having pride in his family. I think you learn by example, and maybe it's why we all have pride in our own families and are so close still," he says.

Dorothy confirms that the children's memories are not exaggerated.

"Yes, Kemmons brought everyone home. Our home was almost a Holiday Inn itself. He didn't bring all of them home for dinner. But he would bring everybody by to meet his family, even if they were going to dinner somewhere else," Dorothy says with a sigh.

"When the kids were little, he would wake them up and I would nearly die. He would come in and wake them all up, pick those little ones up sound asleep, saying, 'I want you to meet all my children.' Then they would go on to dinner and I would be here with all those children wide awake. Oh! I used to scream when he would do that.

"But he always said, 'Momma, if you bring somebody home, they will remember you better.' "

Doubtless, that was true. A trip with Kemmons to his home was probably not easily forgotten. However, as the 1970s began, it became clear that countless people who never visited Kemmons' home were going to remember him.

The golden age of Holiday Inn was at hand. And the world would hear all about it.

CHAPTER THIRTEEN

—INTERNATIONAL CITIZEN—

"Sell your wristwatch and buy an alarm clock."

Kemmons Wilson

.*I*n 1972, Betty and her new husband, Jack Moore, took an apartment in New York City for the summer. Jack, a Vanderbilt law student, was clerking at a law firm on Wall Street during the summer break.

The newlyweds were walking down the street one early-June morning, when suddenly they were struck with an awareness of something extraordinary: Everywhere they looked, they saw the grinning face of Kemmons Wilson.

"At corner newsstands all over Manhattan, Daddy's face was on the cover of *Time* magazine. I'll never, ever forget it, just everywhere we turned. It was so incredible, I was telling people I didn't even know, 'That's my Dad!' " Betty recalls.

It was the June 12, 1972, issue of *Time*, America's news-magazine of record. And there indeed was Kemmons Wilson, with his blue eyes twinkling and his now-famous Holiday Inn sign over his shoulder. The headline above read: "The Man with 300,000 Beds." In the background, an artist's rendition of a highway seemed to stretch off into infinity.

For Kemmons Wilson and Holiday Inn in the early '70s, it certainly did appear the road would go on forever. *Time* assigned two reporters to try and keep up with Kemmons as he raced across two continents, exhausting both of them with 18-hour workdays.

"I had been warned about his pace," wrote *Time's* Alan Anderson. "But I still wasn't ready for it. He worked constantly except for catnaps, and after a while I couldn't believe he was 30 years older than I."

Beginning as early as 4 in the morning, Kemmons put the reporters through predawn-to-afterdusk days that ended with tennis at 10 p.m. On a swing through South America to check out potential Holiday Inn sites, Kemmons and his entourage covered 2,700 miles before heading back for Memphis. Six deals for new Holiday Inns were closed on that trip alone.

The *Time* article opened with a scene of Kemmons leaping out of the car on a bumpy highway outside Sau Paulo, Brazil. "Let's stop right-cheer," he cries upon spotting a sign that reads Vende-Se. "That means 'for sale' and those are the only words I understand in this language," Kemmons says.

Pacing off the dimensions of the property, he fires questions at his aides. "Who owns it? What about the taxes? How many cars pass by this spot?" Then, within minutes, he is sprinting for the car again, impatiently barking, "Let's get going. Daylight is running out, and you can't look at land in the dark."

Actually, Kemmons *could* look at land in the dark. Rudiger Koppen, head of Holiday Inn operations in Asia when it built several hotels there, remembers the time Kemmons insisted on being taken to a potential Holiday Inn site late one night because he was leaving early the next morning. Arriving in a group of three automobiles, Kemmons instructed the drivers to park strategically around the site with their headlights on. What Kemmons saw was enough to convince him on the spot to build a hotel there.

Making the cover of *Time* gave Kemmons international recognition: a portrait of the self-made, hyper-driven tycoon at the peak of his glory years, astride a worldwide corporation he had created with an inspiration, endless labor and borrowed money. At that point, *Time* estimated Kemmons was already worth more than $200 million. He liked to wear a tie emblazoned with the company's motto at the time: "It's a wonderful world."

Kemmons' wonderful world was a product of his own invention, *Time* explained, "because he practically created the modern motor-inn industry. He has transformed the motel from the old wayside fleabag into the most popular home away from home. ... Wilson was among the first to foresee that the fast post-World War II rise in U.S. personal income would lead to a rapid expansion in both business and leisure travel. He also sensed that people on the move would prefer to stay in lodges that offered, in addition to a place to park their car, a standardized level of cleanliness, comfort and food at moderate prices."

Kemmons first saw the *Time* cover at the home of the president of Rhodes College (then called Southwestern), where Kemmons had just been presented with an honorary degree. John Cleghorn, who handled Holiday Inn's public relations, came running up with an advance copy he had obtained just off the presses. Typically, Kemmons responded with an eye on the bottom line: "You can't buy advertising like this."

The day the article appeared, there were 1,405 Holiday Inns in 50 states and 20 foreign countries or territories, serving 72 million guests a year. Holiday Inn was providing more food and lodging than any organization in the world, except the U.S. Army. Kemmons had made his vision of motels for the masses an omnipresent reality. Holiday Inn had become the largest lodging business in the history of the world.

Though other chains like Ramada, Howard Johnson's, Sheraton and Marriott were furiously in pursuit, Holiday Inn still had four times as many rooms as its closest competitor. It was building a new room every 20 minutes and a new Holiday Inn every two-and-a-half days on average. More than 2,000 requests for franchises were coming in every year, but now the company could be choosy enough to grant only about 200 of them.

Kemmons' towering green-and-yellow signs were becoming an inescapable symbol of American business expansion around the globe. From Hong Kong to Casablanca, from Innsbruck to Buenos Aires, from Texarkana to Tahiti, travelers were finding a Holiday Inn to stay in almost anywhere they went. Not even the Iron Curtain could keep The Great Sign out. Holiday Inn had just signed a deal to build Holiday Inns in Yugoslavia, Bulgaria, Hungary and Czechoslovakia.

However, it all remained "Kemmons Kountry" — as one inn's marquee proclaimed. Despite the sprawling, global empire Holiday Inn had become, Kemmons was still running most of the show, "insisting on the last word in most major decisions and many small ones," *Time* said. He was known to veto projects already in the works with a curt "I don't like the smell of it," and to strike sizable deals on the spot before discussing it with anyone else in the company.

It was a period when international recognition was coming to Kemmons more and more often. In 1969, *The London Sunday Times* selected Kemmons as one of the 1,000 Makers of the Twentieth Century. The newspaper's selection placed Kemmons in the company of such figures as Winston Churchill, Franklin Roosevelt, William Faulkner and Elvis Presley.

"The motel reached its apotheosis in Holiday Inns," *The Times* wrote. On the basis of the "primitive research" of his 1951 vacation trip, it said, Kemmons established a lodging chain in which "inexpensive luxury would be absolutely predictable."

Kemmons Wilson, the native of Osceola, Arkansas, who got his start selling popcorn on the street in Memphis, had become a world-famous man.

At times, that fact was demonstrated to Kemmons in ways he found hilarious. One of his favorite occurred when he attended the wedding of Henri Landwirth, the early employee at the Cocoa Beach Holiday Inn who had gone on to become a successful franchisee.

"He was getting married and I went down for his wedding in Florida. After the wedding was over, Henri took me over to meet the rabbi, Aaron Shapiro. Henri said 'Rabbi, I want you to meet my friend, Kemmons Wilson.' And I'll never forget, the rabbi said, "Kemmons Wilson! Why, you are so famous, I wish I had circumcised you.' "

Kemmons would later experience perhaps the ultimate media validation of his renown when a segment of Robin Leach's *Lifestyles of the Rich and Famous* was devoted to him. Kemmons told Leach that his early poverty kept him tight-fisted even after he became wealthy: "I do go out and look for the bargains." Kemmons also made appearances on the most widely watched television talkshows of the day such as *The Tonight Show With Johnny Carson* and *The Merv Griffin Show*.

Kemmons was on *The Merv Griffin Show* with Meshulam Riklis, founder of the conglomerate Rapid American Corporation, and Wally Amos, founder of Famous Amos Cookies. The show was devoted to interviews with self-made millionaires.

Griffin introduced Kemmons as "a fellow who began with a couple of dollars and a couple of ideas, and that's all — all he needed to forge an amazing trail of business successes. His crowning success, the international motel chain called Holiday Inns, showed the self-made man can still pile up great wealth in this complex economy."

Griffin amused Kemmons greatly when he confessed to stealing Holiday Inn towels.

"I have six of your towels at home," Griffin said.

"Well, bless your heart," Kemmons said.

"But why do you print the 'Holiday Inn' so large?"

"I can understand why you would steal a towel that was blank."

"It's not stealing. I borrow them and I keep them clean."

"But I can't understand why anybody would take a towel with a name on it."

"Well ..." Griffin stammered.

"You know, all your neighbors know you took that towel from us," Kemmons said.

Kemmons agreed to send Griffin a dozen new Holiday Inn towels so that he wouldn't have to steal anymore.

By then, Kemmons was moving in circles where encounters with the rich and famous became almost routine. Baseball superstar Mickey Mantle (in Joplin, Missouri) and golf legend Arnold Palmer (in Pennsylvania) were both franchise holders. Kemmons once ran into Muhammad Ali, the heavyweight boxing champion and probably the world's best-known living athlete. Kemmons immediately took the opportunity to persuade Ali to be photographed jumping on a small trampoline that Kemmons was then marketing.

"He was staying in one of my hotels, and I talked him into jumping on one of those trampolines. I didn't pay him anything. He was a very nice guy. I guess he thought I was a big shot because I owned the hotel he was staying in," Kemmons says.

In 1968, while Kemmons was in Rome working on the first Holiday Inn built there, his consultant was Steve Felez. Felez got up a poker game one evening, and one of the players he invited was Monsignor Paul Marcinkus, representative to the Vatican from the Chicago Archdiocese. At the time, Paul VI was Pope.

"We were playing poker, when the Monsignor said, 'Kemmons, did you ever meet the Pope?' I said, 'No, but I sure would like to.' He said, 'I'll arrange it.' So he got on the phone and five minutes later he was back and said, 'You have an appointment at 9:30 in the morning,' " Kemmons recalls.

"When we met Pope Paul VI the next day, he said, 'Mr. Wilson, I have heard of the great work you have done with Holiday Inn. I have heard you are building one in Rome. Can you tell me where it is?' And my mind just went blank. I couldn't think of where it was. If I had had any sense, I would have asked him for a piece of ground right there by the Vatican.'"

Kemmons' most extended encounter with royalty came in the late '60s when he worked out a deal to build a Holiday Inn in Monaco. It also involved a minor gaffe on Kemmons' part, but his relationship with Prince Rainier and the royal family blossomed splendidly all the same.

The prince visited Memphis in 1967, creating quite a stir locally among media and residents. He was flown in on the Holiday Inn jet from the Bahamas, where he had been visiting. Kemmons' son Bob went along on the flight to accompany Rainier on the way into Memphis. They circled the city for an aerial tour, and then landed at Holiday Inn's HI-Air hangar in Memphis, where Kemmons and Wallace were waiting to greet the prince.

"They had been preparing all of us on how to meet the prince and how to speak to him," Bob recounts. "They had told Dad how he should be addressed as 'Your Highness' and all that. They went to introduce him, and Dad goes, 'Hey, Prince, how ya doin'?' All the preparation and etiquette just went out the window."

However, Rainier and later the rest of the royal family would take a liking to the unpretentious Kemmons. At the time, the prince had been reported to have won a power struggle with billionaire Aristotle Onassis for control of the gambling and lodging facilities in Monaco, and wanted to build more affordable accommodations like Holiday Inn.

In Memphis, he was taken on a tour of Holiday City, where he expressed particular interest in its computer center, and other company facilities. Later, he was the guest of honor at a small private party on the top floor of the high-rise Holiday Inn Rivermont, overlooking the Mississippi River. And Kemmons took the prince to Memphis' most famous barbecue joint, owned and operated by his friend, Charles Vergos.

"I always took everybody who came here to the Rendezvous. It's still my favorite restaurant in the world. I said, 'Come on, Prince. Let's get some ribs.' He loved it too, and I sent him two or three orders later on," Kemmons says.

Things went so well in Memphis that Kemmons and Bob were invited to visit the royal palace in Monaco and continue negotiations. "We found Prince Rainier and Princess Grace were just as down-to-earth and as nice a people as you could find," Bob says.

Later the same year, Kemmons returned to Monaco with Bob and other Holiday Inn officials and settled the deal. Holiday Inn got a 99-year lease on about one acre — in a country of only 370 acres — for one franc a year. When Kemmons and his party first arrived at the royal palace, Princess Grace visited with them, served champagne and provided a tour. When Kemmons told her he would like to meet her children, Grace brought in 11-year-old Caroline, 10-year-old Albert and 3-year-old Stephanie. Albert had just returned from judo class and showed Kemmons the punches and kicks he was learning.

After lunch at the palace, Kemmons asked the prince if he had a photographer who could snap a picture for Kemmons. Rainier said it would be no problem and left the room. Kemmons, Princess Grace, Albert and Stephanie arranged themselves on a sofa for the photograph.

"And the prince comes in with his own camera, puts it on a tripod, sets the timer on it and comes around and sits down. So he made that picture himself," Kemmons says.

When construction began on the inn in Monaco, Kemmons sent 23-year-old Bob over to work on the project. Of Kemmons' three sons, Bob has always been the one most interested and involved in the construction business.

"I got to go over there and work with them on the hotel quite a bit," Bob says. "One day they invited me to the palace for lunch. That night was the Grand Ball, the second largest event in Monaco after the Grand Prix. But I had never heard of it at the time. When Princess Grace asked me to be their guest, I told her I didn't have anything but blue jeans to wear. But she said she would take care of that."

Later a royal staffer took him to get fitted for a tuxedo, but when Bob found out it cost $60, he changed his mind, because he believed that was too much to pay just to rent a tuxedo. "I said, 'Just tell Princess Grace they didn't have one left to fit me,' " Bob recalls. But the staffer knew that would never do, and after much consternation managed to arrange for Bob to borrow an extra tuxedo from the bandleader for the ball that night.

"When Princess Grace arrived, she teased me about it, in a real subtle way. She told me I had on a nice-looking tuxedo. But then she said, 'I'm surprised the bandleader has a tuxedo to wear tonight,' " Bob says.

"Later she had a lot of fun calling Dad and telling him about how his son was too cheap to pay $60 for a tuxedo to go to the second biggest event of the year in Monaco. It was something. I still haven't been to anything that big since then."

Kemmons threw a pretty impressive bash himself in 1967 for members of the royal family of Morocco. Kemmons, Dorothy, Wallace and his wife, Alma, hosted a dinner party in New York to honor King Hassan II, along with his sister and brother, Princess Lalla Aicha and Prince Moulay Abdellah. Holiday Inn was building four hotels in Morocco in a joint venture with the lodging division of Armand Hammer's Occidental Petroleum. Among those attending were New York Gov. and Mrs. Nelson Rockefeller, New York Mayor and Mrs. John Lindsey, and Senator and Mrs. Robert Kennedy.

Kemmons had many highly successful dealings with Hammer, who maintained financial interests all over the world. However, one of Kemmons most memorable projects with Hammer was one that fell through. In the early '70s, Holiday Inn was part of a massive economic-development program negotiated between the U.S. and the Soviet Union as part of President Nixon's detente efforts with the communist government. But at the last minute, the Soviets threw in conditions Kemmons couldn't tolerate.

"We made a deal. But when we went to sign the contract, they said the only way they would sign was if they operated the Holiday Inn. I told them there was no way. We wouldn't let them operate it, if it was going to be a Holiday Inn. So we pulled out and left," Kemmons says.

Kemmons has crossed paths with more than his share of American leaders, as well. He has met every U.S. president since Harry Truman. "I guess I talked to President Ford more than any of them," Kemmons recalls. "I had a project I was trying to sell him on."

That project was a recorded history of the United States to be sold as a boxed set of phonograph records. It was packaged to celebrate the nation's 1976 bicentennial, but it turned out to be one of Kemmons' least-successful investments. The records sold poorly, and most remain in a warehouse in Iowa. "I left about a half-million dollars on the table in that deal," Kemmons says.

Kemmons spoke with Bill Clinton many times before he was elected president, during the five terms Clinton served as governor of Arkansas. For some 30 years, Kemmons has served on the National Advisory Board of Little Rock's First Commercial Bank, of which all board members must be born in Arkansas. They have included many prominent natives of the state, such as Wal-Mart founder Sam Walton, Dillard's Department Stores founder William Dillard, Tyson Chicken owner Don Tyson and Dallas Cowboys owner Jerry Jones. Usually once every year, the board members are guests at the Arkansas Governor's Mansion.

Kemmons maintains he never had any favorites among American presidents, nor any interest in politics. "I liked everybody. I always have. I have never touched politics in any way. It just really never interested me. I was too busy to get involved in politics," he says.

"Oh yeah, a lot of politicians ask me to give them money. And I do, if it's somebody I know. I give them $1,000, no more."

Kemmons has also had many encounters with Dr. Billy Graham. "We've been friends a long time with him and his wife, Ruth. He is just a real wonderful guy. Wallace and Bill Walton really got me interested in Billy Graham. We got him to come down to Memphis for two or three Holiday Inn national conventions. He is the only man in the world we ever gave a card that said he could stay at any Holiday Inn for no charge."

Countless people have received some of Kemmons' fake money, the astronomically denominated bills with his picture on them, which he has been handing out at every opportunity in recent years. However, most recipients don't know how this unusual calling-card of Kemmons' got started, or that it had to do with the late Sam Walton.

"I would say I knew him better than most people. I would see him two or three times a year. I don't mean I was a close friend. We lived too far apart. We were on that bank board [for First Commercial Bank] together; that's where we met. We used to play tennis after every one of those board meetings. Real nice fellow," Kemmons says.

"I went with him when he opened his Collierville (Tennessee) store. He made me get up on the counter with him and he introduced me as the man who started all the Holiday Inns.

"He had everybody who worked at Wal-Mart wear a name tag with big letters. He would go up to them and say, 'Hello, Mary, how you doing?' like he had known them all his life.

"The money I give out started with Sam. A guy had given me a fake million-dollar bill and I got the idea that that might be something we could sell. And I got to thinking about Sam and all those stores he had."

So Kemmons had 2,500 fake million-dollar bills printed with the Wal-Mart billionaire's picture on them, and 2,500 printed with Kemmons' picture on them, and shipped a boxful over to Walton. Kemmons' idea was to make an arrangement in which Wal-Mart customers could order a package of 1,000 of the fake million-dollar bills with their own picture printed on them.

"Kemmons, man, this money is wonderful," Walton said when he called Kemmons. "But what in the world am I going to do with it?"

"Well, we are going to make some money," Kemmons replied. "We are going to put it in your stores and print a thousand million-dollar bills with the purchaser's picture and name on them. We'll sell the package for $19.95. I'll give your store $5, and we'll get $14.95."

"Man, that's great. Is it legal?"

"I don't know, but I'll find out."

That's when Kemmons discovered there was a snag. Even though the $100 bill is the largest the U.S. government has in circulation, it was not thrilled to learn of Kemmons' plan to start printing million-dollar bills.

"I didn't think anybody would believe a million-dollar bill was real. But I talked to the Secret Service (the agency that enforces federal counterfeiting laws), and they said, 'Don't print any more million-dollar bills.' And I never have," Kemmons says.

As the Secret Service requested, Kemmons gave them all the fake bills he had printed.

"So from then on, I went to a billion-dollar bill and then a trillion-dollar bill and so on. We never did try to sell any. But I thought they would sell like mad."

Kemmons-currency looks a lot like the real thing, but on the back it says "Non-Negotiable" and "This Certificate Is Backed And Secured Only By Confidence In The American Dream." His business address and phone number are also listed on the back, along with a notation that he is the founder of Holiday Inn. The latest denomination he gives out has reached five hundred trillion dollars.

"Nobody in the government has ever said anything since." Kemmons declares. "And I have sent them to President Clinton, Senator Bob Dole and everybody."

CHAPTER FOURTEEN

—EVERY BUSINESS IN THE WORLD—

"No job is too hard as long as you are smart enough to find someone else to do it for you."

Kemmons Wilson

In August of 1977, the eyes of the world turned to Memphis, Tennessee. Elvis Presley had died at the age of 42. The television images of his funeral procession endure vividly in popular memory. However, to this day, theories abound that the King of Rock and Roll did not really die. Elvis remains alive and well, the stories go, living incognito the normal life he could never have before.

Kemmons knows better. In 1977, he was co-owner of Forest Hills, the funeral home that handled Presley's arrangements.

"I can guarantee Elvis is dead, because we buried him," he says.

"I owned half of Forest Hills at that time. M.N. 'Doc' Murray owned the other half. We buried Elvis and put him in a mausoleum at Forest Hills Cemetery. But then it was just misery for us. So many people were trying to get in the mausoleum, trying to sneak over the fence at night. We were so happy when they moved his body out to Graceland that we didn't know what to do."

It should come as no surprise that Kemmons Wilson owned the funeral home that buried Elvis. The reality is that you could find Kemmons in virtually any business at some point in his life. Perhaps the most consistent theme in his career has been his willingness to try any venture at any time.

"I've been in about every business in the world in some way or another. I'm curious. I like to see if I can do it better than somebody else," Kemmons says.

The *Saturday Evening Post* once described Kemmons as "a good-natured tiger who lives in a cloud of business ideas and constantly itches to get into new things."

The story can still be heard around Memphis that while Kemmons was in the funeral-home business, he once considered burying the coffins vertically. That would require less land per burial and allow more plots in the same space. Kemmons insists that was only a joke that Wallace liked to tell: "He said I would use a big drill to dig the graves."

Whether or not Kemmons really wanted to try vertical burials, there has almost never been a time he wasn't attempting some new twist. Even in Kemmons' busiest Holiday Inn years, he kept dabbling in all sorts of other business endeavors of his own.

For most humans, reaching the chairmanship of a global, billion-dollar corporation like Holiday Inn would be the pinnacle, an all-consuming presence for the remainder of their working lives. However, for Kemmons, not only would heading Holiday Inn not be enough to fill one lifetime, it wasn't even enough to keep him occupied temporarily.

"No, Holiday Inn wasn't the busiest period in my life, to me. I've always been busy. Of course, if I only had Holiday Inn, I wouldn't have been as busy. But I had a dozen other things going on," Kemmons says.

"I'm probably a terrible manager. A guy who is a good manager has more or less a mechanical mind. I've got a curious mind. I want to know how things work. The way I keep from getting bored is to do different things all the time."

Kemmons' curiosity led him to move into business after business, either as a subsidiary to Holiday Inn — which at one time owned everything from a meatpacking company to a lampmaker — or simply as another Kemmons Wilson venture.

All through the Holiday Inn years, he maintained his real-estate, construction and insurance operations. He built housing subdivisions, apartment buildings, condominiums, shopping centers, warehouses, offices and other buildings in cities that included Memphis, Dallas, Nashville, Cincinnati, Louisville, Kansas City and Sarasota, Florida. Other business interests during that time included a company that made fountain pens, companies that manufactured plastic products, a driving range, a commercial catfish and bullfrog farm, radio stations, a mobile-home plant and a coal, oil and gas company.

Dorothy once told Kemmons, "If you died, all your partners couldn't get into the funeral."

She explains, "Kemmons will listen to anybody about a deal. I don't know how they find him. They must know that about him. I tell him, 'Honey, just don't get into anything you don't understand.' And he'll say, 'Well, Momma, it just sounds so good.' So you just have to let him go."

David Sullivan, a hotel developer who worked for Holiday Inn for several years, once told a reporter, "Kemmons will listen to any potential deal, I don't care what it is. I bet that he has listened to more deals than anybody in the world."

"Fortunately," says Kemmons' son, Bob, "Pop has hit on more than he has missed on. What has always surprised me is that he does things he knows nothing about. The ones where he knows what it is about, he usually makes money. The ones he doesn't are the ones he gets in trouble on.

"My brothers and I have always said that any good salesman could sell Pop his own underwear. If a guy comes in and talks a great story, he can sell Pop on it."

Bob says that worries him somewhat, except that no salesman could ever really know how Kemmons' mind works. "There is no rhyme or reason to which deals he does and which ones he doesn't. Sometimes, something I think he would do in a minute, he decides he won't do for love or money. I don't think anybody can outguess what he will do."

It's purely a gut instinct with Kemmons. His friend, Bruce Edenton says, "When he created Holiday Inn, Kemmons did not have consultants, software, training packages or a staff of MBA's. He was and remains a person of vision."

Marion Carden worked for Kemmons in various capacities for 37 years in Kemmons' own business operations before retiring in January 1994. He witnessed how literally Kemmons meant it when he said he had an open-door policy.

"You could just walk in any time his door was open. Anyone could. Anybody could walk in off the street and ask if Kemmons Wilson was in, and if he was and had a minute, you were welcome in his office," Carden recalls.

"But he also had a way of letting you know when he was through talking and wanted you to go. When he was through, he would say something like, 'Well, it's good to see you.' And you knew the conversation was over and it was time to leave."

Kemmons has always made a practice of enjoying his successes and walking away from his failures as fast as possible. Carden recounts an instance when one of their companies had been losing money for years, no matter what they did. Finally Carden found a buyer for it and went in and told Kemmons he was selling it for $50,000 and needed him to sign the contract.

"Why are you selling it for that, Marion? I've got a lot more than that invested in it," Kemmons said.

"I know that," Carden said.

"Well, why do you want to sell it for $50,000?"

"Well, for the last five years, we've lost $50,000 a year, and if we keep it, we will continue to lose that every year. But this year, I'm going to gain $50,000 on the sale and save the $50,000 we're not going to lose."

Kemmons response was immediate: "Where do you want me to sign?"

That was how such decisions were routinely made, Carden says: "Once you told him he was going to lose money or make money, the bottom line was all he looked at."

As for Holiday Inn, Kemmons was the driving force behind adding a multitude of subsidiaries or divisions engaged in transportation, manufacturing, food processing, construction, finance, insurance and services. The various operations were acquired primarily to supply the parent company and franchisees with anything they might need, all at reduced prices through volume purchasing and specialized know-how. However, they also sold goods and services to other firms and individuals. "A dollar made that way is worth just as much as a dollar made renting a motel room," Wallace Johnson liked to say.

When Kemmons first became a homebuilder, he quickly realized he could get his building supplies cheaper if he owned a lumberyard. With Holiday Inn, he took the same principle and multiplied it endlessly.

"Just about everything Holiday Inn used that you could think of, we had a company that made it. And back then, we were building so many Holiday Inns, it was really worthwhile. We could get that stuff out when we wanted it. We saved an awful, awful lot of money," Kemmons says.

Clyde Dixon, who worked for Holiday Inn from 1956 until 1977 and started Inn Keepers Supply for Holiday Inn, liked to say that if it took wood to build something Kemmons wanted, then Kemmons wanted to own the forest.

The vast Holiday Inn operations included companies involved in virtually every business related to Holiday Inn. Inn Keepers Supply company sold room furnishings and food-service equipment. Nat Buring Packing company sold a complete line of meats. Institutional Mart of America packed 300,000 square feet of display space at Holiday City with everything needed to furnish and operate a motel, hotel, dormitory, restaurant, cafeteria or similar institution. Holiday Woodcraft manufactured custom counters and display cases. Master Kraft Manufacturing provided facilities for refrigeration units. Menu Maker Food Services processed meats and other foods. Modern Plastics made lamps and shipping containers. Holiday Containers made corrugated shipping containers. Johnson Furniture made furniture, stereo and television cabinets, living-room and dining-room suites. Champion Lighting made commercial lighting fixtures. Bianco Manufacturing made all types of commercial seating. International Foam made padding for bedding and carpets, upholstery and protective packaging. HI-Air sold small planes, operated a repair station and provided aircraft storage, leasing and rental. General Innkeeping Acceptance Corporation assisted customers of other Holiday Inn divisions with financing.

"At one time, we were in nearly every kind of business. We were nearly self-supporting," Kemmons says.

One of the largest acquisitions was Tco Industries, a $200-million deal representing a trade of about 3 million shares of Holiday Inn stock in 1969. It gave Holiday Inn the 2,500 buses of Continental Trailways, the 11-ship ocean-going fleet of Delta Steamship lines, two insurance companies and a real-estate company. Kemmons' idea was that owning passenger ships and buses would provide fantastic opportunities for steering their customers to Holiday Inns, and vice versa.

However, shortly after Holiday Inn acquired Tco as a subsidiary, it was hit with a series of setbacks. It suffered a costly, year-long driver's strike at Trailways; the IRS ruled Tco owed $12 million in back taxes; and Tco was slapped with huge federal antitrust and customs lawsuits. But in the long run, Kemmons still believes Holiday Inn made money off the deal by the time Trailways was sold in 1979 for $100 million.

The Tco deal was typical of most of the mergers and acquisitions that brought Holiday Inn its array of subsidiaries, in that Holiday Inn stock was traded for it. "I learned I had a money machine. We had all that great stock in Holiday Inn, and we bought all these things by trading stock for them. We bought lots of things with Holiday Inn stock," Kemmons says.

Bill Walton recalls that almost nothing was beyond the realm of possibility in Holiday Inn's merger-and-acquisition drive.

Kemmons even tried to trade stock for the company that makes Tabasco, his favorite condiment. "I was always crazy about Tabasco sauce. I usually had a bottle in my shaving kit or somewhere, even when I was traveling," he says. "I attribute my long life and health to Tabasco sauce: no germ can live in my stomach because of all the Tabasco sauce I have eaten."

So in the late '60s, Kemmons went to see Walter McIlheney, the head of the family that owns the McIlheney Tabasco company.

"I told him I was really impressed with his company and wanted to see if there was some way we could make it a subsidiary of Holiday Inn. I was trying to show him how he could do so much better if I traded him some Holiday Inn stock. He laughed and said, 'Kemmons, we have lots more money than you and Holiday Inn already,' " Kemmons recalls.

"I asked if he made it all out of the Tabasco sauce. He said, 'No, we got rich off of oil.' So he didn't want to make the deal."

Nevertheless, Kemmons made a lifelong friend of McIlhenny when he told him a funny story that developed out of Kemmons' love for Tabasco. Kemmons had been in Calcutta, India, on a site-hunting expedition for Holiday Inn. After he bought some land from an Indian real-estate agent, the agent took Kemmons to dinner.

At the restaurant, Kemmons asked, "You don't reckon they would have any Tabasco sauce, do you?"

The real-estate agent waved his finger, and a waiter brought a bottle of Tabasco sauce, with no cap in it.

"That's funny, this bottle having no cap," Kemmons said.

"Well, Mr. Wilson, over here, it is a great delicacy," the agent said. "If they brought it with the cap on it, people would steal the bottle."

Kemmons and the real-estate agent laughed and finished their dinner. Then as they were leaving, the agent punched Kemmons on the shoulder.

"But Mr. Wilson, I came prepared," he said, pulling a cap out of his pocket, putting it on the bottle and dropping the bottle in his pocket as they walked out.

When Kemmons told the story to Walter McIlhenny, he says, "I thought he would die laughing. And I guess for the next 20 years, until he died, he sent me two big bottles of Tabasco sauce every year."

McIlhenny had custom labels made for the bottles he sent Kemmons. They are signed by Walter McIlhenny and read: "This vintage Tabasco sauce has been especially bottled to become the private stock of Kemmons Wilson. Presented with due ceremony in the best tradition of the McIlhenny Company."

Holiday Inn didn't acquire all its subsidiaries through other companies. Often they were homegrown. One of most successful of the latter was Holiday Press. It was started with one small press in the company basement just to print Holiday Inn's stationery, forms and the Holiday Inn travel magazine. Within a few years, Holiday Press became a national leader in commercial printing, with one of the most modern plants in the world.

Charles Cuneo, who was executive vice president for Holiday Press, says its sales were approaching $30 million annually by the time it was sold in 1978. It started with five employees working in 20,000 square feet of space, and grew into a 540-employee, 300,000-square-foot operation.

"Holiday Press really started as in idea between Lee Yeager and me in Kemmons' living room one night in 1959. We talked it over with him and Wallace Johnson, and a little later Kemmons decided to try it. He believes if you have an idea, go for it. If you make mistakes, you make them," Cuneo says.

Yeager, who was president of Holiday Press, remembers, "Kemmons said, 'You have the job; take it and run. Don't look back. You either sink or swim.' "

Cuneo says Kemmons let them run the operation the way they thought best, as long as it produced results. "I think he pretty much did that with everything he owned. We always made a profit, and when you do that Kemmons leaves you alone. If you had to ask for money, you heard more from him," he says.

"We probably saw him the most whenever we printed the annual reports. He was always bringing in more photographs for us to put in it. He always wanted pictures of everyone in it. As the company got bigger and bigger, the annual reports started looking like a high school yearbook."

Julie Nixon Eisenhower, Richard Nixon's daughter, visited Holiday Press in April 1974, while she was an editor at the *Saturday Evening Post*. She accompanied Frederic Birmingham, the magazine's executive editor, and Dr. Cory Ser Vaas, its owner, to promote the announcement that Holiday Press would begin printing the *Post*. Thus, Kemmons wound up printing the magazine he once sold door-to-door as a boy.

In the early '70s, it was common to see the multimillionaire Kemmons driving around town in a yellow $500 Subaru, a car no one in Memphis had ever heard of at the time. By signing a $1.5 million letter of credit, Kemmons had landed the 10-state Southern distributorship rights for the just-introduced Japanese compact car.

"That was one of those deals where someone sold Pop his own underwear," says Bob Wilson.

"This guy named Mal Bricklin was a real high-roller. Pop didn't know him at all, and he talked Pop into guaranteeing that $1.5 million line of credit in 1969. That would be like someone walking in here now and asking for $10 million. Pop never had to pay any of that, because Bricklin wasn't required to pay for the cars until six months after they arrived, and he was always able to pay everybody off in time. But it could have gone the other way real easy."

Kemmons admits, "Everyone said I was crazy. I said, 'How can I be crazy?' I had driven them. It was a good little automobile. If I had stayed with it, I would have made an awful lot of money, if we had really merchandised those 10 states. I got my money back though."

"All of us drove Subarus for a while," Bob recalls. "It was a great little car, but it was tough to introduce a new car into the market."

What actually made Kemmons drop the deal in the end, however, was another partner who came in as the distributor for Kentucky and part of Tennessee. It turned out he had a wife back in Kentucky at the same time he was introducing another woman as his wife in New Orleans. The last straw came when Bob discovered the man had bought a Lear Jet in the Wilsons' name, without ever mentioning it to them. They won a court judgment against him, but he took bankruptcy and never paid the Wilsons anything, Bob says.

Longtime Memphians probably were too accustomed to Kemmons' eclectic investment habits to be really surprised at his hawking an unknown Japanese automobile. They could remember back in his early Holiday Inn years when he converted a rodeo arena at the Mid-South Fairgrounds into the city's first ice rink.

"I leased it and spent about $300,000 putting in refrigeration. We called it Iceland. We were really doing business for a while with the ice skaters. Everyone wanted to learn to skate. But then every few days, someone would fall and break an arm or a leg. And the newspapers just kept writing it up so much, finally it killed all our business. Everybody was scared to come over. I think I lost some money, but I finally got rid of it," Kemmons says.

While it was open, however, Kemmons also brought ice hockey to Memphis with a 1955 exhibition between two American Hockey League teams, the Buffalo Bison and the Pittsburgh Hornets.

Kemmons had much more success in his ventures that dealt with real estate and construction. One of the most profitable of these during the Holiday Inn years was Wilson Savage Development Corp., in which he was partners with Doyle Savage of Memphis. They built millions of dollars worth of hotels, government buildings and other structures, including the U.S. Embassy in Nigeria.

Bob McCaskill, Kemmons' longtime engineer, was involved in many of the Wilson Savage construction projects. "Africa is a strange, backward country, and it was not uncommon for a building that might take eight months to construct in the U.S. to take five years in Africa. So we would take all our own materials and that way we didn't have to depend on suppliers there. As a result we would get things built as fast as they were in the U.S. People were just amazed, and we had all kinds of people coming to us to do buildings in Africa for them," he recalls.

Still, working in Africa did require some adjustment on Kemmons' part. Savage recalls that on one of their construction projects in Morocco, Kemmons discovered the many Muslim workers would stop five times a day to pray to Allah. Kemmons told the superintendent he would have to do something about that, because they couldn't be stopping the job five times a day. Savage says the superintendent replied, "Kemmons, they have been doing this for centuries, but I will see if I can get it stopped."

Several weeks later when Kemmons returned to check on the progress of the project, he was pleased to find it proceeding well ahead of schedule. He was complimenting the superintendent at great length, when suddenly all work came to a halt. The superintendent — a tough Texan, Savage remembers — turned and went into his office. He returned with a prayer rug and headed off to join his workers in their Muslim ritual.

Savage recalls Kemmons shook his head at the superintendent, but decided the project was going so well that he could live with five-times-a-day prayers after all.

Though Wilson Savage proved quite successful, another of Kemmons own real-estate-development ventures in the Holiday Inn years wound up as his most disastrous. Alodex was a partnership of Kemmons' and Wallace's that ultimately cost them millions of dollars each before it was liquidated to pay off creditors and avoid bankruptcy.

Alodex grew out of Allied Mortgage and Development, which had been run by Cary Whitehead and had done a great deal of subdivision development in Southaven, a Memphis suburb. When Allied Mortgage and Development became Alodex in 1967, Whitehead left the company.

In the late '60s, Kemmons and Wallace merged Allied's operations with those of builder Lloyd Clarke to create Alodex. Clarke was put in charge of the company, and he expanded it greatly from single-family residential construction into government building projects, condominiums and other areas. At its peak around 1970, the company had nearly $90 million of construction under way and a staff of 250. Problems surfaced in 1971 when it was discovered that a stock prospectus did not make clear large losses suffered by the company. Kemmons and Wallace spent $4 million of their own money just to make good those losses.

"Lloyd Clarke had been president of the Home Builders Association. He was a really smart guy. We were going to conquer the world. We had a lot of money, a lot of credit. But it just got in a big mess," says Kemmons, who notes he and Wallace had gotten too busy with other things to keep an eye on Alodex.

"Back then, our credit was so good. How much money do you think Fred Smith [the Memphian who founded Federal Express] could borrow today? Anything he wants, that's right. And that's the way it was with us. First thing we knew, we were in serious trouble."

Fred Jones, a lawyer who became president of Alodex and presided over the liquidation, told *The New York Times* in 1976 that original losses were due to inadequate controls over field construction and later to problems selling housing projects as interest rates climbed in the '70s. All creditors were paid off, he said.

The Times pointed out that Wallace and Kemmons had taken personal responsibility for paying off Alodex's debt. "It's like a nightmare, and I wish I had never heard the name Alodex," Kemmons told the reporter.

A more successful venture of Kemmons and Wallace's outside Holiday Inn was Medicenters of America, which built nursing homes and intermediate-care hospitals across America. They also did well with Walkem Development Company, in which the name was formed from the first syllable of each partner's first name.

"You can't imagine all that Wallace and I had going on along with

Holiday Inn. Alodex. Medicenters. Big homebuilding operations —
and Wallace's was probably bigger than mine," Kemmons says.

Of all the interests Kemmons maintained outside Holiday Inn in
those years, the one that probably sparked his enthusiasm most of all
was pursued on tennis courts around the world.

In the game of tennis he found an instant metaphor that
epitomized his life's philosophy: "Tennis is very competitive, and I
have always been a very competitive person. Absolutely it is important
to win. And don't ever let me have anybody around me who doesn't
want to win, because they are a loser."

He discovered he liked the sport so much that he played it as often
as possible for many years, wherever he found himself and often for
two hours or more without a break. He often closed a business deal by
saying, "And now, gentlemen, one more important thing: Where can
I play some tennis?"

Rudiger Koppen recalls a visit he once made with Kemmons to the
island of Macao, a tiny peninsula off the coast of China. Though it was
pouring rain that day, Kemmons insisted on hitting a few balls so he
could say he had played tennis in Macao. In Poland, Kemmons played
on a tennis court at the bottom of a salt mine, 500 feet underground.

"I was really a nut about playing tennis," Kemmons says. "I usually
played at 10 at night, after everyone else was gone home."

Kemmons' love for tennis led him to build the Wimbleton
Racquet Club (now Wimbleton Sportsplex) in Memphis with
developer Jack Belz. It included 10 air-conditioned indoor courts and
10 outdoor courts. Wilson's friends said he built it just so he would
always have a place to play in his hometown, no matter what the
weather or time of day.

Arthur Muskin, a friend from whom Kemmons once bought light
fixtures, recalls a get-together at Doyle Savage's home. Several people
were taking turns playing tennis on Savage's court, when Kemmons
discovered that Arthur's 16-year-old son, Alan, was a very good player.
Kemmons immediately grabbed the teen-ager for his partner.

"From the afternoon through early evening, they played long and hard, and beat everyone there. There was one court at Doyle's house, so to allow more players to play at one time — yet not stop his winning streak — Kemmons arranged to open his indoor tennis center at Wimbleton. We all went down there and continued to play until about 2 in the morning, with Kemmons keeping Alan as his partner all night," Arthur says.

Charles Cuneo says, "Kemmons always picked the best partner in tennis, which was the same technique he used in business."

However, if Kemmons partners didn't perform according to his expectations, he always set them straight — no matter who they were. Tennis star Ivan Lendl discovered that when he joined Kemmons for a doubles match in an exhibition.

"I always get the best player on my side Lendl insisted I serve first. So we promptly lost the game," Kemmons recalls.

"I said, 'Now, you told me how to play the first time; I'm going to tell you how to play the second time: I am going to get out of the way and you get all of the balls.' So we won the next two games."

Holiday Inn franchisee Henri Landwirth tells of an occasion when he was working late with a company committee in Memphis, when "around 10 p.m., Kemmons walked into our meeting and said, 'You boys have been working enough. Let's go play some tennis.' We tried to explain that we had not brought any tennis gear with us. But he told us to get in the car and let him worry about the rest. He took us to his home, laid out tennis rackets and clothes in all sizes, and we played tennis until midnight," Landwirth says.

Kemmons always kept a couple dozen or so pairs of tennis shoes, sets of tennis shorts and shirts, and other gear on hand.

"I could fit anyone, almost. I remember we had Howard Clark, the chairman of American Express, down here one time. So one night after our meeting, I brought him and all these other guys over, got them all outfitted, and we went out to Memphis Country Club to play tennis," Kemmons says. "And this big dignified guy, the chairman of American Express, was running after a ball. But his shorts were too big, and they fell down to his knees and tripped him flat. I would give anything if I had a picture of that."

Opponents and partners alike recall the various tricks that

Kemmons employed on the court. The late Dr. Cecil Humphreys, former president of the University of Memphis, once explained how Kemmons got the nickname Quick-Service Wilson: "He serves you a second ball before the first one goes off the court. Then when his teammate misses one, he calls timeout to give you a pep talk on how you should play to win."

Irby Cooper, a longtime friend of Kemmons' and a Holiday Inn franchisee, says, "Kemmons is a perfect joy to play with until the ball falls about three feet beyond his range. Then, even though the ball is probably 30 or 40 feet from you, he hollers, 'Get it, partner!' "

Kemmons finally met his match, however, when he found himself on the opposite side of the net from probably the ultimate trickster in the history of the game, Bobby Riggs. The veteran tennis pro is known for winning matches despite giving his opponent ridiculous advantages, and his match with Kemmons was no different.

"He let me put 12 chairs on his side of the court. He carried an umbrella that must have been seven foot in diameter. He wore hip boots. And I still didn't even win a point," Kemmons says.

"I am a guy who would bet you all the money in China that he threw that match against Billie Jean King, because he was just too good."

In 1972, Kemmons fulfilled a long-held ambition when he was able to attend the championship match at Wimbledon, which was won by American Stan Smith that year. However, Kemmons wound up sitting in just about the worst seat in the house.

Kemmons and Dorothy had stopped off in England with Armand Hammer and his wife, Frances, on the way to conduct Holiday Inn negotiations in the Soviet Union. When they arrived in London, they saw in newspaper headlines that the Wimbledon final had been postponed by rain for one of the few times in the history of the English championships. Play would resume the next day.

"I was really a tennis buff at that time. And I wanted to go see that thing so bad I didn't know what to do. We were staying at Claridge's, and I got to asking the concierge and everyone I could about two tickets for the next day. After we had dinner, the concierge came over to me and told me he knew it was way too much but he had found two tickets in not too desirable a location for $100 each. I knew it was probably the only chance in my life to see a Wimbledon Championship match, and I told him to get them for me. I told Dorothy, 'Let's get up early and go out there about 9 in the morning,' We knew the matches did not start until noon, but I thought it would be great to go on out there and watch everyone warming up," Kemmons recalls.

"When we got there, there was absolutely nobody warming up or doing anything at all. We had strawberries and cream, sat around looking and absolutely never saw anyone hit a tennis ball until noon. The seats were very bad, but at least I was at Wimbledon and got to see my fellow American, Stan Smith, win the tournament."

As Kemmons later found out though, his constant drive to charge out of the gate early had cost him on this occasion. "When we returned to Claridge's, I checked to see if I had any messages and found a note and two tickets to sit in Stan Smith's box at Wimbledon! The note said, 'I've heard how badly you want to see the tennis match at Wimbledon today, and I am happy to give you these two tickets in Stan Smith's box.' The time stamped on the envelope was 10:31 a.m. If I had just not been so anxious to get out there, I would have two of the best seats at Wimbledon for free, but instead I had two of the worst seats, and they cost me $200," Kemmons says.

"I met Stan Smith later and we laughed about it," Kemmons says. "I had two of the best tickets in the house, and there I was sitting up in the rafters."

CHAPTER FIFTEEN

—BIG CHANGES AT HOLIDAY INN—

"Do not worry. You can't change the past, but you sure can ruin the present by worrying over the future. Remember that half the things we worry about never happen, and the other half are going to happen anyway. So why worry?"

Kemmons Wilson

*I*n the spring of 1979, Kemmons would retire from Holiday Inn with its annual revenues topping $1 billion. The company had 1,759 inns in more than 50 countries, and twice as many rooms as its nearest competitor.

But on the way there, Kemmons had to see Holiday Inn through some extremely difficult transition years in the mid 1970s. Despite Holiday Inn's dominance of its industry, other motel chains had expanded and were providing stiffer competition. But worst of all, the soaring gasoline prices of the '70s oil crunch caused inflation-driven cost increases and a brutal recession, all of which kept more and more potential Holiday Inn guests at home.

Americans who lived through that era know it was a scary time. The Arab oil embargo in 1973 doubled prices at the pump in the U.S. almost overnight. It led to unprecedented gasoline shortages and long lines at service stations, a Christmas without Christmas lights to save electricity, exorbitant interest rates and skyrocketing price increases on everything from food to homes. Darkening the era further, American troops withdrew from Vietnam without a victory, and the Watergate scandal forced President Nixon to resign.

Though Holiday Inn had record earnings in 1973, profits were slipping in the final quarter. In 1974, profits fell 30 per cent, reflecting an industry-wide trend. Wall Street turned abruptly bearish on the outlook for lodging chains. Holiday Inn stock plummeted from $56 a share to $4.25 between 1972 and 1974.

Many of Kemmons' own businesses suffered as well during the mid '70s recession, and he and his sons had to focus a great deal of their efforts on repairing the damage. The other Holiday Inn cofounders, Wallace Johnson and Bill Walton, also suffered financial setbacks. The Alodex losses hit Johnson particularly hard.

But even during those hard times, Kemmons kept faith that his company and his country would pull through. He was sure the same things that made him successful in the first place — hard work and salesmanship — were still the prescription for overcoming the crises of the '70s.

"As long as the people of this great land are willing to work, I know the American dream is very much alive," he told a reporter. "Somebody is going to have to sell the idea that we have to change our lifestyle to fight this war on inflation, recession and energy shortages. Never in our history has this nation had a greater need for good salesmen than now. I hope and pray that God sends us a lot of them."

In 1974, Kemmons brought in new management for Holiday Inn, but remained chairman of the board until his retirement five years later. Deciding he needed someone more focused on operations to run the company, he called on Roy Winegardner of Cincinnati.

Winegardner was the self-made multimillionaire who had started as a heating and air-conditioning contractor in Springfield, Missouri, then built a motel-development and property-management operation based in Cincinnati that included some 40 Holiday Inn franchises. When he traded 23 inns back to Holiday Inn in a stock swap completed in 1970, Winegardner became one of the largest shareholders in the company.

Kemmons named Winegardner first vice chairman in 1974, and he later became chief operating officer. Winegardner and a protégé from his own company in Cincinnati, lawyer and accountant Michael Rose, set about reorganizing and streamlining Holiday Inn over the next several years.

"By the time Roy and I arrived here in 1974, we were very familiar with the management of the company," Rose says. "When the Arab oil embargo hit in the fall of 1973, the uncertainty around the availability of gasoline had a real dampening effect on travel. Some of the weaknesses of Holiday Inn started to appear. It had had this enormous growth for so many years, but when the tide finally recedes is when you see the rocks for the first time. And I think there were a few rocks."

Rose detailed the major changes that were the focus of turning Holiday Inn around in the mid '70s.

"We sold off a number of hotels that were losing a good deal of money, and we sold off a number of hotels in markets where we had overbuilt the market. Places where the market might be fine for four Holiday Inns, we often had five. So we sort of weeded out, if you will, the weakest performers, and all the others began performing better. Things like that had a pretty immediate impact," he says.

Though many of the changes from that period reversed the way Kemmons had long done things at Holiday Inn — such as personnel changes and selling off many subsidiaries — Rose says Kemmons responded pragmatically to most of the changes.

"During the transition, I thought Kemmons was extremely supportive," Rose recalls. "There was a lot of change going on, and if Kemmons had been defensive or resistant, it just couldn't have happened. But he was the one who asked Roy Winegardner to get involved in the company because he wanted change. He recognized that the management they had in place probably couldn't make the changes that needed to be made, and that Roy had substantial operating experience at actually running hotels. None of the senior management at Holiday Inn had actually run a hotel themselves, or even supervised the running of a hotel. So Kemmons wanted that experience in the company and was supportive."

In the end, Kemmons took a practical approach to the changes, letting the bottom line ultimately guide his decisions. "There were times when we didn't always agree on things. I think of some times where we wanted to come in and sell a hotel that was underperforming or needed to be weeded out of a marketplace. Sometimes Kemmons and Wallace Johnson would sort of reminisce about, 'Oh, remember when we bought that land,' and they would tell a story about how it came about. And Kemmons might say, 'Well, gee, that's a pretty little hotel. I don't know why we would want to sell it.' But then when I would show them even if we put the proceeds of the sale in a savings account, the company would be better off, Kemmons was always quick to put sentiment behind him and get on with the business decision. And I admired him for not clinging to the past. He is very much a man who is always looking forward," Rose says.

"It was the same with a lot of the people changes. Kemmons was very loyal to people, and people had been very loyal to Kemmons. But he also recognized the need for change, and he never stood in the way or tried to protect someone or hold onto someone whose skill level hadn't kept pace with the growth of the company."

Another important move of the mid '70s was Kemmons' decision to assign Bill Walton the almost full-time job of increasing government and public awareness of how significant the travel industry had become in the U.S. economy. Initial government actions early in the oil crunch had hurt tourism, Kemmons felt, and he wanted Walton to work with officials in Washington to avoid further such actions. Walton became a roving ambassador and industry watchdog for Holiday Inn and the travel industry.

"Kemmons called me in and said, 'The people in Washington say the travel and tourism industry is a nonessential industry, and that is the reason our stock went to hell.' Being nonessential, we got no allocation of gasoline during the shortages. And Wall Street was scared the travel and tourism industry was going to be cut out completely," Walton recalls.

"Kemmons said, 'They need to know enough about our industry not to call it nonessential. I want you to go to Washington and do something about it.' Kemmons could make speeches, but he didn't like to. Wallace didn't like to either. So they sent me out to make all the speeches."

However, as part of those changes, Kemmons abruptly moved Walton from his position as president in 1973 and replaced him with Lem Clymer, who would later be named chief executive officer. "We about killed Bill when we made him vice chairman. We said it was a lot higher than president, but I don't think I ever convinced him," says Kemmons.

Though the rest of the '70s were bumpy, circumstances improved steadily through the latter half of the decade. But the struggles of those years led to the biggest changes in Holiday Inn's history: The company was entering the business of gambling.

"After the Arab oil embargo, three things happened at once that really hurt the hotel industry," Rose says. "In the late '60s and early '70s, you had had huge growth in new hotels. Lots of people were building hotels. Holiday Inn was growing rapidly, and a lot of Holiday Inn wanna-be's, like Ramada and Howard Johnson, were growing rapidly. And some new companies like Marriott were getting into the business and growing rapidly.

"And in the middle of this rapid growth, all of a sudden the Arabs turned off the oil. Overnight, the hotel industry realized how vulnerable it was. And another thing that happened, it threw the whole country into a very serious recession, probably the worst since the Great Depression. That hurt the hotel industry of course, because business travel fell off. So even after the oil was turned back on, the recession lasted several more years. The hotel business not only went down, but a lot of people who had been lending money to build hotels stopped lending money.

"So there was a period in 1975 when I really think Kemmons and some others in senior management of Holiday Inn sort of lost confidence in the future of the hotel business. It had grown the company rapidly all these years, and all of a sudden, really for the first time, it was faced with a whole new set of circumstances."

Rose took the position that the difficult era was only a temporary, that would soon pass, and from which Holiday Inn was well positioned to profit.

"I was relatively new to the business, and I thought about all that really as short-term. I thought recessions come and go, and lenders do from time to time turn off the money, and we would cycle through it. I pushed hard in 1975 and '76 for us to be out acquiring hotels and investing more in the hotel business, using our corporate money. Where other people couldn't borrow money, we had the money to go out and buy a lot of hotels," Rose remembers.

"But I never could get Kemmons or Roy to buy off on that. They just turned real sour on the hotel business — just for a short period of time, but it was during a window of opportunity to have really acquired some things that would have come to the fore.

"Instead, they started looking for alternatives, Kemmons and Roy both. They thought, gee, the hotel business has this problem that the Arabs can turn off the oil again, so maybe we ought to look at other businesses."

The two that most caught their attention were restaurants outside of hotels and the casino-gambling business.

"What had happened in that same time period was that MGM, which had always been in the movie business, built a big casino hotel in Las Vegas that was very successful. And Hilton, which had always been kind of a sleepy company in the hotel business, bought two existing casinos in Las Vegas and was very successful with those. So Kemmons and Roy were thinking, gee, this one casino that MGM owns is making more money than our entire hotel business with 1,700 hotels. Maybe we ought to be in that business. So they got real focused on that," Rose recalls.

"They sent me out to talk to a lot of people and investigate the business. It's ironic how it has turned out. I get a lot of credit for taking us into the casino business. But my first reaction was that we ought to be spending that capital in the hotel business, because I knew the hotel business was going to turn around."

In 1978, the board voted to build a casino in Atlantic City. In 1979 it bought a share of Riverboat Casino in Las Vegas. Later that year, Holiday Inn agreed to acquire the Harrah's casino operations for about $300 million. In later years, Holiday Inn's involvement in legalized gambling would be expanded even further.

The move into gambling came only after years of a struggle within the company over the issue. Walton was the most vocal opponent, and his moral objections to Holiday Inn getting involved in gambling would lead him to leave the company. Opposition to gambling also led to the resignation of Clymer and Lewis McKee, a longtime board member and former chairman of National Bank of Commerce.

Winegardner took Clymer's place as chief executive officer. Rose became executive vice president in charge of hotels and casino development. Wallace Johnson was also strongly opposed to gambling, but had retired from Holiday Inn at the beginning of 1977, and would leave the board of directors in May of 1979.

However, Kemmons always saw gambling as simply another business, not a matter of morals. Just as he had persuaded his old partner Wallace many years before that Holiday Inn should serve alcohol because it made good business sense, Kemmons supported Holiday Inn's venture into gambling for the same reason.

"I had no objections to the gambling business, the legal gambling business. But Wallace didn't want any part of it. And Bill Walton didn't either. They were rabid about not wanting any part of it," Kemmons says.

"But you know, we didn't have whiskey for the longest time in the Holiday Inns because Wallace didn't want it. He was one of the finest men I ever knew. I doubt he ever took a drink. He was very religious, very generous to the churches. But I finally had to go to him. I said, 'Wallace, we have never had any arguments at all. And I know you don't want whiskey. But I don't see how we can keep this thing going unless we do have bars in our inns.' And we talked and talked, and he prayed. And he finally said, I guess we have to do it.' But he didn't want to."

Though Holiday Inn did not actually enter gambling until after Kemmons retired, he initiated the move by flying to Reno, Nevada, to discuss the deal with Harrah's.

"Lem Clymer and I flew out in our jet to meet Bill Harrah [who headed the company], and we got pretty close to making a deal, but didn't actually make it at that point. And the next day after we got back to Memphis, Lem told me he was going to resign. I asked him why, and he said, 'I just can't go through with this gambling.' I said, 'Why didn't you tell me that before we flew out there and talked about making a deal?' He said, 'Well, I just thought about it, and I just can't be involved in gambling,' " Kemmons remembers.

A new guard was moving into control of the board in the late '70s though, and it would push the deal through. However, Kemmons would soon discover his board had grown independent of him as well.

In December of 1978, Kemmons was in Miami on business. "I was catching an airplane to come back to Memphis, and I was running to get there on time. All of a sudden I had a big pain in my left side. I thought it was my heart, so I sat down," he remembers.

"After about 10 minutes, I was able to get up and catch the plane, and I thought it was all over. That night I went to bed, and sometime around 2 or 3 in the morning I had the same pain. Dorothy called my doctor, got me in the car and took me to the hospital. They confirmed I had had a heart attack.

He was hospitalized then and in February for his heart problems. On March 8, 1979, he underwent a three-and-a-half hour, open-heart, coronary-bypass surgery.

"When I went into surgery, I told Dorothy I knew everything was going to be all right. I said I loved her very much and I loved all my children, and that I would come through and I would be with them. I had great confidence," Kemmons recalls.

"I have never had any fear of dying. I have a terrible fear of being a cripple, either mentally or physically. I've lived the best life I could and when my time comes, I'm ready to go. I only hope it will be quick when I do go."

Kemmons came through the open-heart surgery well and had a successful recovery. However, while he was still in the hospital, he learned Holiday Inn's board of directors was about to vote on buying the Perkins chain of some 340 restaurants.

"I got them to hook up a speakerphone system where I could talk to the whole board from my hospital room. Roy and Mike wanted to buy Perkins. I thought it was a terrible thing to do. We didn't know anything about the restaurant business, and we had never made any money off restaurants. I told them it was a terrible mistake to even think about buying it. I told them my vote was no, and I hoped they would go along with it," Kemmons recounts.

"But Roy charmed them into going along and buying Perkins. Up until then I had never had any problem with my board. They did anything I wanted them to do. I said, 'Well, if that's the way it is, I'm just going to retire.' That was the main reason I retired. I said 'If I can't control my board, I have no business running this company.' "

Kemmons announced his retirement at the age of 66 on May 16, 1979, at the annual shareholders meeting, effective that June 30. George Falls remembers when he stopped by Kemmons' office to wish him well on the day of his retirement, Kemmons said, "George, it just isn't fun anymore. It's time to move on."

After Kemmons retired, Winegardner was named chairman and chief executive officer, while Rose became president. Rose would continue his rapid rise, becoming chief executive officer in 1981, and chairman in 1983.

"I have a lot of admiration for Kemmons Wilson," Rose says. "We had a lot of success with the company. But Kemmons Wilson was the kind of entrepreneur who could start a company from nothing and grow it to the world's largest of its kind. There are very few people in the world like that, and certainly I am not one of them. Kemmons could do things I could never do, and was successful at things where I would not have been."

"On the other hand, there comes a point in a company's development where it needs a less entrepreneurial style of managing and more of a systems approach as it gets bigger and bigger. And I think with Holiday Inn, that was the time where people like myself were brought in to add more value to the company."

Kemmons maintains that his retiring from Holiday Inn was not an emotional experience for him. "When I realized my board of directors had voted against me, I knew that I never wanted to work another day for that company. I had always been the boss, except for the one time I worked marking stock boards. From that day on, I was the boss and I had to be the boss."

Rose says, "I don't know whether Kemmons was right or wrong about Perkins. It turned out that business was never a real good business for us. We ultimately sold it."

The only public criticism Kemmons ever made of the new

management was over its 1982 decision to replace The Great Sign with a smaller, plain green sign with white lettering and no marquee or star or neon lights.

"A hell of a mistake — it's like if Coca-Cola changed their signs," he says. "Now Holiday Inn's sign looks like any old fast-food sign. They said The Great Sign cost too much to operate, but that's wrong. They could have changed it up, put more neon, less bulbs, a lot of things."

Rose says, "I think there was just a feeling that we needed to modernize the sign, maybe give it a little more of a 1980s kind of look. We did that in the early '80s and it is still a sign that I think is contemporary in the mid 1990s. So therefore I think it was a good decision on the part of the company. Nobody stays in a hotel because of the sign, but they might get an image of the hotel if the sign appears dated. And we felt like The Great Sign that Kemmons had put on the first Holiday Inn in 1952 spoke of an era that had passed. So we moved away from that. It wasn't so much changing the logo so much as getting rid of The Great Sign, which was kind of an icon of the 1950s. I know Kemmons was sentimental about it, and he should have been."

When the sign change was announced, syndicated columnist Bob Greene of the *Chicago Tribune* began his column, "I bring you sad, disheartening news today."

He noted the company's stated explanations. It said the new signs would cost less to build and much less to maintain. And because Holiday Inn was now receiving most of its business through reservations, management felt a giant flashing sign was no longer needed to pull in motorists.

Still, Greene wrote, "I'm one traveler who is going to miss it. ... If you spent a lot of time on the road going to towns where you didn't know anybody, that Holiday Inn sign was like an old pal."

CHAPTER SIXTEEN

—A Fresh Start — Orange Lake—

"Put opportunity ahead of security."

Kemmons Wilson

In the spring of 1979, Kemmons found himself recovering from both open-heart surgery and the fact that he was not working on Holiday Inn for the first time in 28 years. He really did try to take it easy around the house for a while. But he and his family quickly realized retirement would not have the same meaning for Kemmons as it did for most human beings.

"I think he actually stayed retired about half a day, and that was it," says Kemmons' son, Bob.

"I missed the action of having someplace to go," Kemmons says. "I would sit around the house and look at television, but that wasn't for me. My heart attack taught me that I ought to slow down and smell the roses. But the roses for me are business."

Not long after he left Holiday Inn, Kemmons traveled to Sarasota, Florida, where a company of his had been building homes for many years. He was visiting with Billy Springer, his longtime associate there, when Springer asked if Kemmons could stay one more night.

Kemmons said he had nothing else to do, so they headed for the nearby resort of Sanibel Island. Springer had recently bought a two-week time share in a two-bedroom house there for $10,000. Kemmons says it was the first he had ever heard of time shares, which involve purchasing a "share" of a house or condominium for a specified period of time each year.

"I looked at that little place he had; it was a nice two-bedroom, two-bath house. I said, 'Billy, you bought two weeks for $10,000? And other people have done the same thing for every two weeks of the whole year?' I said, 'Man, that means someone is selling a house for $260,000 that probably cost $40,000 to build!' " Kemmons recalls.

Instantly, he was struck with the same kind of revelation he had almost half a century before upon discovering how much money he could borrow on a little house in Memphis.

"I said, 'We're in a new business.' I left there, and I knew right where I wanted to go.' Mickey Mouse was in Orlando, and I knew he was going to be bringing people down there to Disney World for a long time. I decided I was going to find some land over there and build a time share," Kemmons says.

"I didn't find any land that time. But I came back two more times, and the third time I bought 357 acres and started building."

He called it Orange Lake Country Club — the property had once been an orange grove with 22,000 orange trees on it. Within a few years, Orange Lake would be the largest timeshare resort in the world. More importantly, overnight it gave Kemmons the kind of consuming endeavor he needed to replace Holiday Inn in his life. And it proved every bit as profitable as Kemmons had envisioned that day on Sanibel Island.

"For me, it's been the biggest moneymaker I've ever had. Of course, Holiday Inn as a whole made much more money. But I only owned probably 5 percent of Holiday Inn, and I own 100 percent of this," he says.

Dottie Bonds, who has worked at Kemmons Wilson Companies since 1976, and became Kemmons secretary about the time he got busy with Orange Lake, remembers his enthusiasm as he undertook the project. "He thought, 'OK now, I could do this and this, and I know I can build it cheaper than anyone else can.' It really got him motivated as to, 'OK, I know what I want to do.' "

Charles Zanowski, a veteran in the timeshare industry, was the first person Kemmons hired at Orange Lake. They met in the Pennsylvania Poconos, where Zanowski was working at the time, when Kemmons and his sons visited to research the timeshare business there. Zanowski answered many of their questions, and after a couple more meetings, Kemmons hired him as Orange Lake's vice president in charge of sales and marketing.

"Kemmons is a unique person. He called Orange Lake his second dream. It was nice to be a part of helping make that dream come true. It was a major undertaking. He took a raw piece of land and developed it to where it became a livelihood for over 700 people who work there today," Zanowski says.

"I was enamored of Kemmons' integrity and his work ethic. I think he was extraordinarily fair in his business dealings. I always use the phrase 'tough but fair.' I admired his principles and his ethics as they pertained to his family and in the manner in which he conducted his business and personal affairs."

Zanowski quickly learned Kemmons' priorities, such as cost consciousness and attention to detail. "We got a trailer and put it on the property, and I operated out of that in the beginning. I remember he said for my first desk and chair to buy something we could throw away later. So I went to a local Salvation Army store and bought a desk and chair for $10.

"When he was doing the construction of the villas, and it came time to furnish them, he paid the greatest attention to even the slightest detail. I can remember he had me accompany him to the Sealy Mattress Company in Orlando. I was dressed in a three-piece suit with a white shirt and tie. But to make sure he got the right mattress for firmness and comfort, he had me test the mattresses by lying down on them and jumping up and down on them."

For many months, Kemmons flew back and forth from Memphis to Orlando to supervise construction of Orange Lake, spending the better part of most weeks there. "He was always on the job at 7 in the morning, and would work til 7, 7:30 every night. At the end of the day he would invite me into his room, and we would sit around and eat hot dogs and play gin rummy and go over the day's business. They were long days, but they were very productive," Zanowski recalls.

Dottie Bonds remembers the weekly routine. "He would only be here in the office Monday and Friday. He would make the deals and I would send the purchase orders out on Monday. Then all the bills and samples would come in during the week, so when he got back to Memphis on Friday, I would have all the paperwork ready for him."

It marked the first major project in which all three of Kemmons sons were involved with him. Once most of the construction was completed, Kemmons moved on to other things, letting Spence oversee the marketing and operations phase.

Orange Lake opened in 1982. It features more than 1,100 villas, which represent more than 45,000 timeshare owners. It also includes a $6.5-million clubhouse, a 27-hole championship golf course, 11 tennis courts, miniature golf, an 80-acre lake, beaches, an Olympic-size swimming pool and several other swimming pools.

"All the credit should go to Mickey Mouse. Where else in the world can you set up a business and be guaranteed that more than 20 million people will drive past your front door every year? If you've got the right location, you can do no wrong," Kemmons says.

Mickey Mouse indeed brought so many people to town that Kemmons used to drive out to Route 192 just to watch with satisfaction the bumper-to-bumper gridlocked traffic inching along toward the entrance to Disney World. However, John Pettey III, the chief financial officer for Kemmons Wilson Companies, says Kemmons actually deserves more credit than Mickey.

Pettey joined the company about the time Orange Lake construction was beginning in late 1981, and accompanied Kemmons on many of his trips there. He says Kemmons put much of his fortune on the line when he agreed to personally guarantee $20 million in loans for the construction.

"It was a huge gamble. When I started, I don't think I had the understanding I have now of how Kemmons — with a $20 million guarantee in essence — had pushed all the chips out in the middle of the table, saying he was willing to bet it would work. If Orange Lake had not gone well, it could have broken him. And yet, it's been like a grand-slam homerun in almost every respect," Pettey says.

"Kemmons saw he could do something that nobody had ever done like that before, a resort that was nothing but time shares. Previously, time shares were usually a workout for a failed motel or a failed apartment project. They would slap a coat of paint on and get a salesman in there and start selling it. Well, Kemmons had a bigger vision of a first-class resort with the golf course and all the other amenities.

"It was similar to the Holiday Inn idea in that he wanted a middle-class resort. It had never been done before. People say, well, Orlando was a great move. But he picked a site four miles outside Orlando. Back then, we were in the middle of nowhere."

Dick Farley, golf director at Shawnee-on-Delaware, a timeshare resort in Pennsylvania, remembers the first time Kemmons showed him the Orange Like site and asked him if a golf course could be built there. "At that time, it was just an orange grove. I had developed golf courses, and I told him we certainly could build a fine one there."

Farley brought in his partner and fellow golf pro, Rick McCord, and golf-course designer Joe Lee, and built the golf course. "It's a very nice, 27-hole resort complex. I do pro-am golf tournaments around the world, and we were able to hold some prominent pro-ams that helped establish Orange Lake in the beginning as a top property and a really quality establishment," Farley says.

"The golf course is very playable for the average person. It is built for every level of golfer. We asked Joe to make a course playable for the average player and also of the quality to have tournaments. So it is an interesting course. It has quite a bit of water, which makes it challenging, but not excessively challenging. There is one big lake and other manmade lakes we created that come into play. We have an island hole, a par 3 that has been received quite well. Whenever you have water, it makes for interesting shots over and around the water.

"It is an absolutely beautiful course. And the way Kemmons has put the villas on the fairways, people have fairway accommodations, which are highly desirable."

Farley and McCord also established at Orange Lake a Swing's The Thing Golf School, one of a chain of such schools Farley founded.

Dorothy says, "When Kemmons built the Holiday Inns, he wanted all the amenities. And when he built Orange Lake, he did the same thing. He wanted everyone to see what they had there, not what they might be getting in the future. All the big hotel chains are into time shares now, but Kemmons was first, and he gave the timeshare industry a lot of respectability."

Kemmons likes to say, "A time share is the only way the average man can own a second home in a resort area for $10,000, use it for a lifetime and leave it to his children."

A typical week at Orange Lake costs $10,000, and the timeshare owner can either return to Orange Lake each year to vacation, or, through membership in Resort Condominiums International, exchange the week at Orange Lake for a week at one of 2,800 different resorts throughout the world.

Zanowski says, "I think Orange Lake has a wonderful value in the eyes of the purchaser. Kemmons created a great value for anybody who purchased there. He put a lot of time and effort into picking that location, and the fact that he put $20 million in up front to put all the amenities in at the beginning, that gave it a tremendous amount of credibility — along with the credibility he brought because of his background with Holiday Inn."

"It had a mass appeal and it made my job a lot easier to sell Orange Lake because of everything he had done. He established a fair-market value for what he wanted to sell the product for, and it was perceived by the public to be a good deal."

In the first year the property was marketed, some $28 million worth of time shares in Orange Lake were purchased. The buyers eventually included people from all 50 states and 81 foreign countries.

Kemmons believes that Orange Lake is the single prettiest real-estate project he has ever developed. On a promotional video he made about Orange Lake, Kemmons says:

> Orange Lake Country Club — without a doubt a world-class resort. As soon as you enter the resort on Orange Lake Boulevard, you will realize Orange Lake Country Club was designed for you and your family, with all the amenities to make your stay as comfortable and enjoyable as possible. ...

> This beautiful, 357-acre resort contains a championship golf course designed by the famed Joe Lee. The magnificent lobby of the clubhouse overlooks the atrium ballroom. ... The clubhouse has a splendid cocktail lounge and dance floor. ... Just outside the snack bar is a sensational, full-size, Olympic swimming pool, a kiddie pool and two relaxing whirlpools, a

wonderful playground for the children, complete with the latest equipment for their enjoyment.

There is a marvelous 80-acre, spring-fed lake with its own 300-foot sand beach, where you can enjoy windsurfing, paddleboating, waterskiing, parasailing and any other water sport your heart can desire. ...

It is without a doubt one of the finest resorts in the world. And I am really proud of it and want you to see it.

Once he had Orange Lake going, Kemmons bought another 400 acres near there on which the Wilsons may build a second timeshare resort. Again, the process gave Pettey a greater appreciation for Kemmons' vision.

"He found some land selling for $4,000 an acre, while four miles down the road it was selling for $100,000, where the hotels already were. Kemmons felt it wouldn't be long until it was all fully developed. All the way to the closing, I was telling him, 'Please don't buy this land. You don't need it. It's going to cost so much just in interest on the loan, and you have plenty of land here already,' " Pettey recalls.

"So he gave me his rule for buying real estate. You buy it only under two conditions. One, because it is so cheap that you may not know what you are going to do with it, but you can't resist it. Or, two, you pay a good price, but you know exactly what you are going to do with. Never buy if conditions are somewhere in the middle. And he told me that that $4,000-an-acre land was so cheap he couldn't resist it."

Kemmons' instincts proved on target, and the property quickly quadrupled in value. "And it's also provided the basis for doing the next Orange Lake, which will be a huge benefit to the family if they decide to do that. So again, Kemmons had a lot of vision, not only in buying the original land, but also in adding to his holding," Pettey says.

"When he goes out and buys real estate, he is very seldom wrong. He can tell you he makes a lot of mistakes at some of the things he does, but not at real estate. He has done things that have not done well. He's done about everything. But the deals involving real estate have more than paid for all the ones that have not done well."

Spence says he too never saw the opportunity in time shares, even though he was exposed to the idea before his father was.

"It's because of the sheer force of Dad's will that Orange Lake got started," he says. "Once we got it financed and under construction, he practically lived at Orange Lake from 1981 to early '85."

In 1984, Kemmons got back into the hotel business, opening his first Wilson World, a $10-million hotel just a mile from the Disney gates. "The whole time Orange Lake was under way, his mind was percolating on building that Wilson World Main Gate," Pettey recounts. "We drove all up and down the highways; we were going to buy this, going to buy that. Finally he found a piece of land he liked, and the way he swapped off that land was just brilliant. I thought he was making a terrible mistake."

Kemmons bought 10 acres for $100,000 an acre, making it a $1-million package. But then he decided to swap an acre of his highway frontage for some less-valuable land at the back of the property. The man he was making the swap with, Lee Smith, owner of the local sewer system, needed highway frontage so he could build a road back to his land — where he wanted to build a hotel of his own.

"I said, 'Well, you are just creating a competitor. Please don't do that.' He said, 'Oh no, I want to do that. It's the right thing to do.' He had several things in mind. One, Lee was a good friend to have, because Kemmons realized your sewer permits had a lot to do with what you could do with your property," Pettey says.

"And he wasn't worried about Lee's hotel. Lee ended up selling it, and somebody else built a Radisson, and it really hasn't hurt us. Then when Lee built his road, it created a strip of real estate that we sold to a man who built a T-shirt shop, who paid us a million dollars for one acre of land. So, in effect, Kemmons got nine acres there for free."

Around the time he left Holiday Inns, Kemmons also launched

other ventures that took off in the early years of his retirement. One was Factory Outlet Malls.

At a time when outlet malls were located out in the boondocks in converted warehouses and even old barns, Kemmons helped introduce the concept of an outlet mall designed from the start for factory-outlet stores only. It was kicked off in Memphis, then expanded to other cities.

When Kemmons, in partnership with Doyle Savage and Jack Belz, began construction on Factory Outlet Mall at Interstate 40 and Canada Road in Lakeland, Tennessee, just east of Memphis, it was considered the first venture of its kind. Rather than placing an outlet mall in a building designed for something else, they built a facility from the ground up specifically tailored for an outlet operation.

The location was selected on the basis of two key factors: proximity to an interstate highway, but with enough distance from established retail centers that the merchandise sold would not directly compete with retailers handling the same merchandise.

The industry practice of selling off at a steep discount goods that had been overproduced or had not sold well was already established. What Kemmons and his partners sought to do was to provide a more effective means of marketing such products.

"We're not trying to get the manufacturer into something he's already in," said Savage during construction in 1979. "The factory outlet already exists all across the country in one form or another, whether it's a converted grocery store or maybe even the corner of the manufacturer's own factory. We're simply updating his facilities."

That was done through a "cluster concept," Savage said. The concept involved bringing a number of manufacturers' outlet stores together under one roof, in a building that would look essentially like a retail shopping mall.

John Ellis, a former vice president with First Tennessee Bank, was chosen by Kemmons and Belz to spearhead the new outlet concept. He emphasized, "Convenience and comfort are just as important in the retail business as in the hotel business. This new outlet center will be designed to be easy to access and easy to shop, with real values. People will seek us out if we follow this approach."

The concept proved successful, and the partnership built similar outlet malls in Williamsburg, Virginia, and Orlando, Florida, while Kemmons was still involved. Belz Enterprises continued to develop the outlet malls in other cities.

An ad for Factory Outlet Malls in *The Wall Street Journal* announced, "Kemmons Wilson got 327,616,503 people to sleep in Holiday Inns. Now he's building factory outlet malls that are waking up a lot of manufacturers."

The $2.5 million, 120,000-square-foot Factory Outlet Mall outside Memphis included tenants like Arrow Shirts, Munsingwear, Wrangler, Vanderbilt Fashions, Pilgrim Draperies, Ambassador Luggage and several footwear outlets.

Prices at the various outlet stores in the mall were marked down 25-75 percent off retail. At the grand opening in 1980, Kemmons was so impressed with all the great deals that he bought several wine-colored turtleneck sweaters himself. Later, he said he couldn't figure out why he bought them, except that they were such a good buy.

Still another early '80s success for Kemmons was GranDaddy's nachos and dip.

"I was out in California and I found some tortilla chips I thought were the best I had ever tasted. I was curious and I went to see the guy who made them," Kemmons recalls.

"I told him who I was and said I would like to take his formula back to Memphis. He said Memphis was too far for him to be involved, but if I would buy his equipment at a fair price, he would give me the formula. I bought it for about $100,000, and moved it to Memphis and started making tortilla chips."

Kemmons also began marketing under the GranDaddy's label the salsa he had been making at home for years. Although it got off to a slow start, GranDaddy's soon caught on. Within a few years, a $100,000 original investment had turned into a $12-million-a-year operation. He later sold it for $9.5 million in 1987.

Kemmons says the key element in GranDaddy's success was his hiring of Leonard Peek, who had been working in the snack-food business since 1948. He had worked all over the country, but was working in Terre Haute, Indiana, when a mutual friend introduced him to Kemmons in 1981.

"Anything in the salty-snack field that is manufactured — potato chips, cheese stuffs, pretzels, popcorn, tortillas chips, corn chips — I had been involved in it. Kemmons needed some help, and my expertise and his resources made a perfect marriage. We had a 50-50 ownership deal. Some people say 50-50 doesn't work, but it did with Kemmons," Peek recalls.

"When I joined the company, they were making a good product but didn't have any sales. That is what I focused on — sales. Kemmons had Orange Lake on the drawing board, and very soon after I came in he started spending most of his time there. He would just give me a call now and then to see how things were going."

Peek said most of the company's sales were in grocery-story delis, particularly in the eastern U.S. In the delis, they sold chips under the GranDaddy's label, and also under the label Nachos. A third label, Papa Grande, was also introduced to sell on regular grocery-store shelves. All three labels are still on the market today, primarily in New England, New York and the upper Midwest.

Kemmons got so enthusiastic over GranDaddy's that employees recall him feeding them samples of nachos and dip at 7:30 in the morning to get their opinion on the taste. Henri Landwirth, the onetime Holiday Inn employee who became a successful franchisee in Florida, recalls meeting Kemmons at the Orlando airport to find him traveling with two huge boxes.

"I asked him what in the world he was carrying around. He told me they were nacho chips he planned on selling to the Winn Dixie Grocery people, and he asked me to take him to their headquarters," Landwirth says.

"So with no appointment, and with Kemmons lecturing me on the importance of trying everything possible and necessary to accomplish one's goals, we headed off to find the Winn Dixie offices."

They found Winn Dixie's offices, but since the company had not been contacted beforehand, no executives were available to meet with Kemmons on the matter.

"Kemmons simply began distributing bags of nacho chips to every person working in the offices. He told me that at least we had tried, and he guaranteed that once they had tasted the chips, they would be calling."

Whether promising to build 400 motels, or risking all on a timeshare dream, or selling the world on a better nacho chip, Kemmons simply never knows doubt. Life is a game he plays by his own rules. His relentless confidence applies to every aspect of the world according to Kemmons.

Kemmons' brother-in-law, Albert Owings, recalls driving through the Rocky Mountains one summer with Kemmons on a Holiday Inn site-hunting trip. Despite the warm weather, many mountain peaks at high altitudes were snowcapped.

Everyone in the car marveled at the sight, except for Kemmons. He took one glance and announced that it wasn't snow but white paint applied by the local Chamber of Commerce. Then he matter-of-factly resumed his nap.

Charles Zanowski, Kemmons' director of marketing at Orange Lake, can testify to what extraordinary lengths that Kemmons' certainty extends. The two of them were driving about Orlando on business one day, when they stopped for gasoline. A pleasant young man with a beard filled the tank. As they left, Kemmons asked Zanowski what he thought about people with beards.

"I don't guess I have an opinion, one way or the other," Zanowski said.

"Well, I've got a bit of a problem with people who grow beards," Kemmons said.

"Why is that?"

"It seems to me that people with beards want to hide something. They don't want to show their true identity. I have a problem trusting people with beards."

"Why, that's not like you at all, Kemmons. You're a God-fearing Christian. How do you reconcile that opinion with Jesus Christ having a beard?"

Kemmons gave the matter a few moments' thought, then conceded that, yes, Christ did have a beard.

"But," Kemmons added, "I guarantee God didn't like it."

CHAPTER SEVENTEEN

── SECRETS OF GREATNESS ──

"You can do anything if you just work hard enough."

Kemmons Wilson

*A*t a spring banquet in Pittsburgh in 1982, Kemmons received an award that brought back memories of the glory days with Holiday Inn. Dinah Shore presented Kemmons with the award from Junior Achievement and *Fortune* magazine honoring him for induction in the Hall of Fame for U.S. Business Leadership.

In an article profiling Kemmons and other Hall of Fame inductees that year, *Fortune* magazine wrote, "In every age, some businessmen recognize the opportunity of a lifetime where others see nothing. ... Whether one calls them mavericks, plungers, visionaries or geniuses, the crucial fact is that such people are rare." With Holiday Inn, it said, Kemmons Wilson and Wallace Johnson "smashed the competition, transformed the industry, and built the world's largest lodging chain."

When Kemmons was a subject of Sybervision System's video *Profiles of Achievement* a few years later, it asserted that one can trace Kemmons' success through several "key elements" that Sybervision considers common to all leaders and achievers. The profile concluded that Kemmons is a model of achievement we can all learn from because:

• Ever since childhood, Kemmons has had a *strong sense of purpose* — never to be hungry again. That is what drove him to work so hard throughout his life. As a means to that end, he became a leader, not for the sake of leading, but to fulfill his purpose.

• Another key factor is his *persistence*. From the days when he first peddled *The Saturday Evening Post* as a youngster, through his founding of Holiday Inn, up to his creation of Wilson World and Orange Lake, he has stuck to his goals. And to this day, Kemmons is fulfilling his dream.

• *Knowing his strengths and weaknesses* is one of Kemmons' strongest characteristics. He freely admits that he did not have a good education. But he makes up for it by positioning the right people around him. Kemmons says finding those key people has been critical to his success.

• Kemmons has an *insatiable curiosity* about the way people live and work. He credits that curiosity for some of his best and most valuable ideas.

• Above all, Kemmons really *loves his work*. He says he is the happiest man who ever lived. And he is quick to remind us, if you are doing the things you like, it's really not work after all.

• Kemmons has a natural talent to attract, motivate and unite people toward a common goal, by using a *charisma* — if not a *power* — *to lead*. As a youngster, he soon had 10 boys selling magazines for him. And today, he energizes his forces with a zeal that makes each individual realize they are an integral part of the organization.

• Kemmons' ability to interact with people, his people sense, is an obvious trait. He realizes that leadership is a human skill. He *thoroughly enjoys people*.

• When it comes to taking risks, Kemmons is a *high-roller*. For instance, when Holiday Inn was first trying to finance a computerized reservation system, Kemmons had to sign for the $8 million loan personally. He knew the computer would be critical to his vision of the future of hotels. He says he could have lost everything, but he was not afraid. Looking back, Kemmons remembers that day as the turning point when Holiday Inn took control of its destiny.

• Kemmons' ability to take risks stems from a fail-safe attitude that views a momentary setback not as a mistake but as a long-term learning experience. The fact is, Kemmons *does not believe in failure* at work or at play.

• Kemmons' winning ways extend to his ability to *recognize a need* and then make a profit from it. When the nation's highway system was being built back in the 1950s, Kemmons realized that traveling families needed affordable hotels with a name they could trust.

• Behind all of Kemmons' creations, there is *remarkable common sense*. He is quick to compare his own experiences with those of others, cross-referencing and evaluating information to stay in touch and deal with shifting circumstances.

• When it comes to meaning, *the family is the center of Kemmons' life.* As the patriarch of a 26-member family, he thrives on the give and take, and the heartfelt rewards of developing warm and lasting relationships.

According to Sybervision, Kemmons achieved his great success through what it calls *The Four Keys to Power:*

• *Vision* — After taking a frustrating family vacation, Kemmons had a vision to build a chain of hotels for a changing world, where there would never be a separate charge for children and there would be a brand name travelers could trust.

• *Communication* — Kemmons had to communicate that vision, translating it into a goal that others could believe in and improve upon through the exchange of ideas.

• *Positioning* — Kemmons created an environment that promoted his vision. He put his plan into action. First he set the standard of high quality and hard work. Then he positioned his company for success, franchising each Holiday Inn and locating them one day's drive apart, structuring a common-sense plan for future growth of his hotel chain.

• *Self Management* — Kemmons has a very positive outlook on life and he is able to bring that to his organization, creating an atmosphere where everyone wants to do their best.

On another television special in the 1980s called *Living Legends,* Kemmons credited his success to a sense of self confidence instilled by his mother. He said he gets so many great ideas, because "I guess I am probably the most curious guy you ever knew. I want to know what makes everything work. I want to know why it works. ... I was always hustling, always trying to find a way to make a dollar."

He said the success he has known is still possible for young people today: "Absolutely, it is just as possible as it was back in my day. But you've got to give up a lot of things. You've got to give up the 40-hour-a-week job that you want. You've got to work after you get through with that job and go on somewhere and make some money for yourself. Anybody can be a successful entrepreneur if you work hard enough. You can do anything if you just work hard enough. Most people are not willing to work hard enough."

Kemmons said he never had much faith in relying on business consultants. "A consultant is a man who knows a hundred ways to make love but doesn't know any women. I think you have to have your own ideas, believe in your own judgment and go ahead. I'd rather trust my judgment than anybody I know."

He spelled out his philosophy of leadership as leading by example: "I am always leading. I feel the boss has got to lead. I never ask anybody to do anything I wouldn't do myself."

In 1982, a roast of Kemmons was held at the Holiday Inn Rivermont in Memphis as a fundraiser for the Big Brothers/Big Sisters organization. Many friends and longtime business associates told tales of Kemmons' that highlighted his genius and his heart, as well as his stubborness and pecularities — secrets of greatness revealed on that evening to entertain as well as illuminate.

John Martin, Kemmons' longtime attorney, recalled the time Kemmons wanted to put in a commercial development next to the exclusive Chickasaw Gardens residential area. Martin warned Kemmons he would have opposition from Chickasaw Gardens residents in the hearing before the zoning board over the matter. Kemmons said he wouldn't, because he was bringing in busloads of his own supporters early to fill up the meeting room so there would be no space for opponents. According to Martin, it worked so well that opponents never got anywhere near the meeting room, and Kemmons got the vote he wanted out of the zoning board.

Martin also said that after the trouble Kemmons had building houses on other peoples' lots, it led Kemmons to adopt his habit of asking to be given land for free for Holiday Inns. He said Kemmons once made progress persuading the Argentine government to give him some very choice land, until he also asked to be given the money for building the Holiday Inn as well.

Martin highlighted Kemmons' constant borrowing habits by recalling a time when *The Tennessean*, a Nashville newspaper, reported Kemmons was one of the parties in the largest real-estate deal in state history. "That statement may have been true, but the only money that passed hands that day was the 50 cents I had to lend Kemmons to buy some cigarettes after we closed the deal," Martin said. He remembered once asking Kemmons what he would do when he began getting competition for his Holiday Inns from other motels. Kemmons told him, "There isn't going to be any competition. I'm going to build them all."

Sam Phillips regaled the large crowd gathered with the story of how Kemmons gave Sam the famous advice to sell Elvis Presley's contract to RCA for $35,000. "Kemmons is still my friend. But I checked on it today, and if I had just held onto 1 cotton-picking percent of Elvis on just the records he sold at retail list price, I would be worth $100 million without having to get up in the morning!" Phillips cried.

Then he pulled out a recent edition of the *Midnight Globe* tabloid newspaper. Among articles headlined "Joan and Jackie Fight for Prince's Love" and "Thin Thighs in 30 Days," was an article Phillips wanted to tell the audience about as an example of Kemmons' "sustaining power."

It was headlined: "If You Think You Have Goofed, Consider These World-Shaking Bloopers." No. 1 on its list of bloopers was "The college admissions director who turned down Albert Einstein on the grounds that he showed no promise." No. 2 was "All 21 New York publishers who rejected the manuscript of a Korean War novel titled M*A*S*H."

And No. 3 on this list of World-Shaking Bloopers: "Sam Phillips, the recording executive who for $35,000 sold to RCA all future rights to a young singer named Elvis Presley."

Cecil Humphreys, president emeritus of the University of Memphis, said the audience should take note of Kemmons' reputation as an international diplomat. When the Marrakech Holiday Inn was dedicated, Humphreys said, the ceremony was conducted in front of the Holiday Inn, with top officials from the government, Holiday Inn and Occidental Petroleum, a partner in the hotel. Within five minutes after the speeches began, Kemmons was sound asleep and had to be awakened by Dorothy when it was his time to speak. "I'm sure this greatly aided relations with the government," Humphreys said.

George Falls, who was then vice president for government relations at Holiday Inn, said he was very comfortable participating in the fundraiser for Big Brothers/Big Sisters: "Working for a volunteer organization reminds me of workng for Kemmons — and the pay is approximately the same. Bill Walton used to call Kemmons and say, 'So-and-so needs a raise.' Kemmons would say, 'Give him a title.' Bill would say, 'He's already up to senior vice president.' And Kemmons would say, 'Well, think up a new one, or start him all over.'"

Falls, who started working for Holiday Inn in 1960, told about playing tennis with Kemmons in Tokyo against executives from a large securities company there. The match came down to one point, with Falls serving. "Kemmons came over to me, looked at me with those steely-blue eyes, and put that big paw on my shoulder and said, 'George, you got to get this one in. And remember this, *this is Japan versus the United States.*' Talk about pressure. If you think that first serve didn't go in, you should have seen the second one. It ended up in Nagasaki.' But Kemmons liked it because he had someone to blame the loss on."

Falls continued, "Whenever Kemmons went into a town, he was never looking for property, never looking for real estate. He was always *looking for ground.* Now that's OK in Forrest City or Wichita, but it's a little disarming in New York or Washington." He recalled they once spotted a piece of land in New York that looked great for a Holiday Inn. The real-estate agent told Kemmons it was a state bird sanctuary, but Kemmons wanted to buy it anyway. It took Falls and the agent all day to convince Kemmons they could not build a Holiday Inn on state property.

Falls also detailed one example of Kemmons' "scientific research methods." He recalled once, during a meeting, someone from the advertising department at Holiday Inn announced that they wanted to buy time on the *Huntley-Brinkley News Show,* then the most dominant evening-news program on television. Kemmons said, "Have you lost your minds? Nobody in the world we'd want to reach gets home from work early enough to watch the 5:30 news, and I can prove it. How many people in this room get home in time to watch the 5:30 news?"

Falls said, "Well if you think a hand went up, you are dead wrong. If Kemmons had asked if anyone got home by 7, not a hand would have gone up. So that was the end of the advertising plan for *Huntley-Brinkley*."

Hugh Chatham, a Holiday Inn franchisee and furniture manufacturer from California, said his first association with Kemmons had come in Chicago 29 years before when they met at a furniture trade show there. Chatham claimed Kemmons was staying at the Chicago YMCA to save money. He said he sold Kemmons $50,000 worth of furniture, but didn't find out until after he wrote up the order that Kemmons intended to buy it on credit. And before it was ever shipped, Kemmons ordered another $50,000 worth on credit.

Chatham said Kemmons once stopped at Chatham's home in California on his way to Asia. He talked Chatham into going with him, telling Chatham's wife they would be gone eight days. It turned out they were gone 29 days. While they were in Asia, they attended a luncheon in Taiwan in Kemmons' honor, because he was negotiating to build a Holiday Inn in Taipei. The first course was pickled fish; the second was squid. "You've never seen such a face on Kemmons," Chatham recalled.

The general hosting the luncheon could tell Kemmons was not enjoying the food, and expressed his disappointment, asking if they should adjourn the luncheon since Kemmons was not pleased. Kemmons said to Chatham, "What should I do?" Chatham replied, "Just keep your mouth shut," and then stood up and said to the interpreter: "Please tell the general that Mr. Wilson suffers from a bleeding ulcer and cannot eat this food." So when the general asked what Kemmons would like, Kemmons said, "Could you get me a hamburger and a Coca-Cola?"

Chatham also recalled a fishing trip with Kemmons to Manitoba in the mid '50s when Chatham blew a chance to land the greatest Holiday Inn franchise deal in history. On the trip, they played gin rummy, and Kemmons wound up owing Chatham $47. When Kemmons said he didn't have the money on him, Chatham told Kemmons to give him a check. Kemmons pleaded that he didn't have a check either, but Chatham told him to borrow the money from someone. Finally, Kemmons said, "If you will cancel out this $47, I will give you the Holiday Inn franchises for Virginia, North Carolina and South Carolina." However, Chatham replied, "I don't want it, I want my $47." He got home from the trip with an I.O.U. for the $47

Chatham also recounted Kemmons' legendary audience with the Shah of Iran at the Shah's summer palace. Chatham went to the meeting with Kemmons, a representative from Intercontinental Hotels who also wanted to build a hotel there, and a former classmate of the Shah — who was then a large rancher in California and had arranged the meeting to discuss Kemmons' interest in building a Holiday Inn in Tehran.

Before the meeting, an emissary was sent over to brief the Americans on how to conduct themselves before the Shah. They were sternly instructed to bow from the neck down; never to offer their hand to the Shah unless he offered his first; never to sit down unless the Shah requested it; and if asked to sit down, never to cross one's legs and show the Shah the bottom of one's shoes. And above all, they were cautioned, always address the Shah as "Your Majesty."

When Kemmons' group arrived at the magnificent palace in the mountains, they were escorted into a huge room with Persian rugs on the walls and gold furnishings everywhere. Chatham said he picked up a small gold ashtray and put it in his pocket as a joke. The others in their group laughed, but Kemmons "just about died," and told Chatham to put it back because they were being watched on security cameras. Chatham did return the ashtray.

When they were escorted single-file into the Shah's chambers, Chatham said the order of their entrance should have been: the Iranian friend of the Shah's first, the Intercontinental representative second, Kemmons third and Chatham last. However, for some reason, Kemmons entered first and walked straight up to the Shah. Kemmons stuck out his hand and said "How do 'ya do, Your Majestic? My name is Kemmons Wilson and I'm an American." Then he walked over and sat down in a chair and crossed his legs.

Fortunately, the Shah found Kemmons' entrance amusing. The meeting went well, with the Shah agreeing to everything Holiday Inn and Intercontinental wanted. But as they were walking down the steps outside, Chatham said, "Kemmons, why in the hell did you call him 'Your

Majestic'?'" Kemmons at first said he didn't do it, but when the others confirmed that he had, Kemmons scratched his head and said, "I guess the reason I did that was when I was a young man, I sold Majestic stoves."

Memphis real-estate developer Philip Belz said that when he was first asked to participate in the roast, he had to check with his rabbi, because "roast has to do with food and Kemmons is not kosher." Then Belz told the story of how Kemmons once ordered all the Holiday Inn franchise owners to install trampolines, because he thought they were great recreation. Belz said Kemmons told the franchisees, "Don't worry about the insurance. Nobody can get hurt, especially if you build them level with the ground." Many of the franchisees grumbled about it, but the trampoline program went ahead because Kemmons insisted upon it.

"Well, one of the trampolines was installed just outside Kemmons' office at Holiday City. And one day, as chance would have it, a young man jumping on the trampoline came crashing through Kemmons' window in the middle of a business meeting. The young man recovered, but the trampoline program did not. You would have thought there was a gravediggers' convention at all the Holiday Inns the way they were covering up the trampolines the next day," Belz said.

Kemmons' dearest partner, Wallace Johnson, concluded the roasting. He recounted the oft-told story about Kemmons coming over to see him in 1953 to persuade Wallace to become his partner and take Holiday Inns national. Wallace claimed the letters he sent out to homebuilders around the country said, "We invite you to come to Memphis, and we will show you how to make a million dollars. Don't ask any questions, just get on the next plane."

Wallace said Kemmons was the first person he ever met who shared Wallace's habit of always saying "I love you" to his wife before hanging up at the end of every phone call. He said that as they traveled around for Holiday Inn, whenever Kemmons called home, he also would say "I love you" to each of his children and to his mother.

Wallace said that on one occasion, Kemmons was flying the Holiday Inn company plane through a turbulent storm caused by Hurricane Diane, with Wallace and a prospective lender as passengers.

They were trying to make a very difficult landing when Wallace turned to the lender and asked, "If we make this landing, do we get the money?" He said, "Man, you get the money if you just get me back on the ground safely." According to Wallace, Kemmons landed the plane on his second pass at the landing strip, with less than enough gasoline in the tank to go 10 more miles. And they indeed got the loan.

Wallace also told one of his favorite yarns, about a time Kemmons and Wallace and other Holiday Inn executives supposedly went on a bear-hunting expedition. When Kemmons and Wallace got up the next morning, the others told them they had already been hunting. So Kemmons and Wallace went out by themselves. They spotted a bear and shot at it, but both missed and the bear began chasing them.

Kemmons and Wallace ran back to the cabin and charged through the front door, leaving it open as the bear pursued close behind. Then they ran out the back door and Kemmons slammed it shut, yelling back to the other executives still inside, "You boys skin that one! We'll go get another one!"

CHAPTER EIGHTEEN

—STILL CLIMBING AFTER 80—

"When I want your opinion, I'll give it to you."

Kemmons Wilson

$\mathcal{T}$hough Holiday Inn was sold to a British conglomerate in 1989, it remains the world's largest lodging chain. As a brand name and icon of American popular culture, it ranks alongside Coca-Cola, McDonald's and Chevrolet.

As for the man who invented Holiday Inn, he could have quit working decades ago and just had fun for the rest of his life. Kemmons has had fun. He just hasn't quit working. Even in his 80s, nearly two decades after he officially retired from Holiday Inn, Kemmons refuses to spend his days doing anything except work.

"I just like to work. I enjoy what I do, and I never do anything if I don't enjoy it," he says.

"I won't ever retire. I would go absolutely crazy, and I would drive my wife crazy. I've got to do something."

Vacations remain rare. Dorothy recalls persuading Kemmons to join her on a cruise ship from Vancouver to Alaska in the late '80s. "He was like a raving maniac. He looked at me and said, 'You have taken your first and last cruise with me,' " she says.

"I loved the cruise. But Kemmons was miserable because there wasn't any land to buy. Kemmons is just a workaholic. He always has been and always will be. And that's OK. He's happier doing that than anything else."

After all these years, Kemmons still carries a tape measure in his pocket everywhere he goes, just as he did on the famous trip that resulted in Holiday Inn. "If I have my clothes on, I have my tape measure. I use it every day," he says.

Dorothy says, "He measures everything the minute we walk in a hotel. He always has to know what size the rooms are, what the floorplan is and how far it is from the commode to the dressing table."

Kemmons does sleep a bit more these days, getting in bed most evenings about 9 to flip through the channels with his remote control until he dozes off. Dorothy gave him a T-shirt that says "King of the Remote."

But he has yet to take up a hobby or pastime — not even golf. Kemmons has lived across the street from Galloway Golf Course for almost 50 years, but has never played on it. He has in fact only played golf three or four times in his life. "Golf is for people with lots of time," he maintains.

David Sullivan, a hotel developer who worked for Holiday Inn, told a reporter a few years ago, "I sometimes see Kemmons in the airport when I'm taking a 7 a.m. flight. I'm thinking, 'I'm tired, why am I doing this?' And then I run into Kemmons catching a flight to who knows where. I don't know how he does it, but he's still at it."

Kemmons' ventures today include the Wilson Graphics printing operation, his W&W's candy operation, real-estate holdings, shopping malls, homebuilding, Wilson World and Wilson Inn hotels, Federal Savings Bank, an oil-drilling operation in Rapides Parish, Louisiana, developed by Occidental Petroleum, a deep-mine coal operation near Fort Smith, Arkansas, and Orange Lake Country Club. His company still owns or manages eight Holiday Inns.

"Orange Lake has not only produced a lot of money on its own, it's produced the money that bought the banks the Wilsons own now, as well as the money that built the 20 or so hotels Kemmons has built since the 1980s," says John Pettey.

"He would start building a hotel, and I would go out and start trying to get a bank loan. But he wasn't going to be slowed down in his building. He was just going to use Orange Lake's money until we got the loans. At one point, he had 12 hotels under construction but I only had six loans, so I was really scrambling. But Orange Lake brought in enough money, and we got it all done."

Kemmons has had only three personal secretaries in his long career. The first was Fairie Morris, the second Sue Todd. Dottie Bonds has been Kemmons' secretary since 1982. She finds working for him "challenging, frustrating, fun, maddening — it runs the gamut. He's not patient by any stretch of the imagination. Everything has to be done immediately. Unless you're geared toward that, it's real frustrating. He is fun though. He has a good sense of humor."

After working for Kemmons for so many years and learning to deal with his demanding, all-consuming approach to life, she believes, "I've gained an education here ... I can do anything with anyone at any time."

Dottie takes care of anything that comes up in Kemmons' business dealings. She writes all of his speeches and handles his personal correspondence, visitors and calls. She manages the shipping, receiving and purchase orders on operations such as Kemmons' candy business. She helps make selections for interiors and furnishings for his hotels.

One of the trickiest parts of her job is juggling Kemmons' schedule, because he never works off appointments, and he maintains his lifelong habit of seeing anyone who drops by his office any time he is free. When people request appointments, Kemmons tells them to just call and see if he is in before they come by. Even out-of-town businessmen must come in without an appointment.

"We try to make all the allowances we can to make sure that Kemmons will be free. But if somebody walks in five minutes before a scheduled visitor from Atlanta gets here," Dottie says, "Kemmons is going to sit down and listen to the guy who just walked in, because his idea may be that one that's really going to jump."

Kemmons has always been fascinated with gadgets, and in recent years with computers and electronic equipment. He doesn't understand how much of it works, however. "He calls me his engineer," Dottie says, "because I am mechanically inclined and I can program everything he buys."

Once, during a trip to Asia, Kemmons was very impressed that many businesses there had intercom systems so employees could easily speak to each other from office to office. So, he had an intercom system installed between his office and Dottie's adjoining office. However, Kemmons has never used it, and still communicates with Dottie by yelling for her through his open door.

In her nearly two decades with the company, Dottie says, the Wilsons have made her feel she is part of the family. "I have free rein to speak my mind. ... I feel I can go to any of them at any time."

Spence, Bob and Kem Wilson have all been working for their father's company since about 1970. Kemmons is chairman of the board. Spence is president. Kem and Bob are executive vice presidents.

"But, we brothers don't worry much about titles," says Spence. "We all know how things get done, and we have our own way of doing it. Sometimes we think alike, sometimes we think differently. We do sometimes disagree very strongly, but we don't ever draw lines in the sand."

A few years ago, Kemmons' sons had a poster made for him. It features Kemmons in a godfather-like pose, wearing gangster pinstripes and wide-brimmed hat, with his sons arranged behind him. "When I want your opinion, I'll give it to you," the caption reads.

"It was my idea to give him that poster. He has always been in total control, and is reluctant to relinquish that super-final authority," says Bob.

"Dad has always been willing to let others run with the ball in in areas where he is not particularly interested in dealing with the details," says Spence. "But, in the area of construction and purchasing, he is an expert and keeps most of those jobs for himself."

"But probably the best thing about him is how he instilled in us the ethic that we *always* do what we say we will do," Bob adds. "I think you could work with us and never have a legal document. Pop has always done a lot of things on a handshake. He is a really tough negotiator, but once you reach an agreement with him, his word is his bond with all of us."

The makeup of the Kemmons Wilson Companies continues to reflect the eclectic mix of interests that has always characterized Kemmons.

"It's a complicated organization to explain," Spence says. "I tell people we are an entrepreneurial organization with a focus on five or six key businesses. First, we are in the resort timesharing business, with our Orange Lake Country Club development. We are major hotel operators, now owning and operating 25 properties. We are in the banking and financial-service business, with bank operations in both Arkansas and Tennessee, and a large property and casualty insurance agency based in Memphis. We develop subdivisions and build homes in Memphis and in Sarasota, Florida, and we own and operate a number of miscellaneous real-estate properties in Memphis, including retail, warehouses and office properties. And then we have a venture-capital focus: We invest in different kinds of businesses, both existing and start-up ones. Over the years, much of this investment focus has been in the manufacturing area.

"Both Orange Lake and our hotels make up the largest part of our business activity in terms of revenues and profits. My brothers and I and other partners own several of our hotels, and Dad owns a number of them individually. Many of his hotels are Wilson Worlds or Wilson Inns, but he also owns several Holiday Inns. I have always found it interesting that the man who really developed the hotel franchise concept should now be a franchise holder of the company he started."

At the company's headquarters in the airport area of southern Memphis, the three brothers occupy a triad of offices arranged around a small courtyard. Kem's features a collection of LeRoy Neiman prints, many of them athletes such as Joe Namath and Muhammad Ali. Spence's walls display western art, wildlife photographs by his wife Becky and some of the most prized signatures from his autograph collection, such as those of Einstein and Churchill. Bob — the most active pilot in the family — works in an office dominated by models of all sorts of aircraft. Bob loves flying so much he commutes to work by plane from his home near La Grange, Tennessee, where he lives with his wife, Susan, reducing a 70-minute trip by car to 15 minutes.

"We each have specific parts of the business that we are responsible for. Kem is chairman of the board of the banks. He looks after Wimbleton Sportsplex. He oversees much of the hotel development activity," Spence says.

"Bob focuses on major construction and renovation work that we have, and now is responsible for the development of our new fixed base operation for private aircraft in Memphis, which will be known as Wilson Air Center. Securing the approvals to build and operate this center was a 10-year personal effort on Bob's part.

"I look after a lot of Dad's personal interests and investments, in addition to being very active in our venture-capital arena. I'm the point man on Orange Lake for the family, as well as on a couple of other businesses in which we have invested. With John Pettey's help, I try to be certain we have enough money to maintain and operate our many different businesses. I spend a lot of time on our capital allocation and capital budgeting decisions."

Bob has always been the son who loved construction as much as his father. "I always liked that end of it. I like the tangible deals you can put your finger on. Spence or Kem, they can do the projections and all that, but I like to deal with the actual structure," he says.

"We all have different likes, so in the company we do different things and we don't step on each other's toes. Pop kind of does his own thing."

Spence finds Kemmons' continued active presence in the family companies a mixed blessing. "When Dad says he is going to go build a hotel in Florida and will need $8-9 million that you hadn't planned on, he can make life difficult for a while," he says.

"But, all in all, I'm glad he can still do the kinds of things he loves. I think Dad's work is his life force. It's really where he gets his energy: by being focused on a project, it takes his mind off any ills he might have."

Kem says, "I'm a little surprised he still works so hard, and somewhat disappointed that he doesn't stop to smell the roses more. He has probably missed out on a few things, but work is his hobby. It's amazing someone his age could not only still have the desire but the capacity to work like he does. He always has a lot of balls in the air.

"He gets here about 8 every morning. He has more of a special-projects mentality now. It's more our responsibility to run the company day-to-day. And many things Dad does — calling contractors and things like that — he does himself. He doesn't have a big staff helping him.

"He is still a tough negotiator. We call him the best purchasing agent around. He drives a hard bargain, and he generally finds someone who will accept what he wants to pay."

As a reminder of one of Kemmons' classic negotiations, Spence keeps on his wall a framed contract Kemmons wrote out on a single sheet of paper in pencil several years ago. It involved Philadelphian John McShane who, among other things, was the contractor that built the Pentagon in Washington, D.C. In his later years, McShane gave most of his assets to charity, except for a Holiday Inn in Philadelphia.

"The hotel had developed problems and it was using up what cash John McShane had left," Spence says. "Holiday Inn was operating it for him, but it was not doing well. He felt that since Holiday Inn had encouraged him to build it there, the company had some moral obligation to buy it back. Dad became very intrigued with the idea. But he talked to Holiday Inn, and they didn't want the hotel back. So he asked them for permission for him to buy it personally. They said whatever he wanted to do on his own was fine. I didn't think we ought to do it, but Dad really wanted to."

"So we are up there on our third trip to see Mr. McShane. It was a complicated transaction. Mr. McShane had a foundation that was leasing the land to him, but Dad was not willing to buy the hotel on leased land. We are talking about the deal structure, and I'm throwing out a lot of ideas and thoughts, all of which Dad sees as obstacles to getting the deal done. So finally, he sends me out of the room."

About 15 minutes later, Kemmons came out with a single piece of paper, signed by him and John McShane and providing the basis to conclude the deal. By themselves, the two legendary entrepreneurs had written out a bottom-line agreement in pencil on a plain piece of stationery.

"I really didn't think we would make a nickel off it," Spence admits. "But I told myself if we ever made any money, I would frame it. And we finally did."

Kemmons works today at a desk cluttered with paperwork, merchandise and other evidence of his many ongoing ventures. The walls are covered with family photos and memorabilia of every sort. But the most dominant item in the room is a large portrait of Doll, watching over Kemmons from behind his desk.

"A very big part of Dad's drive was always his desire to take care of his mother," says his son, Spence. "She sacrificed so much for him in his childhood, raising him by herself. He recognized very early that life was a tremendous task for her, and how caring for him was number one in her life.

"It became his ambition to succeed for his mother's sake. And once it was part of him, it went on all his life. Those formative years shaped the rest of his life."

So Kemmons just keeps working. In recent years, he has taken great pride in the development of his Wilson World and Wilson Inn hotels. It offered him the chance to get back into the business that made him famous. And he still believed he could succeed on his original formula of offering travelers first-class amenities at a budget price.

Billy Mills sells Kemmons the carpets for the Wilson Worlds and Wilson Inns. Mills is a longtime friend of Kemmons' as well as owner of Billy Mills Carpets, in which Kemmons and Kemmons' brother-in-law, Albert Owings, were partners until Mills bought them out in the early '70s.

Mills recalls flying down to Orlando with Kemmons when he built his first Wilson World there. Kemmons wanted Mills to stay with him about three weeks, Mills says, "to push my carpet installers. They would push the painters and the tile people putting in the bath tile. And he told them if they didn't get out of the carpet men's way, they'd have to work on top of them. And if they ruined the carpet, they would have to pay for it," Mills recalls.

The first Wilson World in Memphis opened in 1986, with Kemmons proclaiming it "the prettiest hotel I have ever built, by far." Today, there are six Wilson Worlds and eleven Wilson Inns. The largest number are located in Tennessee, but others are located in Texas, South Carolina, Mississippi, Louisiana, Kentucky, Florida and Arkansas.

Kemmons is building a 250-room hotel, the first Wilson Suites, on a choice site on Stemmons Freeway in Dallas. It is scheduled to open in 1996 and will cater to business travelers. And he recently sketched out the plans for another Wilson Suites for Cape Canaveral, Florida.

The rough-sketching of plans remains something Kemmons still does every time he builds anything. Dottie Bonds notes that he has on occasion drawn plans that were architecturally impossible. However, after more than 30 years of engineering projects with Kemmons, McCaskill can usually resolve such problems.

"It's like anything Kemmons does. He comes up with some wild ideas sometimes. He is an idea man, with a real fertile, creative mind. He has a lot of common sense, but occasionally he goes astray with some ideas that are not realistic," says McCaskill.

"Fortunately he takes these ideas and bounces them off the people around him. If you can come up with good reasons why they won't work, he will usually back off and see your point. But occasionally he will force it on through, and even then, sometimes he turns out to be right. Everybody was really opposed to him doing Orange Lake, but he went ahead anyway, and it turned into a virtual money machine."

McCaskill also remembers having doubts about Kemmons' site selection for the first Wilson World in Memphis, built just off American Way in the southeastern part of the city: "I didn't think that site was a good one at all when he built it. But now it is one of the most successful hotels in the city."

Every hotel Kemmons builds today is different than the last. "From the man who cookie-cuttered every Holiday Inn, now nothing is the same," Dottie says. "As soon as he finishes one design, he figures out something he wanted to put in that one, so he'll add it to the new one.

"And he'll change a hotel in the middle of construction. It's nothing unusual for him to add a floor, or take out a wing, or say, 'Let's move the building back.' "

One of Kemmons' most thriving operations today is Wilson Graphics. The way it was launched illustrates how Kemmons prefers to invest in people rather than established businesses.

Bill Holcombe, who is now president of Wilson Graphics, called on Kemmons one day in 1984, with no appointment or prior introduction, in hopes of landing some of Kemmons' printing business. Holcombe remembers that Kemmons talked to him for more than an hour, not only questioning him about his business but asking questions like "Where do you go to church?" and "Do you know your pastor?" and "Does he know you?"

After that one meeting, Kemmons proposed that he and Holcombe form a partnership in which Kemmons would put up all the money for the building and equipment, and Holcombe would run the business. They did, creating Wilson Graphics. Holcombe says Kemmons has an uncanny way of sizing up people and judging character, and that once he is impressed by an individual he puts a lot of trust in them. Kemmons likes to find people who are trustworthy and whose word is their honor, and then invest in them.

Holcombe says there is nothing about Kemmons that he distrusts, and that he does not even know if they have a contract. He says Kemmons inspires loyalty, and as long as people working for him make more right decisions than wrong ones, he is satisfied.

However, Kemmons expects his people to do whatever is necessary to get the job done. And if they don't, they can expect him to scold them. However, even while Kemmons is "fussing at you," Holcombe says, he always seems to be doing it out of personal concern. And once the scolding is over, the issue is left in the past and Kemmons moves forward.

When Kemmons is displeased, he tends to be quick tempered, Dottie agrees. "But he has a very short memory when it comes to arguments or anything like that. He doesn't hold a grudge. He will flare up at a moment's notice, sometimes totally unexpectedly. But once the flare's gone, it's over and he's calmed down," she says.

Dottie says Kemmons has not mellowed with age in the least. He is disappointed that everyone is not as obsessed with working as he is, because his mind is constantly working on new business ideas, new products, new ways to make money.

"It's always interesting to wonder what's going to be around the corner, because you know he is always going to get into something," she says. "You know there's going to be something else coming up, and it's just, 'What's it going to be? What's he getting into now?' "

After more than half a century as one of the most active customers of area bankers, Kemmons became one himself.

He recalls that his venture into banking originated in 1987 when a young salesman named Ted Gammill called on Kemmons in an effort to get him interested in buying West Memphis Federal Savings and Loan. Gammill said 100 percent of the stock in the savings and loan could be acquired by investing $5 million in the company.

Kemmons looked over the figures and talked with his three sons. He was impressed with Gammill and learned he was a CPA and happily married, with two children. Kemmons decided here was a man he wanted on his team.

The third time Gammill returned to discuss the matter, Kemmons and his sons met with him. Kemmons told Gammill that he wanted to buy West Memphis Federal on one condition: that Gammill quit his job with T.J. Raney and Sons, a Little Rock brokerage, and become president of the savings and loan. Ted asked if Kemmons was serious, and Kemmons said he had never been more serious about anything in his life. Gammill asked if he had to give an answer then, and Kemmons told him to go home and talk to his wife first.

Gammill did accept the offer to become president of West Memphis Federal, which was renamed Federal Savings Bank of West Memphis. Eight years later, he is still president of Federal Savings Bank, now almost a $400 million company with offices in Rogers, Bentonville, Fort Smith and Little Rock, and a branch office in Memphis. The Memphis bank, in fact, is located on the same property on which Kemmons built his mother's first house on Poplar Avenue. However, Kemmons no longer owns the property.

Visitors to Kemmons' office in recent months have grown accustomed to finding his conference table covered with bags, jars, bottles and other containers of his various candy concoctions. Seldom has he had more fun with one of his ventures, even if it has yet to become a moneymaker. First he tried Krazy Knuts, a roasted corn kernel. Next he decided to try covering kernels of roasted corn with chocolate and a smooth, eggshaped candy-coating colored red, green, brown, orange or yellow.

He called them W&W's. However, because he placed a cameo-shaped photo of himself in the middle of the two W's, the name is often taken to be WOW's, which Kemmons doesn't really mind. He is planning to add a sugarless version of W&W's, as well as a new version of Krazy Knuts in which the corn will be toasted instead of cooked in oil. Leonard Peek, who helped make GranDaddy's a success for Kemmons, has recently joined the candy operation and says he expects big things from it before long.

Kemmons attempted to persuade President Clinton to help promote W&W's. "I sent him about 500 small packages and two quart jars, one for him and one for Hillary. I said, 'Pass these around and see if you don't like them.' You know how Reagan got the country started on jelly beans. When he wrote me back, he just said he received them and appreciated them very much. His letter started 'Dear Kemmons,' and he did spell my name right. But he didn't say he ate any of them or gave any away or what."

Recently, Kemmons got involved in a venture aimed at producing an engine that runs off the hydrogen in water. While he waits for it to pan out, he isn't giving up on fossil fuels.

"We have about 95 million tons of coal if we can ever get it out. It's over in Arkansas. We are trying to get someone to get it out for us. We did some strip mining, but it needs to have somebody with big bucks to go in there and bring in $20 million worth of machinery or something. It might be a great big asset someday," Kemmons says.

The Wilsons also have a share in the mineral rights from an oil field in Louisiana. That asset resulted from a purchase Kemmons and Wallace Johnson made more than 30 years ago of a mortgage company in Alexandria, Louisiana. The mineral rights that came with the deal were considered insignificant at the time.

"It wasn't a big deal at all. It was on the books at something like $5,000 or $10,000. Nothing happened until Gulf and somebody else drilled some wells. They drilled three, but they were more water than oil, and they couldn't control them, so they had to cap them," Kemmons recalls.

Then about two years ago, Occidental contacted the Wilsons and said some new studies they had made of the Wilson site had them interested in trying the field.

"So they spent all the money. We spent nothing, but we get 5 percent of what they bring in," Kemmons says.

"And they were successful. Occidental told us it was the biggest well they had hit in 10 years inside the United States — 2,000 barrels a day. Now they are getting ready to drill two more wells. It's just found money for us."

CHAPTER NINETEEN

——FAMILY IS EVERYTHING——

**"We don't use the term 'in-laws.'
We introduce them all as our sons and daughters."**

Kemmons Wilson

Whatever happens with his oil wells, Kemmons knows he will never strike it richer than he has with the love of his family. He calls it "a miracle" that every one of his children and grandchildren continue to reside in Memphis. The boy from Osceola who grew up without a father or brother or sister now finds himself the patriarch of a large, loving and remarkably close-knit clan.

"I think Kemmons is one of the most fortunate men I have ever known," says Bill Walton. "He without a doubt has the most wonderful family. All his children are just fine people in their own right. And each one of them married someone with character who was going somewhere. And then he has all these beautiful grandchildren."

Rather than striking off in search of fulfillment somewhere else, Kemmons and Dorothy's children have always found true happiness at home within the Wilson family circle. The Wilsons simply like being with each other, a feeling that has been passed down from generation to generation.

Says Kem, "Family has always been a top priority in all we do. There is a real special closeness between my brothers and sisters, and this was fostered by Mom and Dad. The grandchildren are in clustered age groups, because we all had children around the same time, and now it is heartwarming to see them become best friends as well."

Jack Moore, Betty's husband, says Kemmons and Dorothy raised all their children with the same "core Christian values," emphasizing the important things in life. "That has resulted in a family where the shortest marriage has lasted 24 years, everyone lives in the same city; they all vacation together; and all the grandchildren are good kids. Everyone has followed the plan as to what a family ought to be, as outlined by Christian ethics. Christianity is a strong component in everyone's life," Jack says.

When Kemmons was invited recently to speak to a singles group at his church, he wondered why they had asked him. How could he have anything to say that would be meaningful to single people? By Kemmons' own calculations, if you added up the number of years himself and Dorothy and each of his children and each of their spouses have been married, the total comes to 356 years of marriage. And if you include Kemmons' late parents, you have three generations of Wilsons who have spanned almost the entire 20th century without one divorce.

Someone pointed out to Kemmons, however, that he could be a great source of inspiration to a generation of disillusioned people afraid to hope, in this age of the deterioration in family values, that long-term success in relationships is possible. Kemmons continues to be the embodiment of this principle, both professionally and personally. He believes in the institutions of church, marriage and family; they have always sustained, supported and encouraged him

"My family has always been the most important thing in my life — from the time I watched my mother working all her life to raise me, to the time I married Dorothy and had our five children and saw our grandchildren come along. Nothing is closer to me than my family," he says.

"From the day I was born, I had the most loving mother anyone ever had, and I think I was probably one of the most loving sons. All my children love each other, and all their families love each other. I don't think there is any doubt they are all best friends.

"There was never a mother or father who was more proud of their five children than Dorothy and myself. They have never given us one ounce of trouble in any way. They are all happily married and all active in their churches. I have always said, the only thing in the world that is wrong with my children is that they did not grow up poor."

Bill Holcombe, who has spent a lot of time with Kemmons over the past decade as president of Wilson Graphics, says that even today there are few conversations with Kemmons in which he does not mention his mother.

Among Kemmons' favorite memories are the many times he and Dorothy would have all five children gathered with them in their bed.

"The kids were always joining us in our bed. We started out with a double bed. Then we got a king-sized bed, and I was still getting kicked out in the morning. So I finally went to Jim Patton at National Bedding Company. Of course I was buying hundreds and hundreds of beds for the Holiday Inns, so he said he would make me anything I wanted," Kemmons recalls.

"I said I wanted one that was the width of two double beds, which are 4 1/2 feet by 6 feet, but I wanted it longer. So it would be 9 feet wide by 6 1/2 feet long. He said, 'How are you going to get sheets and blankets for it?' I said, 'That's simple — just sew two double sheets or two double blankets together and you got it.' We had that bed, I guess, 15 years."

In 1955, when Kemmons was president of the Memphis Home Builders Association, the local newspaper took a photograph for a special National Home Week section. It featured the Wilson family posed together on the front steps of a model home, and provided the impetus for a family tradition that continues to this day: the Wilson family Christmas card.

Since first using that newspaper shot on a Christmas card, the Wilsons have been posing together for similar photos each year. The series of shots provide a family scrapbook of sorts. Over the years in the Christmas card photos, the five Wilson children grow up, are joined by spouses and then children — who in turn grow from babies to young adults. The Wilsons send out more than a thousand of the cards each Christmas. Some of their friends have collected every one.

"I never knew a man who loved his family more than Kemmons," says Guilford Glazer, Kemmons' longtime associate in California. "He probably was tough on those boys at times, but love was never in doubt. Kemmons could be tough. But Dorothy always caused him to mellow."

Kemmons says, "Even though I had to drop out of school at an early age, I've always understood the value of a good education. I was very proud when Spence made Phi Beta Kappa at Vanderbilt and went on to get his MBA from Harvard.

"I'm also glad to see my children giving back to the Memphis community that has been so good to us for so many years. Although I didn't grow up with a father and didn't have a role model, I admire my sons for how they've balanced being good businessmen with being good husbands and fathers. They spend a lot of time with their families."

Spence has been a trustee at Rhodes College and now chairs the finance committee. He chaired a major fundraising campaign for Dogwood Village, a foster home for troubled youth that is now a part of Youth Villages. He is director of the Thomas W. Briggs Foundation, a charitable foundation in Memphis, and retired as a pilot with the Air National Guard in 1984 after completing a 20-year tenure.

Kem has been president of the Liberty Bowl Classic, king of the Memphis Cotton Carnival, chairman of the Young Presidents Organization Rebel Chapter, chairman of the Memphis Emmaus Community, a board member and capital-campaign chairman at St. Joseph hospital, a board member at Presbyterian Day School and Hutchison Day School, and chairman of the Board of Visitors at the University of Alabama.

Bob is on the board of trustees at Christian Brothers University and on the business school board at Southern Methodist University. In April of 1996, he will complete 30 years as a pilot in the Air National Guard. However, what his wife Susan admires most is simply his caring approach to life.

"I'm most proud of his genuine goodness. He freely shares himself on a daily basis with his family and friends. During the day, he may call his college roommate in Fort Worth to visit, stop by the hospital to see a friend, advise a young pilot, attend a board meeting at Christian Brothers, or finish the day with a finance meeting at Mullins United Methodist, our church," Susan says.

"He cares about people and easily demonstrates his love. Just like his father, Bob never ends a conversation with me without saying my favorite words: 'I love you.' "

After their five children married, whenever Dorothy and Kemmons met someone who asked how many children they had, they would reply: "Ten. We don't use the term 'in-laws.' We introduce them all as our sons and daughters."

So they now have 10 children and 14 grandchildren. For more than two decades, the entire family got together every Sunday night for dinner. As a result, everyone knows each other like one big family.

"Once they started marrying, I started out having everybody over every Sunday night. So everybody got to see each other at least once a week. I think that's one reason they are all so close. Their families all grew up together, and I think a big family is a happy family," Dorothy says.

Becky says, "Kemmons was an only child who never knew his father. It is natural that he would want a big family. The fact that for over 20 years, all the 20 or more members of the family got together for Sunday supper almost every week is remarkable and almost unheard of today.

"Often on these Sunday evenings, (Memphis businessman) Abe Plough would come over and eat dinner with the family. He and Kemmons and the older children and their spouses would often discuss a very wide range of business and political matters."

The Wilson family dinners on Sunday evenings continued for some 23 years. For about the first 20, the dinners were at Dorothy and Kemmons' house. The dinners continued for so long, Becky says, because everyone liked each other and there was a commitment on everyone's part to maintain an extended family.

The family still gets together often. But in recent years, as more of the grandchildren have reached college age, it has become harder for the Wilsons to gather as regularly. Carole and Betty have begun a new tradition of trying to take their father to lunch at least once a month to catch up on things.

"Everybody's lives are so crazy and so busy now. It's gotten harder for the Sunday night dinners at their house to pan out. So we try to get together with Dad, just the three of us. We see Mother all the time, but it's harder with Dad because he is still away from the house so much," Betty says.

"Most of the time he takes us to Wilson World. Sometimes we treat him and go somewhere else. But I think it has really touched him. We get stories out of him we have never heard before. It blows us away to discover all the things he's done that we don't know about."

"He's not one to get into, 'Well, how's your life?' and all that," Carole says. "If you need him to talk to, you can get his attention. But if you don't get his attention, his mind is going in a million directions."

"I know he must have been a hyper kid," Betty says. "He has just always been on the go. But as my husband says, if people don't have that kind of drive, nothing gets done.

"Both my husband and Carole's are very much like our Dad, very driven individuals. I think I always wanted to marry someone like my father, and durned if I didn't."

Becky Wilson, a native of Jackson, Tennessee, recalls meeting Kemmons when she was first dating Spence at Vanderbilt, where they were both undergraduate students in the '60s. Becky was a sophomore working at the Vanderbilt psychological counseling center when Spence came in to take a vocational-aptitude test. Becky had heard Spence speak a few days before at a vespers service at the Christian Student Association, so she commented on how much she enjoyed it. A few days later he asked her out, and they dated platonically for three months, because both were involved with other people at the time.

But during that period, Kemmons, Dorothy, Carole, Betty and Kem visited Spence in Nashville, and Becky joined them all for dinner. Afterward, they went to see the movie *The Longest Day*, and Kemmons fell asleep in the middle of it. "We were seated about the third or fourth row in this re-enactment of World War II, with all the howitzers and the guns going off, and he was able to sleep through most of that, which I just found astounding — that he could relax anywhere," Becky says.

"But that has proved true through the years. He catnaps, and everybody else is running with their tongues hanging out trying to catch up with him after his catnaps."

Spence and Becky began dating again, this time romantically, a few years later when he dropped in on her while she was living in New York and he was on his way to Harvard Business School. They dated two years and were married after his graduation in 1968. They have four children.

After selling real estate for Kemmons Wilson Realty, Becky attended law school at the University of Memphis. She practiced as an assistant U.S. attorney for the Western District of Tennessee, but is not in practice presently. Like her husband, she is a licensed pilot. She is a trustee at Vanderbilt, and also like Spence, a deacon of Second Baptist Church.

Becky is an accomplished amateur photographer who has traveled extensively to photograph wildlife. The Memphis Zoo sells postcards and posters of her photographs of zoo animals. She has been involved with the zoo for 12 years, and was a member of the Breakfast Club, the small group of people who met at Shoney's for two to three years planning long-term development of the zoo.

In 1988, Becky founded Bridge Builders, a youth leadership program in Memphis, in response to the admonitions of County Mayor Bill Morris that unless the private sector got involved with the public sector, there would soon be no money left for amenities in Memphis such as the zoo. Becky realized that the societal problems her children were going to have to face were much different than those she faced as a girl, yet their upbringing was the same. Like her, they had little or no contact with children who were different racially and culturally.

To address this separation, Becky came up with the idea of pairing the private Briarcrest and public Northside schools, and in July of 1988, the first Bridge Builders Camp was held. Today, Bridge Builders includes students from 40 different high schools, with 200 participants enrolled for July of 1995. Some 700 students have gone through the program.

Becky says Kemmons has been very supportive of her work with Bridge Builders, and has come to hear the speakers at the organization's fundraising programs. Kemmons has recognized Becky's entrepreneurial efforts and her involvement with the community.

She says her first impression of Kemmons was that he was always very friendly. He loved to dance, and would always mix everyone up on the dance floor to get people to meet one another. She says both he and Dorothy have always been very gracious. "They have accepted the spouses and called us their children and made us feel that way too. That's not something that's just lip service," Becky says.

She says Kemmons is very proud of his "10 children," and particularly later in life has become more appreciative of the fact that all the marriages have been successful and none of the grandchildren have had any major problems. "I think in large measure it is because the grandchildren have grown up in an extended family where they regularly were together and surrounded by people who love them," Becky says.

"I think Kemmons probably always intended to have a big family to compensate for the fact that he didn't have one growing up. And Dorothy must be given a lot of credit for keeping the family together. She is indefatigable — tireless and patient."

Susan Wilson, Bob's wife, grew up in Memphis and went to Southern Methodist University, where she earned a degree in biology and chemistry. She met Bob there in 1965, when she was a sophomore and he was a senior. They married in 1969.

She remembers that Bob introduced her to Kemmons the same way Kemmons used to introduce people to the Wilson children — by waking them up at night. She and Bob had just begun to date and had driven to Memphis from SMU for Christmas vacation. They arrived between 2 and 3 a.m., and Bob pulled in the Wilson driveway and woke Susan, telling her she was going to meet his family.

He took her inside and proceeded to wake Kemmons, Dorothy, Doll, Betty and Carole. "They were in their pajamas and they were just wonderful, very welcoming and warm. I have never not been welcomed by them — and not just welcomed, but welcomed with loving arms. They are just a loving family," Susan says.

The next summer, Susan recalls, she was riding back to Memphis early on a Monday morning after spending a weekend away with the Wilsons. Dorothy and Kemmons were in the front seat of Kemmons' Cadillac, while Susan, Betty and Betty's boyfriend were riding in the back. They had a flat tire, but it happened near a Holiday Inn, so they pushed the car into the inn parking lot. Kemmons walked in and said to the desk clerk, "Honey, I am Kemmons Wilson." At first she didn't believe him, but then she looked at a copy of the Wilson family Christmas card and exclaimed, "It is him!"

Susan enjoys hiking, rafting, birding, gardening and canoeing. She and Bob are very involved in environmental issues in Memphis and Shelby County, and have made financial commitments to many of them. They also raise horses and rescue animals. They pick up stray animals and try to find homes for them, and have cared for up to 41 animals at a time at their rural home. Susan is a licensed physical therapist, with a degree from the University of Tennessee, Memphis, and is attending Memphis Theological Seminary.

"I got to see a lot of Kemmons when I moved my physical-therapy practice over to the company office. We shared the same common wall, and of course I had babies and young children who would cry. It never bothered him. He would just come wandering in and offer everybody candy. He would ask why the children were crying, but he never complained at all," Susan recalls.

"He is extremely intelligent, very entrepreneurial. I think he is a man who keeps a lot of thoughts to himself. He can be a very silent man, and I think that's probably a real asset in how he has been able to achieve so many things. I think he very much cares about all of us as a family. I think sometimes it is probably difficult for him to express it."

Over the years, Bob and Susan have taken their nieces and nephews on vacation trips to ski in Colorado, attend theater productions in New York, and hike and raft in Montana, Maine and Oregon.

Kem's wife, Norma Wilson, grew up in Memphis and met Kem in the 10th grade at East High School. They dated for seven years, through high school and college, and married in 1969. They have five children.

Though Kem and Norma also dated others in high school and college (Norma went to the University of Mississippi), Kem remembers that as 10th-graders they first talked about someday getting married and having five children. As it turned out, that is exactly what came to pass.

"Norma is an unbelievably good mother. She is very talented and could have done a lot of other things, but she made a conscious decision to be there for our children. And she has still been able to get involved with other activities. A few years ago, she completed a triathlon. I don't think there are too many mothers of five who have accomplished such a feat," Kem says.

Norma was honored as one of the 1994 Women of Distinction by

Baddour Memorial Center, a center for the mildly retarded in Senatobia, Mississippi. Norma plays tennis, is involved with several Bible-study and prayer groups, and for some 25 years has been teaching her own swimming classes to 4- and 5-year-old children at the beginning of each summer. At first, Norma taught the classes in the backyard pool at Kemmons and Dorothy's house. After Kem and Norma built a house with a pool of their own, Norma continued the lessons there.

Norma also has known Kemmons and Dorothy since she was in high school. She says she has always felt welcome in the family and feels close to Kemmons and Dorothy.

"I love being with them. They are very fair. They treat us all the same. There's just never any jealousy with any of the other in-laws. It is amazing. It's an unconditional love that you really feel," Norma says.

"They don't demand that the family be close, but yet it is, because you know you're doing it on your own. We have the freedom to do what we want, and we choose to stay close. Because they've let go is why we stay."

Norma describes Kemmons as a gentle grandfather who always wants to interact with the grandchildren when they are around.

"He loves the attention and the affection of the grandchildren. He's not the type that would go out in the yard and throw the football with my boys when they were little. He didn't play, but he was always there," she says.

Norma is proud of the working relationship between Kemmons and his sons, and hopes it will continue in the next generation. "I think Kemmons expects a lot from his boys. I hope that our children will work with their father like Kemmons' boys work so well together with him. He's really blessed to have three boys that work as well together and want to please him," she says.

"I bet Kemmons could be hard to work for, because I'm sure he demands a lot. But I think with me, he's easy. I feel like I could probably say just about anything to him, or ask him just about anything, or come to him with any needs I had, and he definitely would treat me like a daughter."

Carole's husband, Dr. William West, is an oncologist who is chairman and chief executive officer of Response Oncology, Inc. which provides healthcare for cancer patients. He earned his bachelor's degree at Harvard and graduated from medical School at Johns Hopkins. A Memphis native, Bill met Carole when they were students at East High School. They married in 1970. They have two children.

Bill grew up with two brothers and a sister. His father was a fine physician in Memphis, and Bill and both his brothers followed in their father's footsteps to become doctors as well.

After Bill's mother died of cancer, he decided to devote his medical career to cancer research and treatment. After completing his medical studies at Johns Hopkins, he took a position with the National Institutes of Health in cancer research in Bethesda, Maryland. He later opened his own practice in Memphis and created Response Technologies.

"I first met Kemmons when he visited my family home to discuss a business issue with my parents. I was 10 or 12 years old, and I was enormously impressed that he remembered my name and was so personable and energetic," Bill recalls.

"Four or five years later, I met him again through my dating of Carole. From the start, he has been the perfect 'father of the bride,' interested but never intrusive, always anxious to include his in-laws as genuine family members. Carole and I became engaged while I was in medical school, and Kemmons was keenly interested in how I planned to pay the bills. As I recall, he wasn't too satisfied with my answers."

Bill frequently plays gin rummy with Kemmons, along with Betty's husband, Jack Moore. They keep running totals of their winnings and who owes what to whom.

Jack grew up in the small Alabama town of Clanton, where his family owned the bank. Betty met him on a blind date while they were in college at the University of Alabama. It was her first date there, and it took place on "Squeal Night," when all the sorority pledges receive their bids. They dated for four years and were married in 1971, after Jack's first year of law school. They have three children.

Jack says Betty's greatest accomplishment has been "raising three wonderful Christian children and maintaining a wholesome, caring, loving home environment." Betty is a very active volunteer at their church, Christ United Methodist, and has been a member of the board of directors at the Shepherd School and the Memphis Museum

System. She has also been active in other Christian organizations and with Community Foundation issues.

Jack remembers being somewhat in awe of Kemmons when they first met, and for some time thereafter. Though they became good friends, Jack at first found it a challenge relating to Kemmons because they had grown up with such different frames of reference.

"It is beyond my comprehension that anyone I know as well as I know Kemmons literally grew up hungry — did not have food to eat. I grew up with all the luxuries and all the financial security and the security of my parents and my friends. It was just so secure, and to try to believe that here's the guy that's the father of my wife that I see week in and week out, and have known for 25-30 years who came from that frame of reference and had that experience, it's very difficult to understand the impact that would make on someone. I have no way of ever understanding it. And the same would be true of him having grown up without a father," Jack says.

"But he and I have always had a very, very good relationship. We both like to have a good time. The biggest difference I think that he would have from maybe all the rest of us is that I don't think he ever separates his business and work life from anything. He came up hustling from the time he was old enough to understand you have to have money to eat, and you have to get it yourself. He never knew anything else, and it is very difficult for him to separate work from the rest of his life. But that's one of the things that has made him as successful as he is and as unique an individual as he is.

"There is no sense of competition within the family because I don't think anybody ever tried to compete with him. I don't think anybody wanted to compete with him, because you can't outwork him. That's his playing field. So don't get in a game that you don't have a chance of winning, because you're going to lose."

After finishing school at Alabama, Jack got his law degree at Vanderbilt. He then worked for John Martin, Kemmons' lawyer, at the firm of Martin, Tate, Morrow and Marston. After a few years there, Jack joined the Memphis firm now called McDonnell-Dyer, which represented Union Planters Bank Corporation. In 1989, Jack became president of Union Planters.

Before he won Betty's hand, however, he had to make a vow with Kemmons. Kemmons recounts the day that Jack came to him and said, "Mr. Wilson, I'm in love with your daughter, and I want to ask your permission to marry her."

"Jack, you are one of my favorite guys. I would love for you to marry Betty, on one condition," Kemmons replied.

"What is that?" the young man asked.

"On the condition that when you graduate from law school, you will practice in Memphis."

"Oh, I like Memphis, and I'll sure do that. I could never make a living in my little hometown. I'll practice in Memphis."

Jack did go into practice in Memphis after law school, and built a successful career at his firm. However, after about 15 years there, he went to have another serious talk with his father-in-law, Kemmons recalls.

"Pops, I'm kind of bored with my practice now. I think I've gone about as far as I can here. I have a chance to go to Nashville and go with a big firm over there. What do you think about that?" Jack asked.

"Jack, do you remember when you asked me about marrying Betty?" Kemmons said.

"I sure do."

"Do you remember what you told me?"

"Yes, I do."

Jack thought about it for a few seconds, then shook Kemmons hand and said, "I'll honor that."

In the spring of 1995, Betty and Jack, along with Kem and his wife, Norma, contributed $200,000 to the University of Alabama to equip a computer facility there and have it named in honor of Kemmons and Dorothy. During his comments at the ceremony, Jack told the first part of the story. Kemmons was not scheduled to speak, but he stood up and told the second part of the story.

"I wanted them to know what a man of his word he really is," says Kemmons, who by then could also add a postscript.

"While he was working at the law firm, he represented Union Planters for several years. And then they asked him to become their president. He's the happiest guy you ever saw. That shows you how life can be. If I hadn't said anything, he probably would have gone over to

Nashville, and he might have been happy there. But I guess it was just a year or so after he came and talked to me that he got this position with the bank instead," Kemmons says.

___

Betty says...How do you leave a gift to honor your parents who have everything they need and have given so much of themselves to their children and their community?

Oddly enough, the answer came as a name gift opportunity presented by Doug Noble, director of the Memphis Museum System, to Spence Wilson, the eldest son of Kemmons and Dorothy Wilson. The Memphis Pink Palace Museum & Planetarium was involved in an ambitious $16,000,000 capital fund-raising campaign in 1991 when Doug first approached Spence about a gift honoring his parents.

Spence approached his brothers and sisters with the idea of making a gift of $500,000 available to name the first floor, east Wing, in honor of his parents, Dorothy and Kemmons Wilson. This substantial gift allowed the Memphis Museum System, which is headquartered at the Pink Palace, to not only renovate the aging mansion spaces but prepare exciting history exhibits highlighting Memphis history from 1900 to 1960. The Pink Palace Mansion East Wing would serve to recognize the achievements of Mr. & Mrs. Wilson as loving parents who have made Memphis, Tennessee a better place to live. Kemmons Wilson is featured as a legendary entrepreneur in the Hall of Honor.

The children of Kemmons Wilson take enormous pleasure in sharing the rich history of Memphis, Tennessee and the Mid-South with the nearly 200,000 visitors who enjoy the Pink Palace Mansion and the Unique Entrepeneur Hall of Fame each year.

___

Also in the summer of 1995, Spence's oldest son, Spence Jr., became the first of Kemmons' and Dorothy's 14 grandchildren to marry. Though his bride, Stephanie Beard, is from Troy, Alabama, they will continue the Wilson tradition of making their home in Memphis.

Shortly after the wedding, Spence Jr. also became the first grandchild to go to work for the Kemmons Wilson Companies, after working two years at Boatman's Bank. When the grandchildren began nearing employment age, the Wilsons set up some guidelines for younger members of the family interested in joining the family business. One requirement is that they must first work elsewhere for two years.

"I don't really know how many of the grandchildren will ultimately end up working within the family organization," Kem says. "We would be delighted to have any one or all of them involved, but there is absolutely no pressure to do so. We have in place the proper planning to ensure a smooth entry, transition and succession. It is obviously our hope and desire that the family business will pass from generation to generation to generation."

Kemmons and Dorothy still attend Christ United Methodist, as do Carole and Betty and their families. The boys and their families have joined other congregations, but all are active in their churches. Kemmons and Dorothy contributed the funds to build Christ United's Wilson Chapel, a striking facility used for weddings and smaller services. Kemmons also contributed the money for the chimes in the church sanctuary, in honor of Doll.

"Daddy has always been very generous to his church and had a great love for it," Betty says.

Old friends are also dear to Kemmons and Dorothy. Lee Yeager, who worked for Kemmons for many years at Holiday Press, and later retired in Hot Springs, Arkansas, says Kemmons has helped him through many difficult times.

The most recent occurred after Sybil, Yeager's wife of 58 years, died in 1993. Kemmons called to offer his help, then attended visitation, the church funeral services and the graveside services, Yeager remembers.

"After the service was concluded, Kemmons came up to me and put his hand on my shoulder and said, 'Lee, go home and pack your belongings and come back to Memphis. We will find a place in our organization for you to spend some time.' I know he wanted to keep me from being lonely and isolated," says Yeager, who later did decide to move back to Memphis.

"Kemmons and Dorothy are as dependable as any friend can be," says Kemmons' longtime pal and business associate Irby Cooper.

"Never an invitation declined, never failing to show for any event, be it sadness or happiness. Be it a death in the family, a wedding, a Bar Mitzvah, an anniversary, Kemmons and his bride are always there. Set their places at the table; they will be there."

CHAPTER TWENTY

A WORKING MAN WHO WALKED WITH KINGS

**"It is not how much you have,
but how much you enjoy that makes happiness."**

Kemmons Wilson

$\mathscr{A}$ visitor to the site of the first Holiday Inn today will find only a vacant lot grown up in weeds and a for-sale sign. Only the furniture from one guest room has been preserved at the Pink Palace Museum in Memphis.

The original Holiday Inn remained in operation on Summer Avenue until April 1973, when it was sold and turned into the Royal Oaks Motel, a locally-owned operation. It was sold for $720,000, and was still profitable. But Holiday Inn had a company policy that after 20 years, each inn must be either sold or brought up to current Holiday Inn standards, so Kemmons okayed the sale.

After the sale, a state historical marker was placed there. It marked the site for many years, but was later removed. It read: "First Holiday Inn. The original Holiday Inn was opened here August 1, 1952, by Kemmons Wilson. He undertook to do better than motels he had experienced the year before on vacation with five children. Within months, he was building on other highways into Memphis. He was joined by Wallace Johnson, and 20 years later they had the world's largest hotel-motel system. The first inn was retired, by sale, in 1973."

In 1994, the Royal Oaks was torn down and the land put up for sale. Kemmons did not mourn its passing, viewing the whole matter strictly in business terms.

"A lot of people criticized me for not keeping that first one. But to renew the franchise after 20 years, the holder had to bring the hotel up to present-day standards. Well, that first Holiday Inn was a wood-frame motel, and it was not on the expressway. I said I would rather go out east (toward suburban Memphis)," he recalls.

"So I bought land at Sycamore View and Interstate 40, and we sold the old Holiday Inn. We couldn't have brought it up to present-day standards for $10,000 a room. And we built a new one that was a lot better for less than that."

Kemmons' children, however, hated to see the historic old Holiday Inn go. "Dad is not a sentimental person. I kept saying, 'Well, Daddy, you need to keep it. It needs to be a landmark.' I think it would have been nice not to let it be torn down, since it was the first one," says Carole.

But, Bob recalls, "When they were going to tear it down and someone asked Pop about preserving it, he just said, 'You can't make any money off it. Bulldoze it.' "

As for the rest of the Holiday Inn operation, it was sold in 1989 to Bass PLC, a British conglomerate best known for its beers, for $2.23 billion. However, the sale did not include the spinoff corporate entity, Memphis-based Promus Companies, created to run what until then had been Holiday Inn's casino operations and the other hotel chains it started in the 1980s: Embassy Suites, Hampton Inns and Homewood Suites.

In 1991, Bass moved Holiday Inn headquarters to Atlanta. In 1995, Promus spun off its hotel operations into Promus Hotel Corp., and renamed the gambling operations Harrah's Entertainment.

Kemmons thinks highly of the men who took charge of Holiday Inn after the sale. Sir Ian Prosser is Chairman and Chief Executive Officer of Bass PLC, the United Kingdom's largest brewer and exporter of beer, reaching 80 international markets. Bryan D. Langton was named Chairman and CEO of Holiday Inn Worldwide when Bass bought Holiday Inn in 1990. He remains Chairman of Holiday Inn Worldwide today.

"I had the pleasure of meeting Bryan when he first came to Memphis and took over Holiday Inn for Bass in February, 1990," Kemmons says." I did not meet Ian Prosser until the convention in New York in October,

1990. He had invited Dorothy and I to be his guest at the first convention under their leadership. Since that time, Dorothy and I have been invited by them to attend every convention. They have never failed to introduce us to the entire convention delegation.

"I have been very pleased with the aggressive way that Ian and Bryan have handled the business. They have been very innovative in coming out with Holiday Inn Express, Holiday Inn SunSpree Resorts, Holiday Inn Garden Court, Holiday Inn Select and Holiday Inn Hotel & Suites.

"When I retired as Chairman in 1979, there were 1,759 Holiday Inns in 50 different countries. As of January, 1996, there were 2,104 Holiday Inn properties in 63 different countries. So Holiday Inn just keeps getting bigger and better all the time. I know that will continue."

When Holiday Inn was sold, Kemmons' children again had to express the sentimentality that eluded Kemmons. "When they sold the company to Bass, we boys wanted to keep certain things for the family that they had, like the first stock certificate and the first ticker tape when they went public. But Pop said it was just pieces of paper, no big deal. So we finally wrote them a letter requesting those things under his signature, and that's why we have them now," Bob says.

Kemmons again viewed the sale strictly on business terms. "When Mike Rose sold the company, he called me about a week before it was announced and said, 'Kemmons I don't want you to have to read it in the paper.' He said, 'I sold Bass all the Holiday Inns. We are keeping all the Embassy Suites, Hampton Inns, Homewood Suites and all the gambling. And they are taking over all the debt,' " Kemmons remembers.

"I said, 'Let me repeat that.' I did, and he said, 'That's right.' And I said right there, 'Mike, you just made the deal of the century.' So how could you say they didn't do a good job with Holiday Inn? They did the greatest job in the world. I would have rather it stayed in Memphis, but there was nothing I could do about that."

Rose, the last man to head Holiday Inn while it was a Memphis company, recalls the sense of relief and gratitude he gained from Kemmons' response.

"I was real worried about that telephone call. Kemmons had obviously devoted a large part of his life to Holiday Inn. And I was younger than he was, but in terms of percentage of my life, at that time I had probably devoted about the same percentage of my life to Holiday Inn as he had. So we both had a lot of emotion, I think, around Holiday Inn," says Rose.

Many Memphians were outraged when Holiday Inn was sold and moved. For decades, it had employed thousands and become a part of the city's identity. Many people believed that, with the exception of Elvis Presley, nothing had ever brought more favorable attention to Memphis than Kemmons and his Holiday Inns.

By taking a purely business view of the matter, however, Kemmons spared Rose from being painted with the villain's role in the sale, Rose recalls.

"It was the right decision for the company. And I was really grateful to Kemmons for supporting that decision. Because he could have been critical, and there were people in the community who didn't look at the business aspects of the deal, but just looked at the emotional aspects and wondered how we could do something like that," he says.

"But the fact that Kemmons was so vocal in his support, I think, made it a lot easier for me to walk around this community and hold my head up. I will never be able to thank Kemmons enough for his support then."

Kemmons held only about a thousand shares of Holiday Inn stock by the time the company was sold. Though he has long since gotten too busy with other ventures to follow Holiday Inn's business closely, he and Dorothy still enjoy attending the annual convention for franchise holders.

Looking back on eight decades of life, Kemmons confesses he flew by the seat of his pants all the way.

"I never had a master plan. I just went with the punches. The thrill of doing something and creating something kept me going, being able to give my family the things they wanted.

"I have always been the most contented man you know. I take everything as it comes. I have some good luck and some bad luck. But there is nothing I would change about my life."

While working alongside Kemmons for 25 years, Bill Walton

observed him more closely on a day-to-day basis than almost anyone alive today, outside the family.

"I don't think money is the driving force in his life. Kemmons is a doer. He has a new idea every other day. Sometimes I would fuss at him about it and try to tell him a lot of these things just wouldn't work. And he would say, 'Well, Bill, I only have to be right half the time.' Obviously, he doesn't have to work today. But he is still working as hard as he ever did. It's just his character," Walton says.

Charles Cuneo, Kemmons' longtime vice president at Holiday Press, says simply, "Work is Kemmons. It's what he is. He loves it like other people love golf or fishing."

Billy Mills, who has supplied Kemmons with carpet for many years, says that on the day that legendary football coach Bear Bryant was buried, Kemmons said he wanted to go the same way — to work until he couldn't anymore, as Bryant essentially did.

Dorothy still knows exactly what time Kemmons will be home for dinner: whenever he is finished working. But she never knows whether he will arrive alone or not.

"He will still call at 6 o'clock from his car and say 'I've got two men I'm bringing home for dinner.' And I will say, 'Kemmons, I don't have a dinner for guests tonight.' And he'll say, 'We'll be there in 15 minutes — I love you,' " she sighs.

Kemmons' health, as would be expected at 83, is not perfect. His doctors try to manage his diabetes and heart ailments. But Kemmons doesn't worry about any of that much. He never exercises except for a little tennis, he says, and his legs are no longer in condition for him to actively play the game he loves. He pays only passing attention to dietary advice.

"Kemmons just will not take care of himself," Dorothy says. "Since he has gone into the candy business, he eats candy all day long. I tell him it is foolish, but what are you going to do? At 83, he is going to do what he wants."

The things that Kemmons wants remain astoundingly modest, given his financial success. He still lives in the same house he did before he ever started Holiday Inn. He drives a late-model Mercury that is comfortable but hardly opulent. He still loves to eat at the

Wilson World on Cherry Road, where he says his chef Ron Brinkley prepares the greatest food in the world. Bill Holcombe, president of Wilson Graphics, says Kemmons does not really even know how much money he is worth.

"I live probably the simplest life of anybody you ever knew who had the money that I have," Kemmons says. "I don't care about expensive things. Every one of my five children have much, much better homes than I do, much better cars than I do."

"I've had anything I ever wanted. I've always said that money is the most unimportant thing if you have enough to live the way you want to live. For some people that is $10,000 a year; for others it's a million dollars a year. But anything else is just a fun way of keeping score."

Bob McCaskill says Kemmons has walked with kings, but never stopped thinking like a working man.

"Mr. Wilson doesn't recognize people by their position in life. To him, they are all people. I have seen him many, many times stop and talk to someone who might be cleaning toilets or something like that. He will engage them in conversation, ask them their name, ask about their family, what kind of soap they are using," he says.

"Most of us don't even notice the guy cleaning the toilet. But Mr. Wilson sees them. He has something in common with the richest and the poorest. And he has never forgotten how poor he once was."

Kemmons lost his closest business partner in 1988 when Wallace Johnson died. Walton, Kemmons' other early partner in Holiday Inn, lives on his longtime lake estate in Collierville.

Kemmons and Walton had their differences over their quarter-century together. But Walton was there when Holiday Inn was nothing but a dream. And he was there each day along the way, until it became a reality in every corner of the planet.

Bill Walton has contemplated few subjects as much as he has the subject of Kemmons Wilson. Ultimately, he comes back to one thought, bigger than all the rest.

To this day, he marvels at the power of an idea. The idea that struck that ambitious young homebuilder as he motored his way across America with his family in the summer of 1951.

"At our peak, we had a payroll of $25 million, with 150,000 people working for Holiday Inn and its franchises. We had 2,500 working at Holiday City alone. Just because Kemmons had an idea, and Wallace joined him, and I left my law practice to help put it together," Walton says.

"We hired a lot of people. And a lot of people made a lot of money. Millions upon millions upon millions of dollars. And some of those millions were given to churches and hospitals all over the world.

"All because Kemmons had an idea. And that's what it's all about."

CHAPTER TWENTY-ONE

——A LIFE WORTH LIVING——

**"The important thing is to take your idea
and see it through."**

Kemmons Wilson

$\mathcal{O}$n October 12, 1994, Kemmons was guest speaker in the Conrad Hilton College Distinguished Lecture Series.

He could have easily been speaking to the world instead of just the students in attendance that day. His words provide appropriate closing comments for this volume.

After recounting the story of Holiday Inn, Kemmons said to the audience:

"This was the idea and this was my dream. This is how it all began in 1951. When I retired 28 years later, after a heart attack and open-heart surgery, we had 1,759 Holiday Inns open and a Holiday Inn in 50 different countries.

"Sometimes, the first step is the hardest — coming up with an idea. Getting an idea should be like sitting on a pin. It should make you jump up and do something. I've had a great many ideas in my life. And some were good, some were great, and some I'd prefer to forget about.

"The important thing is to take your idea and see it through. Not all of your ideas are going to be good ones. But just remember, 'A man who wins may have been counted out several times, but he didn't hear the referee.'

"Of course, my rise was not without some failures. But it's a mistake to worry too much about making mistakes. A man who never makes mistakes is also the man who never does anything.

"I guess I've made as many or more mistakes than anyone in the world. But I try to learn from my mistakes and profit from my failures. And of course, it is stupid to make the same mistake twice. However, I've done that too.

"My good friend, who is now deceased, Norman Vincent Peale, wrote a book: *Enthusiasm Makes The Difference*. This is so very true. Also the lack of enthusiasm makes all the difference in the world in a person's life. It has been said that enthusiasm is the most contagious thing in all of the world. Personally, I think the lack of it is. Both are like the measles — highly contagious. Very little has been achieved without enthusiasm. And any individual is very old if he has outlived enthusiasm. All we need to be really and truly happy is to have something to be enthusiastic about.

"Attitude towards life determines life's attitude towards us. Many games have been won or lost simply by the attitude of the players and the participants. Many lives have failed because of the wrong attitude of the individual. As long as the people of this great land are willing to work, then we can know that the American dream is very much alive and there's still hope for us.

"I firmly believe that attitude is one of the most important things in a person's life. Attitude is a magic word in every language. Learn to smile and be happy. Make the most of whatever comes to you in your life. Whenever there's a smile in your heart, you just can't keep it a secret, for your face and your actions will reveal it.

"In fact, the smile on your face is the light in the window that tells people that you are at home. Although there are hundreds of languages in the world, a smile speaks all of them. In fact, a smile is a curve that can set a lot of things straight. It is not necessary to know a person's name to greet him with a smile.

"You know, success is built by doing everything the best possible way. If you really want to be happy in your life, you must learn to enjoy and even love your work. If you can't, then it's high time for you to be looking for another job.

"Success may not be yours just for the asking. It can certainly be yours if you are willing to work hard enough for it. Decide now that you're going to be successful, and then put every ounce of physical and mental energy into the effort of making that prediction come true.

"I've always been a firm believer in hard work. I believe the freedom to work is second only to our religious freedom. Work is the master key that opens the door to all opportunities.

"If a person truly knows what he wants out of life and is willing to work hard, then he can rest and be sure that life will pay its richest dividends to the person.

"I believe that work is not a man's doom, but a man's blessing.

"A 40-hour week has no charm for me. I'm looking for a 40-hour day.

"I have worked in boom times and in recessions, in the Great Depression and in time of war. Our government has had Republicans and Democrats and conservatives and liberals. Through all of this I have seen our free-enterprise system survive and provide the economic means to build the greatest society in the history of the world.

"My feeling is that the free-enterprise system is in good shape for the 1990s. And this is because the system provides rewards for the entrepreneur who recognizes opportunities and acts on them.

"I've seen a lot of changes over the span of my business career and I guess the only perfect science is hindsight.

"There's no question that either you take charge of change, or change will take charge of you."

A Pictorial History

of

KEMMONS WILSON
AND HOLIDAY INN

COMPILED AND EDITED BY KEMMONS WILSON

These pictures capture some of the highlights of my life—my family, friends and partners, as well as many internationally known celebrities. The photographs show me building a business and growing a family.

While I will always remember everyone who has made a difference in my life, not every one of them could be included in these pages.

I hope you will enjoy reliving these memories as much as I enjoyed living them.

A special thank you to two of the Kemmons Wilson Companies who made it possible for these pictures to appear—Wilson Graphics and Vance Commercial Color Lab.

Kemmons' mother
Ruby Lloyd "Doll" Wilson

40–42 S. Cox, which rented
for $25, but Kemmons paid
only $2 per month

Grandmother's boarding house at 336 N. Watkins—
Kemmons' first home in Memphis

Doll Wilson

Kemmons' father
Charles Kemmons Wilson

First job: model for local
bread company ads

Kemmons selling war
bonds in 1918

At this age Kemmons was
selling magazines door-to-door

Who could say no to
this young salesman

Second grade class picture at Maury Grammar School—
Kemmons, third row (from bottom), second from left

The crew of Airways Theater at opening: Dorothy, ticket seller;
Kemmons, ticket taker; and Doll, candy seller

Kemmons and Jack Embry paid $800 for their
first plane, which included flying lessons for both.
(photo inserts of Kemmons and Jack)

Newlyweds Kemmons and Dorothy and wedding party at
The Peabody Hotel, Dec. 2, 1941

Lt. W.H. "Bud" Barron
A great test pilot

Ben Gaines, Kemmons'
partner in Gaines
Manufacturing Company

Galloway United Methodist Church where Kemmons and
Dorothy were married, at 1015 South Cooper in Memphis

Dorothy's home at 1076 Blythe, during "courting days"

Kemmons' sweetheart—
Dorothy

Mamie Eisenhower
congratulates Dorothy as 1970
American Mother of the Year

Dorothy with Bob (l.)
and Spence (r.)

Dorothy—8 months old

This is the first house that Kemmons built at 6241 Poplar, the
first of two that were built on the wrong lot

Carpenter Kemmons at
work on first house

Bill Bond
Main Holiday Inn architect

The lot for Kemmons' first house now has Federal Savings Bank at 6209 Poplar (bank owned by Kemmons) and Poplar Towers at 6263 Poplar Avenue

6256 Poplar Avenue: Home of Charles G. Smith, who sold Kemmons the lot for his first home. The lot Kemmons bought was exactly across the street from the home

All of the Wilson first cousins: (from left) Heard Sutton,
Kemmons, V. O. Sneed, Sidney Gennette, Lucille Sutton,
Milton Fletcher, James Sutton, Bill Ramsey,
Rowlett Sneed and Charles Sutton

Fred Barbee, Kemmons, Lawrence Welk, Clarence Camp:
Kemmons won $10,000 for selling more phonographs,
per capita, than any other salesman

Kemmons with first born,
Spence, in 1942

Kemmons while in military
service—1943

Kemmons, Elton F. Duncan and Leo W. Mitchell in front of their
happy home: Dum Dum Airport, Calcutta, India

Spence, Kemmons, Kem and Bob at summer home at
Pickwick in 1946

Kemmons' second favorite photograph, taken in 1951

Kemmons, Kem, Spence and
Bob scootin' around

Three young cowpokes,
Spence, Bob and Kem

Daddy's little girls—Betty, Kemmons and Carole

Dorothy, Louie Weaver,
Kemmons and Bob Hope
on movie set in 1941

Look where these two
clowns ended up

Largest bed ever made (9' wide x 6'6" long)
Big enough for the entire Wilson family

The Wilsons visit Tijuana, Mexico; (l.–r.) Kemmons, Carole,
Bob, Dorothy, Spence, Doll, Betty and Kem (foreground)

Dorothy's parents: Allen and Alleen Lee

Kemmons and family enjoying favorite snack—popcorn— in their Galloway home

Kemmons with the $50 popcorn machine that started it all

The Wilsons show off their new Samsonite luggage—
the results of another Wilson "deal"

Elmer C. (Jack) Ladd, senior
vice president of francise sales

Kemmons and his daughters
Betty (l.) and Carole (r.)

Kem graduates from the University of Alabama.
Kemmons delivered the commencement address and received an
Honorary Doctor of Laws degree

Kemmons receives Honorary Doctor of Business Administration
from Rhodes College. Dr. Burnet C. Tuthill, Dr. William L.
Bowden, Dr. O. G. Henry, Dr. Athelstan Spilhaus,
Dr. David L. Stitt, Kemmons Wilson and E. H. Little

Dorothy being honored by President and Mrs. Nixon as
American Mother of the Year, 1970

Chosen American Mother of the Year in 1970, Dorothy and
family, including her mother, Mrs. Alleen Lee, appear on the
Ed Sullivan Show

Queen Dorothy

Kemmons and his Queen
Sandy Seeman

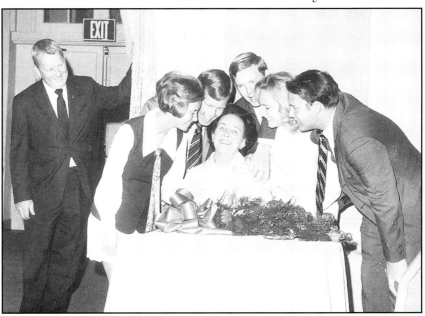

Dorothy's children congratulate her upon being selected American
Mother of the Year—1970 as a proud Kemmons looks on

The first grandchild, Spence Jr., and part of the Wilson family at home in living room of Galloway residence

Kemmons and Dorothy's home of almost 50 years

Kemmons and Doll—the inspiration and driving force
behind the young entrepreneur

Holiday Inn executives taking off for opening
of 200th Holiday Inn in Palm Springs, CA

COMPLIMENTARY
PASS

Issued to   ROBERT KERR

Stay at the Holiday Inn FREE

Courtesy *Kemmons Wilson*

(Subject to conditions shown on back)

ASK THE INNKEEPER FOR A HOLIDAY INN DIRECTORY

"Complimentary" pass that was freely distributed by Kemmons and Wallace

NOT GOOD ON WEEK DAYS

NOT GOOD ON SATURDAYS OR SUNDAYS

NOT GOOD AT THIS HOLIDAY INN

NOT GOOD AT THAT HOLIDAY INN

IN FACT, JUST NO GOOD AT ALL ! !

Do you have a Holiday Inn Directory? If not, ask the Innkeeper for one.

Keith Funston, Bill Walton, Kemmons, Doll Wilson, Dorothy, Alma and Wallace Johnson when Holiday Inn stock first traded on New York Stock Exchange in 1963

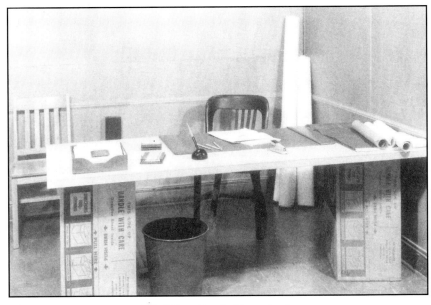

Holiday Inn's first desk

Wallace and Kemmons wearing Christmas vests made by Mable Fry

Kemmons and Jack Kelly—opening of 200th Holiday Inn
in Palm Springs,Califorina

Kemmons Wilson, larger than life

Swimming in money; bankers John Brown (l.), chairman of
Union Planters National Bank, Allen Morgan (r.),
chairman of First National Bank and Kemmons

Kemmons keeping an eye on Holidex System

Barney McCool, Kemmons and Wallace

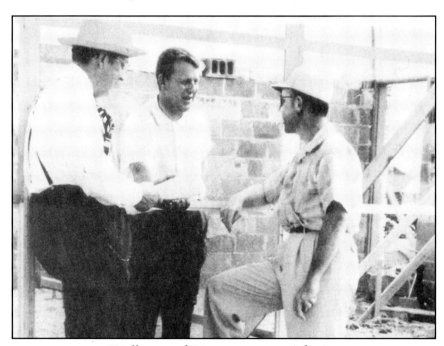

Wallace and Kemmons on a job site

Kemmons and Wallace inspecting model of a new Holiday Inn

Doll, Kemmons, Alma, Dorothy and Wallace

Historical plaque in front of
first Holiday Inn

Kemmons showing Doll a
great Holiday Inn location

Walker Gray—one of the early Innkeepers—in front of the first
Holiday Inn, 4985 Summer Avenue, Memphis, Tennessee

"Podners" Kemmons and
Wallace Johnson

"PODNERS"

Wallace and Kemmons
surveying for a new
Holiday Inn

Wallace Johnson,
Bill Walton and Kemmons
in the early days of
Holiday Inn

Doll Wilson and Kemmons

Doll, Kemmons and his first secretary, Fairie Morris

Kemmons and Mother

Kemmons and Wallace prove
they can skin a bear

(From l.–r.): William Clarke, Jimmy Ross, Lem Clymer, Charles Collins, Bill Walton, Kemmons Wilson, Wallace E. Johnson, Barney McCool, Raymond Williams, Howard Carlson, Allen Gary and J. B. Temple

"No job is too hard as long as you are smart enough to get someone else to do it for you." —Jerry O'Roark, T. George Harris, Kemmons and Jim Hansen

KEMMONS WILSON
Chairman, Board of Directors

WALLACE E. JOHNSON
President

WILLIAM B. WALTON
Executive Vice President

E.B. McCool
Senior Vice President
Manufacturing

CHARLES M. COLLINS
Senior Vice President
General Counsel

Holiday Inn® BOARD OF DIRECTORS 1969

L. M. CLYMER
Senior Vice President
Mergers & Acquisitions

JEROME B. TEMPLE
Senior Vice President
Inn Operations

CLYDE H. DIXON
Senior Vice President
Product Distribution

FRANK W. ADAMS
Senior Vice President
Finance

WILLIAM W. BOND, JR.
Architect

JOHN E. BROWN
Former Chairman,
Board of Directors
Union Planters National Bank

WILLIAM N. CLARKE
Partner, Cadwalader,
Wickersham and Taft

FREDERICK G. CURREY
Vice President, Finance
TCO Industries, Inc.

C. BENNETT HARRISON
Chairman, Board of Directors
Union Planters National Bank
of Memphis

R. A. LILE
President
Transportation Properties, Inc.

LEWIS K. McKEE
Chairman, Board of Directors
National Bank of Commerce
in Memphis

MAURICE E. MOORE
Chairman of Board
TCO Industries, Inc.

ALLEN B. MORGAN
Chairman, Board of Directors
First Naitonal Bank
of Memphis

RALPH OWEN
Presidernt
Equitable Securities,
Morton & Co., Inc.

ROY M. SCOTT, JR.
Attorney

ROBERT E. SLATER
President and Chairman
John Hancock Mutual Life
Insurance Company

Holiday Inn had a most prestigious board. Pictured above are four chairmen of the three largest banks in Memphis; John E. Brown, Chairman Emeritus—Union Planters Bank; Bennett Harrison, Chairman; Lewis McKee, Chairman—National Bank of Commerce; Allen B. Morgan, Chairman—First National Bank (now First Tennessee Bank). Other board members included the president and chairman of John Hancock Life Insurance Company as well as Ralph Owens, president of Equitable Securities, who did Holiday Inn's first underwriting. Equitable Securities, second only to Merrill Lynch, was the highest capitalized brokerage company in 1969

Doll and Kemmons in front of first Holiday Inn sign

A young Kemmons with Sam Phillips, owner of
Sun Recording Studio

John Martin, Kemmons, John Brown and Ben Harrison

Kemmons and Spence Jr. celebrate the purchase
of Trailways Bus Line

Grandmother and Granddaddy Wilson showing support for
Kemmons Wilson III, McLean Wilson and Wilson Moore during
Grandparent's Day at Presbyterian Day School

The Wilson women leave their worries (and their men) behind for their annual "girls trip." They travel to a different location each year. Pictured at the Snow Den Inn in Vermont are: (l.–r.) Carole West, Dorothy Wilson, Norma Wilson, Betty Moore, Susan Wilson and Becky Wilson

Wilson family celebrates discovery of oil in Rapides Parrish, LA. The family owns the mineral rights on the property. (l.–r.) Bob, Spence, Kemmons, Carole, Kem, Dorothy and Betty

Kemmons and Aero Commander 500

Kemmons and Sue Todd (r.), his second secretary,
leaving in Holiday Inn Twin Cessna 310

Kemmons and his first
Lear Jet

Kemmons with Cessna 172

Kemmons and General Tom Stafford

Kemmons in his new Citation Jet

Kemmons on wing of 70 KW Citation Jet

Kemmons, Merv Griffin and Meshulam Riklis

Here's Johnny and Ed McMahon advertising Holiday Inn

Kemmons and Jack Klugman

Julie Nixon Eisenhower, Betty Wilson, Dr. Cory Ser Vaas,
John Cleghorn and Dorothy

Charles Duke, *Apollo 16*

Muhammad Ali testing
"Jumping Jack" trampoline

Apollo 10 astronauts presented Kemmons with flag and patch that
was carried to the moon

Maurice Moore and Kemmons celebrate the Holiday Inn
acquisition of Continental Trailways

Kemmons and Maurice Moore in car owned
by Continental Trailways

Herbert Humphreys and Kemmons on business trip to far East

Kemmons—hard at work

Kemmons, Armand Hammer and Sargent Shriver
negotiating for Holiday Inn in Moscow

Kemmons and Archie
Bennett in front of Leaning
Tower of Pisa

Prospective franchisees tour
Portobello, Brazil
with Kemmons

At the groundbreaking ceremony of the Holiday Inn—
Nathan, Road, Hong Kong: (l.–r.) Hari & Padma Harilela and
their family. Dorothy looks on while Kemmons breaks ground

Opening of Holiday Inn with Mr. Shoin Umemura owner—Kyoto,
Japan. Built on 1-1/2 acres, the hotel contained a driving range, two
tennis courts, a McDonald's, Kentucky Fried Chicken, 16 bowling
lanes and 270 rooms

Mr. and Mrs. Rudiger Koppen, Billy Graham, Ruth Graham,
Kemmons Wilson and Dorothy Wilson

Doll Wilson, Spence Wilson, Betty Wilson and
Carole Wilson (with back to the camera)

Kemmons and Tom Voight at opening of first Holiday Inn
in Europe—Leiden, Holland

Kemmons and Dorothy at opening of Holiday Inn—
Leiden, Holland. This was the first Holiday Inn built outside
the United States, changing forever the chain's motto of
"The Nation's Innkeeper" to "The World's Innkeeper"

Mr. and Mrs. George Harilela, Dorothy and Kemmons, Padma
and Hari Harilela and Clement Chen (groundbreaking of
Holiday Inn—Nathan Road, Hong Kong)

Lem Clymer, President

Mayor of Viernhein,
Germany welcomes
Kemmons and Holiday Inn

Mr. Lui Che Woo and
Kemmons in front of Wilson
Suite in Holiday Inn—
Harbor View, Hong Kong

Victor Yamagishi, with C. Itoh of Japan, enjoys dinner with
Kemmons and Dorothy in Tokyo

Frances and Armand Hammer (l.), Princess and Prince of Morocco (center) and Dorothy and Kemmons in New York City

Groundbreaking for Holiday Inn in Lagos, Nigeria; General Gowan, Kemmons and Armand Hammer

Kemmons and Dorothy with President Ferdinand Marcos
of the Philippines

President Kenyatta of Kenya meets with Kemmons

Kemmons as guest of Prince Rainier, Princess Grace and their
children, Prince Albert and Princess Stephanie

Rudiger Koppen, Billy Graham, Kemmons and the Rev.
Swami Satchidananda, Grand opening of
Holiday Inn—Golden Mile, Hong Kong

King Norodom Sihanouk of Cambodia presents Kemmons and
Dorothy with welcoming gift

A thrilling moment in Kemmons' career —an audience with Pope
Paul VI in Rome. Making the introduction is Monsignor
Marcinkus as Jerry Sims looks on

Ray Kroc—founder of
McDonald's

Happy Trails!! Kemmons,
Dale Evans, Wallace
Johnson and Roy Rogers

Ruth and Billy Graham with Kemmons and Dorothy in Malaysia

Geneva Walton, Bob Hope, Kemmons, Mrs. Arthur Grant,
Dorothy Wilson, Bill Walton and Arthur Grant

Kemmons visits South Africa

Kemmons, Bill Walton and
Pat Boone

Albert Owings, Bill Van Hersh, and Shek Usif Timel
of Saudia Arabia negotiating for Holiday Inn franchise

John Martin, Kemmons' lawyer and friend for 40 years

Kemmons, Wallace Johnson and Warren Andrews, president of Merchants Hotel Supply, Inc.

Morgantown Factory Outlet Mall
Dorothy and Kemmons using "son power"—Bob and Kem

President Jimmy Carter and wife, Rosalynn

Kemmons presents President Gerald Ford with
"History of the States" record collection

Dorothy and Kemmons with President George Bush

A great president—
Ronald Reagan

Kemmons applied the
phrase "Two for the
Price of One" to the
Clintons when Bill was
Governor of Arkansas

President Reagan visits
Founders Hall at Holiday City

Kemmons and
President Reagan

Kemmons peeking into
Presidential limousine

Kemmons and
Queen Dorothy

The beautiful Debbie Reynolds with Dorothy, Kemmons,
and Hugh and Ann Chatham

Alma (Mrs. Wallace) Johnson, Ann Landers, Dorothy and
Geneva (Mrs. Bill) Walton

Kemmons and Dorothy with friends, including Norm and
Avis Jansen, visit with Don Ho in Honolulu, Hawaii

Kemmons with Wendy's founder Dave Thomas

Wal-Mart founder, Sam Walton with Kemmons
in Bentonville, Arkansas, Walton's hometown

Well known for his love of Tabasco, Kemmons received his own private
stock from McIlhenny Company president, Walter McIlhenny

Holiday Inn celebrates
25th Anniversary

Kemmons and Dorothy at
Holiday Inn retirement party

Holiday Inn's Chairman of the Board; Kemmons shaking hands
of successor Roy Winegardner, Mike Rose (center)
followed Winegardner.

Not all hunts were for land—Kemmons enjoying some time off at the "Quack Shack" hunting lodge. (l.-r.) Kemmons, Everett Dobbins (World's Best Duck Caller), Brick Lile and Lem Clymer

Kemmons and Tom Wells visit the birthplace
of Elvis Presley in Tupelo, Mississippi

Kemmons, Philip Belz and Abe Plough

Kemmons and Tom Wells
the greatest interior
designer—ever

Kemmons with mentor
Bob Bostick

World's best secretary—Dottie Bonds

Kemmons and Dorothy Wilson with Bill and Sara Holcombe at
the Wilson Graphics Christmas party, 1994

Kemmons at 83 years is still climbing

Wilson World Suite Hotel under construction in Dallas, Texas—
Stemmons Expressway and Wycott across the street
from the Loews' Anatole Hotel

Kemmons' calling card—from $1 million to $500 trillion in four years

(The Godfather) Kemmons with three sons, Kem,
Spence and Bob

Kemmons in Kracow, Poland, at Tennis Club
located 2,000 feet underground

Jeff Mann, Bruce Edenton and Kemmons

Kemmons with Danny
Thomas and Colonel Sanders

Kemmons and Stan Smith

Kemmons with Senator John Glenn, Terry Henson-Whaples, Henri Landwirth,
Alan Beychok and John Quinn, the proud owners of Holiday Inn—
SunSpree in Kissimmee, Florida. Landwirth is founder of
Give Kids the World

Kemmons and Ivan Lendl

Kem, Kemmons, Bobby
Riggs and Tom Samuels
playing tennis at Wimbleton
Racquet Club shortly after
opening in Memphis

John and Sally Greene having dinner at Wimbleton
Racquet Club shortly after it opened

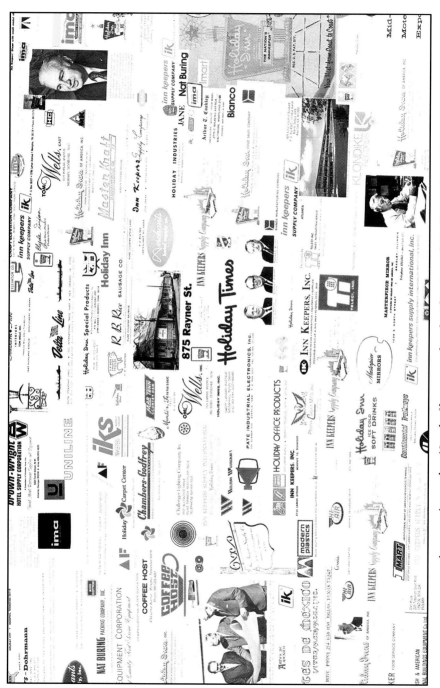

Approximately 40 wholly owned subsidiaries of Holiday Inns, Inc.

Kemmons' likeness appears on a wall in the bar of the
Holiday Inn—Grand Cayman Island.
Pictured: Jane Edenton, (l.) and Martha McGuire, (r.)

Eikichi Itoh and Kemmons.
C. Itoh and Co. was Holiday
Inn's partner in Japan.
C. Itoh and Co. was world's
largest trading company in
1980; company now called
Itochu Corp.

Kemmons and Vawad
Bokhartseen, Holiday Inn
owner in Kuwait

Wilson Inn—Cherry Road, Memphis, Tennessee

Wilson World—Cherry Road, Memphis, Tennessee

Kemmons with Ron Brinkley, chef, and Bert Clauson, manager, of
Wilson World Hotel, Memphis, Tennessee

Eight-story nurses dormitory given to Methodist Hospital
by Kemmons Wilson in honor of his mother Doll Wilson

Portrait of Doll Wilson in lobby of nurses dormitory

Art Linkletter presents Kemmons
with Methodist Hospital's Living Award

Dinah Shore presents Kemmons with the Fortune Magazine/
Junior Achievement National Business Hall of Fame Award

Kemmons received Horatio Alger Award from the Rev. Norman Vincent Peale in 1970

Kemmons with Easter Seal Poster Child

Kemmons received National Business Hall of Fame Award, 1982

Shalom Award presented
to Kemmons by the
government of Israel

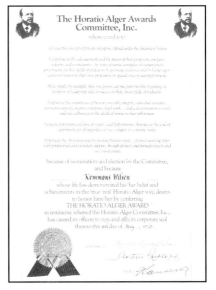

Kemmons received Horatio
Alger Award, 1970

Eight great success stories.

Adolph Simon Ochs (1858-1935)
Though bankrupt, he scraped together $75,000 in 1896 to buy a loser called the *New York Times*. In an age of scurrility, he proved a newspaper could thrive on thorough, unbiased news coverage.

Jacob Henry Schiff (1847-1920)
A German immigrant, he turned the little investment-banking house of Kuhn Loeb & Co. into the leading banker to the railroads. By 1900, he was the one financier in a class with J. P. Morgan.

Charles Michael Schwab (1862-1939)
By 35, he was president of the Carnegie steel empire. But, he later explained, "I wanted to be a czar." So he bought control of a small, failing enterprise called Bethlehem Steel and turned it into a giant.

Edward Crosby Johnson II (born 1898)
This mystical, swashbuckling Brahmin transformed the way Americans invest. Through his Fidelity mutual-fund complex, he was one of the chief architects of the modern mutual-fund industry.

Charles Kemmons Wilson (born 1913)
On a 1951 family trip, the $2-a-head charge for kids by motels got him so angry he vowed to go home and start his own motel chain. Today, there are 1,750 Holiday Inns around the world.

Malcom Purcell McLean (born 1913)
He was first to ship containerized cargo by water on a commercial scale—an idea that revolutionized the shipping industry. In 1969, he sold his Sea-Land to R. J. Reynolds for $157 million.

Tonight at the Pittsburgh Hilton Downtown, eight business giants will be inducted into Junior Achievement's Hall of Fame for U.S. Business Leadership.

Each year, at the request of Junior Achievement, FORTUNE magazine's board of editors selects a group of past and present business leaders who have made "outstanding and enduring contributions to improving the products, the processes, the efficiencies, or the human relations of business."

The Business Hall of Fame provides high school students with models of the very best the free-enterprise system has to offer.

The 69 leaders chosen in past years range from Eli Whitney and Andrew Mellon to Walt Disney and Donald Regan.

We believe the success stories of the eight to be honored tonight, as told in the current FORTUNE, stand as an inspiration to us all.

We are proud to salute them.

Charles Franklin Kettering (1876-1958)
A technical genius, he accumulated more than 140 patents and contributed mightily to General Motors' success during the nearly three decades he ran its R&D. The company insured his brain for $4 million.

Howard Joseph Morgens (born 1910)
As head of Proctor & Gamble for 17 years, he saw the potential of TV advertising better than any other businessman. He used the new medium to boost P&G profits from $67 million to $316 million.

FORTUNE
How to succeed.

©Time Inc. 1982

Men Who Help Make Memphis Great

by David A. Lehmann

A Medium-Sized City Makes a Big Impact on the World.

1000 Makers of the 20th Century

The first 73 years of the 20th century produced more technological advances than in all previous recorded history of mankind. Men have been sent to the moon; vital human organ transplants are commonplace; the airplane was invented and perfected; the atom was conquered and harnessed; thousands of other dreams have been realized.

Who has been most responsible for the incredible changes of this century?

The SUNDAY TIMES MAGAZINE of London set out to answer this question with a series called "The 1000 Makers of the 20th Century." The purpose was to name the 1000 persons throughout the world who have done the most to make the 20th century what it is. In selecting names for the list, the TIMES consulted specialists in many fields of expertise.

In the study of the final list, one of the unexpected facts to surface was that a city in the southern United States — perhaps best known worldwide for its position on the Mississippi River, its cotton and as the birthplace of the blues — placed four residents on the TIMES' list. This was more than any other city of its size in the world and more than many cities much larger. The four were from the diverse fields of medicine, retailing, food and lodging and music.

The city: Memphis, Tennessee. Once a robust river town and regional agricultural center, Memphis today is a major capital for not only agriculture, but business, industry, the arts and medicine as well.

The first history-maker is Kemmons Wilson who has probably done more than anyone else to shape the international food and lodging industry. Board chairman of Holiday Inns, Inc. Wilson opened the first Holiday Inn only 21 years ago on the outskirts of Memphis. Today, Holiday Inns is a globe-girdling chain which includes 1600 properties in 35 countries.

In 1951, Wilson and his family left Memphis for a vacation in Washington, D.C., a trip which he later described as the "most miserable of my life." They found accommodations along the way to be uncomfortable, often unclean, expensive and inconvenient. On his return to Memphis, he decided to start his own chain of motels, with unheard of standard features, such as swimming pools, television and no charge for children under 12.

The rest is history. Today there are not only 40 Holiday Inns in Memphis, but Wilson's inns can also be found in all 50 states and from London to Lesotho. In every location, travelers can expect features such as restaurants, carpeting, comfortable beds and baths, which have made Holiday Inns one of the most important chains in the food and lodging race.

Kemmons Wilson, board chairman, Holiday Inns.

Clarence Saunders, father of the modern supermarket.

Dr. John Shea, pioneering surgeon for deafness.

Elvis Presley, no further identification necessary.

39

DELTA AIRLINES SKY MAGAZINE
MARCH 1974

Kemmons with Clarence Saunders, Dr. John Shea and Elvis Presley

Covering the world's most successful inn keeper is frenetic business. That was the first fact learned by Correspondents Alan Anderson and John Tompkins as they followed Kemmons Wilson, board chairman of Holiday Inns, across two continents to gather material for this week's cover story. Anderson, based in our Rio de Janeiro bureau, accompanied Wilson on a swing through Brazil in search of new motel sites. Beginning as early as 4 a.m., Wilson, with Anderson in tow, visited with local officials, toured local marketplaces and even traveled the Amazon. "I had been warned of his pace," says Anderson, who is 29. "But I still wasn't ready for it. He worked constantly except for catnaps, and after a while I couldn't believe he was 30 years older than I."

After dawn-to-dusk days in search of real estate, Wilsonspent evenings in search of lighted tennis courts so he and his aides could squeeze in a set or two before bedtime. One 18-hour stretch of land hunting ended at the Tenis Clube Do Para in Belem, Brazil, where Anderson found himself whacking back Wilson's forehand drives at 10 o'clock at night. After four sets of tennis, Wilson again turned his attention to real estate. How much did the courts cost? he asked. The fence? The club pool? In all, they covered 2,700 miles before Wilson headed home to Memphis. There the chase was taken up by Tompkins, who is based in New York and covers business news. From the company's headquarters in Memphis to the Holiday Inn University being completed in Olive Branch, Miss., Tompkins observed Wilson at varied work and play for three days.

The tour ended three days later with tennis and gin rummy on a Wednesday evening. While Tompkins prudently took the spectator's role, Wilson played tennis with a group of his Memphis business acquaintances, then challenged a friend to cards. Tompkins shuffled as Wilson dealt his way to victory in five straight games. Says Tompkins: "Wilson never claims to be "just a country boy" or pretends not to be smart."

Contributing Editor James Grant, who wrote the story, chose a less exhausting approach to the Wilson phenomenon. On an inspection trip, he decided to sample the service at a pair of Holiday Inns outside New York City. In Kingston, N.Y., he found the staff conscientious; the motel manager phoned every name in the registry late one night until he finally matched Grant to the car in the parking lot with its lights left on.

Henry Luce III, Publisher
Time Magazine
June 12 1972

The nation's best-known innkeeper hasn't been dozing in retirement. At age 71 he is set to make a new mark in Central Florida.

William Souder
Florida Trend Magazine
March 1984

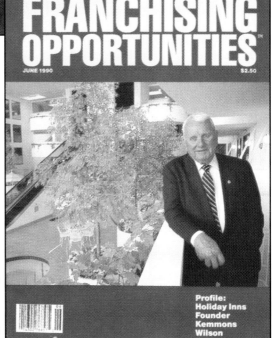

Kemmons Wilson:
The Deal Maker
The name Kemmons Wilson may not sound familiar to many people, but to the franchising world, he is a legend. A high-school dropout, Wilson built the world's most popular lodging chain, Holiday Inns. Today, at 77, he is worth hundreds of millions of dollars and is still too busy to do anything but work.

John P. Hayes
Franchising Opportunities
June 1990

As a young businessman in a hurry, Kemmons Wilson would dash into a sandwich shop and order a hamburger and a piece of pie—then eat the pie first so he wouldn't waste time waiting for the hamburger. Things are not all that different now that he's a millionaire at least 60 times over, for he's still a man "In Pursuit of the Golden Egg."

Mid-South *Magazine*
February 8, 1970

Kemmons Wilson is making a comeback on the highways of America. And he's offering Orange Lake a deal...

Nancy Long
Orlando *Magazine,*
August 1985

Kemmons Wilson, founder of Holiday Inns, is the current winner of the International Franchise Association's Hall of Fame Award. Still building dreams at 77, he's highly active in the lodging industry with two growing lines—and also directs a wide array of companies in other fields, from manufacturing to banking.

Susan M. Reagor
Hotel & Resort Industry
February 1990

The man who invented the Holiday Inn has just turned 65 and has no apparent intention of relinquishing his hold despite pressure from younger executives; Kemmons Wilson is still in control of every detail.

John Mariani
Enquirer
March 26,1978

For Kemmons Wilson, founding Holiday Inn wasn't enough. Now in his 80s, this legendary entrepreneur still can't tell the difference between work and play.

Carlo Wolff, Associate Editor
Lodging Hospitality
November, 1994

"A hell of a mistake," says Wilson of management's decision to change the famous Holiday Inn sign.

Taken from Memphis Magazine *cover story, September, 1985 Ed Weathers, writer*

THE COVER. The beautiful Alice Faye and the ebullient Phil Harris, who were among the famous couples who maintain homes at Palm Springs, were among the stars who turned out for the opening of the 200th Holiday Inn in the California desert resort. Cover photo by Eugart Yerian, director of Holiday Inns' visual aids department.

THE SUNDAY TIMES *magazine*

1000
MAKERS
OF THE
TWENTIETH
CENTURY

century Britain assumed office at an average age of 60; he was 48 and has 20 years at the top if he wants the job that long. G. S.

Kemmons Wilson (U.S., b. 1913) hotelier. The motel reached its apotheosis in Holiday Inns of America, Inc., the first of which went up in Memphis in 1952. Motor hotels, lodges and inns sprang up in America as the motor car became the over-whelmingly dominant form of transport, but many of them at first were shabby shacks. By the late 1940s a better class of motel had still to take pot-luck, both in the quality of his accommoda-tion and in the price he had to pay. Wilson changed that. Born poor, he started up in business with slot machines, afterwards owning a small cinema chain. The legend is that he returned from a lousy vacation and decided from that piece of primi-tive market research that the motels were wide open for development. Right from the start he planned a nation-wide chain, with exactly the same standards in each Inn. "Inex-pensive luxury" would be abso-lutely predictable; each room would have two double beds, one for Mom and Pop, the other for the kids (for whom there would be no extra charge). Today a new Holiday Inn opens every 2½ days it is the largest hotel group in the world, with over 1100 units at the last count. G. P. G. N.

Kemmons Wilson (U.S., b. 1913): hotelier. The motel reached its apotheosis in Holiday Inns of America, Inc., the first of which went up in Memphis in 1952. Motor hotels, lodges and inns sprang up in America as the motor car became the overwhelmingly dominant form of transport, but many of them at first were shabby shacks. By the late 1940s a better class of motel had begun to appear, but the long distance traveller had still to take pot-luck, both in the quality of his accommodation and in the price he had to pay. Wilson changed that. Born poor, he started up in business with slot machines, afterwards owning a small cinema chain. The legend is that he returned from a lousy vacation and decided from that piece of primitive market research that the motels were wide open for development. Right from the start he planned a nation-wide chain, with exactly the same standards in each Inn. "Inexpensive luxury" would be absolutely predictable; each room would have two double beds, one for Mom and Pop, the other for the kids (for whom there would be no extra charge). Today a new Holiday Inn opens every 2¹/xdays—it is the largest hotel group in the world, with over 1100 units at the last count.
G.P.G.N.

Travelers throughout the North American continent have enthusiastically accepted the invitation to use their Gulf Credit Cards in charging food and lodging at all *Holiday Inns* (In Canada, both Gulf and British-American cards are always honored.)

View of the Gulf station next door to Holiday City. If you look behind the car, you will see the executive offices of Holiday Inn

Holiday Inn was the first national firm to have a national and international credit card. Holiday Inn made a deal with Gulf; in return for building Gulf stations on Holiday Inn property, they would let Holiday Inn use their credit cards for food and lodging. At this time, there were no major credit cards other than oil company cards.

Orange Lake Resort and Country Club,
Kississimmee, Florida

Main entrance to Orange Lake

Five-story Orange Lake condominiums

Aerial view of Orange Lake

High-rise Orange Lake condominiums

Atrium of Orange Lake clubhouse

Roomy interior view of an Orange Lake villa.
All villas open onto the golf course

Every villa at Orange Lake has two bedrooms,
two baths, kitchen, dining room and den

Orange Lake golf pros Dick Farley and Rick McCord

Orange Lake owners enjoying the 27-hole golf course

Kemmons at Orange Lake's 7,000-seat tennis stadium

Kemmons' second dream: Orange Lake Country Club—a time-share resort in Kissimmee, Florida. (aerial photo of golf course's island hole surrounded by villas)

Sir Ian Prosser
Chairman, Bass PLC

Bryan D. Langston
Chairman Holiday Inn
World Wide

Wallace Johnson, Bill Walton and Kemmons Wilson presented
with the Changemaker Award
by *Institutions*, October 15, 1973

As senior vice president of facilities, John Greene's job wasn't an easy one—but it was challenging. He was in charge of construction, remodeling and interior design for both parent and franchised inns

George Falls, 37, and senior vice president of the franchise sales division

Ray Schultz came to Holiday Inn from IBM after helping developing Holidex—and was vice president of information systems

Kemmons and Doyle Savage, partners in Wilson Savage
Construction, a worldwide development company

Kemmons and Frank Jemison in front of Holiday Inn, Montgomery,
Alabama—the first Holiday Inn decorated by Tom Wells. It was so well done
that Kemmons hired Tom to be in charge of all Holiday Inn decorations

Kemmons Wilson Family Center, Whitehaven YMCA

Pictured (l.–r.): Spence, Kemmons, Kem, Barbara Hamilton, Bob and
Pete Davin at the groundbreaking ceremonies for the
Kemmons Wilson Family Center—Davis YMCA

Kemmons' new Chocolate Flavored Corn, manufactured
by the Wilson Candy Company

Special postage stamp issued in October, 1970, featuring tourist
attractons in Maseru, Lesotho. The stamp shows a panoramic view
of the Holiday Inn complex

Wilson Chapel at Christ United Methodist Church

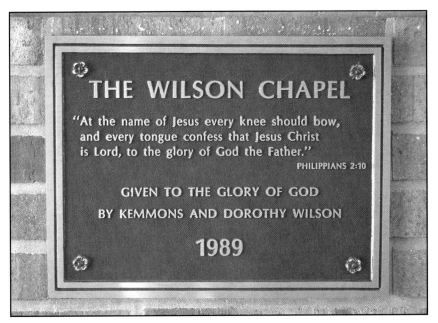

Dedication plaque in chapel

Wilson Chapel—Christ United Methodist Church

William Bone

Robert Wilson

Moon Astronaut Jim Irwin Visits Wimbleton

AFTER THE BATTLE—In the picture, standing, are Tom Samuels (l.), and Ambassador Ghorbal. Seated, from left: Eldon Roark, Jacob Saliba, Col. Jim Irwin, Kemmons Wilson, Tom Saliba

Diane and Guilford Glazer

Kemmons and his chief structural engineer, Bob McCaskill

Charles Zanowski,
vice president and sales manager,
Orange Lake Country Club

Billy Springer and Kemmons—
Billy has run Kemmons'
Ridgewood Homesites and
other companies in Sarasota,
Florida, for the past 30 years

Leonard Peek,
Kemmons' partner
in Nachos

John Pettey (standing), C.F.O. of
Kemmons Wilson Companies—
Spence (l.) and Bob (r.)

Greetings...
from our house
to your house

1957

1958

1959

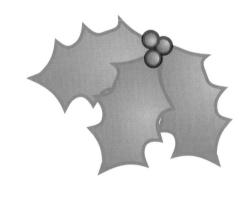

1960

1961

1962

1963

1964

1965

1966

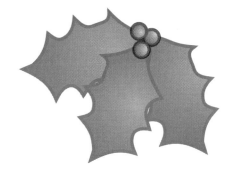

1967

1968

1969

1970

1971

1972

1973

1974

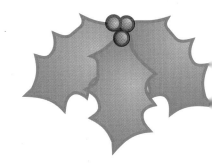

1975

1976

1977

1978

1979

1980

1981

1982

1983

1984

1985

1986

1987

1988

1989

1990

1991

1992

1993

1994

THE KEMMONS WILSON FAMILY 1994

1. Kem Wilson, Jr.	8. Lee West	15. Santa	22. Jackson Moore, Jr.
2. Norma Wilson	9. McLean Wilson	16. Webb Wilson	23. Spence Wilson, Jr.
3. Kem Wilson, III	10. Kemmons	17. Susan Wilson	24. Betty Moore
4. Carole West	11. Katherine Wilson	18. Lauren Wilson	25. Jack Moore
5. Dr. Bill West	12. Elizabeth Wilson	19. Wilson Moore	26. Becky Wilson
6. Carey Wilson	13. Dorothy	20. Rebecca Wilson	27. Spence Wilson
7. Meg West	14. Bob Wilson	21. Shellye Moore	

The Kemmons Wilson Family 1995

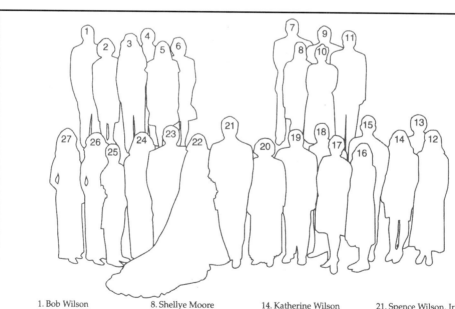

1. Bob Wilson
2. Susan Wilson
3. Lee West
4. Dr. Bill West
5. Meg West
6. Carole West
7. Jackson Moore, Jr.

8. Shellye Moore
9. Jack Moore
10. Betty Moore
11. Wilson Moore
12. Carey Wilson
13. McLean Wilson

14. Katherine Wilson
15. Kem Wilson, III
16. Elizabeth Wilson
17. Norma Wilson
18. Kem Wilson, Jr.
19. Kemmons
20. Dorothy

21. Spence Wilson, Jr.
22. Stephanie Wilson
23. Spence Wilson
24. Becky Wilson
25. Webb Wilson
26. Rebecca Wilson
27. Lauren Wilson